LEGENDARY LOCALS

OF

ASHEVILLE

NORTH CAROLINA

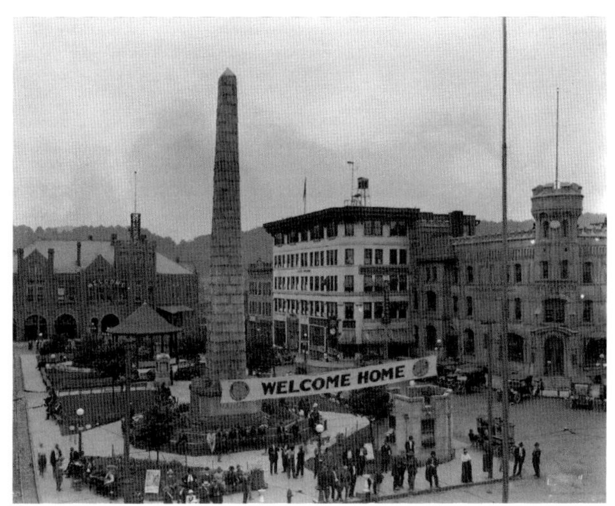

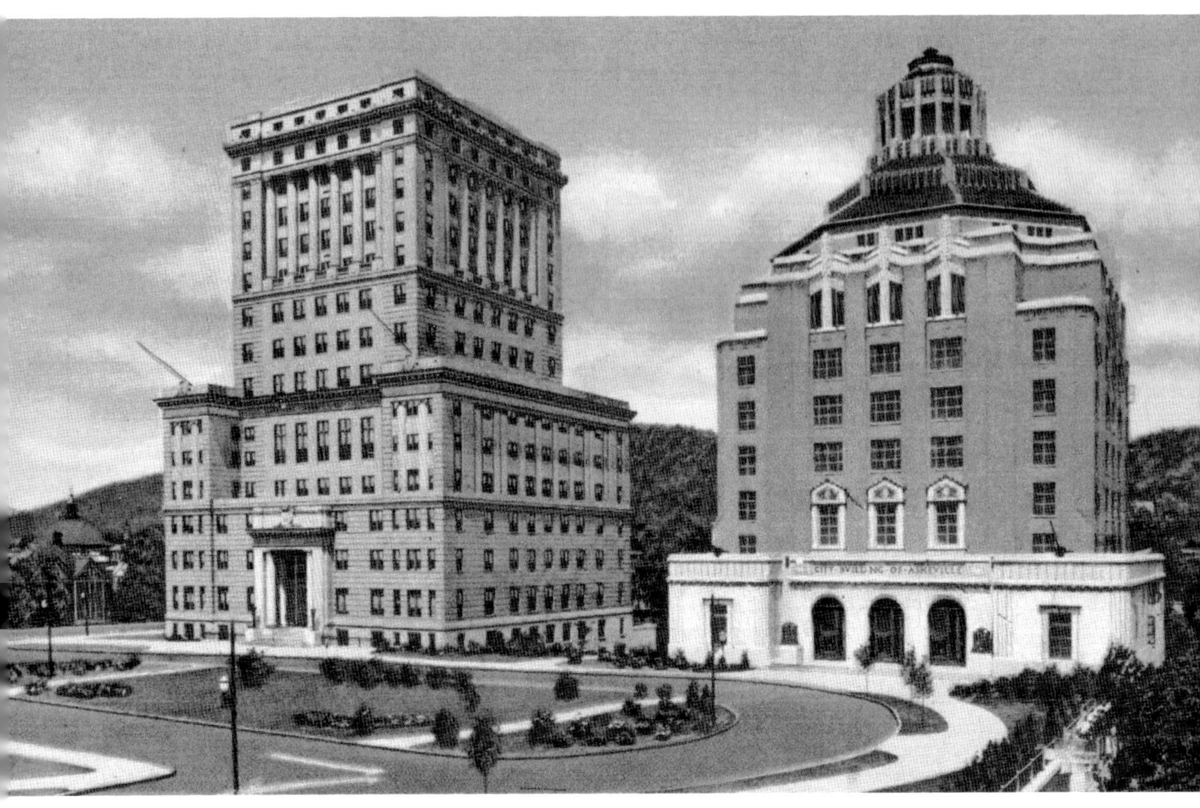

Buncombe County Courthouse and Asheville City Hall

When the courthouse and city hall were completed in the late 1920s, they were believed to be the largest of any city in the Southeast, a great accomplishment for a city of some 50,000 people. They were symbols of Asheville's prominence and, as the Great Depression commenced, signs of its excess. After a half century of struggle, Asheville reemerged from its financial crisis; today, these buildings are once again symbols of Asheville's triumph as one of the country's great downtown revitalization success stories. (Courtesy of the North Carolina Collection, Pack Library.)

Page 1: Pack Square

Asheville's historic city center, Pack Square, is festooned to welcome the troops back from World War I. (Courtesy of Ramsey Library Special Collections.)

LEGENDARY LOCALS

OF

ASHEVILLE

NORTH CAROLINA

KEVAN D. FRAZIER

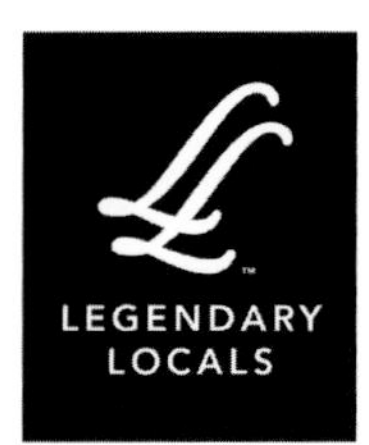

ISBN 978-1-4671-0167-7

Legendary Locals is an imprint of Arcadia Publishing
Charleston, South Carolina

Printed in the United States of America

Library of Congress Control Number: 2014933971

For all general information, please contact Arcadia Publishing:
Telephone 843-853-2070
Fax 843-853-0044
E-mail sales@arcadiapublishing.com
For customer service and orders:
Toll-Free 1-888-313-2665

Visit us on the Internet at www.arcadiapublishing.com

Dedication
To the women and men whose leadership, dedication, and civic-mindedness have made Asheville an extraordinary community in which to live.

On the Front Cover: Clockwise from bottom left:
George W. Vanderbilt II, builder of Biltmore Estate (courtesy of the National Archives and Ramsey Library Special Collections; see page 32), E.W. Pearson, community leader (courtesy of the North Carolina Collection, Pack Library; see page 22), Capt. Robert Morgan and the crew of the *Memphis Belle*, World War II heroes (courtesy of the North Carolina Collection, Pack Library; see page 106), Zebulon B. Vance, governor (courtesy of the North Carolina Collection, Pack Library; see page 17), Irene Hendrick, librarian (courtesy of the North Carolina Collection, Pack Library; see page 70), Thomas Wolfe, author (courtesy of the North Carolina Collection, Pack Library; see page 89), William Jennings Bryan (left), secretary of state (courtesy of the North Carolina Collection, Pack Library; see page 103), Pack Square (courtesy of Ramsey Library Special Collections); and Lillian Exum Clement, the first female North Carolina legislator (courtesy of the North Carolina Collection, Pack Library; see page 23).

On the Back Cover: From left to right:
Bascom Lamar Lunsford (right), musician (courtesy of Ramsey Library Special Collections; see page 84), Asheville Student Committee on Racial Equality (ASCORE) reunion, civil rights leaders (courtesy of the *Urban News*; see page 28).

CONTENTS

ACKNOWLEDGMENTS

I would like to thank the staff of the North Carolina Collection at Pack Memorial Library for their tireless efforts at preserving our city's history. I offer my thanks, too, to Gene Hyde and Colin Reeve of the D. Hiden Ramsey Library Special Collections at the University of North Carolina at Asheville. Their colleagueship has been invaluable in this endeavor. Thanks as well to the curatorial staff at Biltmore Estate for their gracious assistance.

I am thankful to my parents, Asheville natives Donna and Nelson Frazier, for their loving support; my copyeditor and friend Griffin Payne; my graphic designer and friend Courtney Crawford; photographer and friend Aaron Dahlstrom; and my friend and fellow historian Darren Poupore. I offer my thanks, too, to Steve Green and Chris Allen, who have had my back throughout the entire process. I am fortunate to have an extraordinary group of friends who are so generous with their love and support. To each of them, I am deeply grateful.

I would also like to thank the individuals, families, institutions, businesses, and professional photographers that provided photographs. Acknowledgments are noted with each one. Photographs from Ramsey Library came out of several collections, but space does not allow each to be listed. The photographs can be easily found through the university's catalog. A special word of thanks to Grovewood Galleries, the Omni Grove Park Inn, the Black Mountain College Museum, and Jim Stokely for permission to use photographs from their collections at Ramsey Library. I also want to thank the UNC Asheville Communication and Marketing Department for their numerous photographic contributions, as well as the Biltmore Company and Biltmore Farms for the use of their photographs.

INTRODUCTION

In 1794, John Burton, a land speculator, received a 203-acre land grant from the state of North Carolina. The land lay at the center of the newly created Buncombe County on a site that had been a crossroads of ancient Cherokee trading routes. To curry the favor of William Morrison, a nearby member of the general assembly, Burton called the new settlement Morristown, in hopes of his new town becoming the county seat. Within a year, however, the name was changed to honor the new governor, Samuel Ashe, and in 1797, the general assembly officially chartered the town of Asheville.

As the county seat, Asheville became a center for government and commerce as more settlers moved into the area. Pioneer families such as the Davidsons, Pattons, and Bairds began to grow their businesses in the new village. In the early decades of the 19th century, especially after the completion of the Buncombe Turnpike, Asheville became a stopover point for livestock drovers from other parts of the mountains bringing animals to market in South Carolina.

While Asheville would grow, its remoteness kept the town fairly small, with less than 1,000 residents in 1860. Soon after the guns fired at Fort Sumter, South Carolina, in 1861, starting the Civil War, one of Asheville's own, Zebulon Vance, was elected to lead the state as its governor during the war. Vance had not favored secession, but he supported the will of the convention as North Carolina reluctantly seceded. Though the loss of life in North Carolina would be among the highest of all the states, Asheville's remoteness would spare it from the physical ravages of the war. General Sherman was never going to climb the mountains and march through Asheville. But like many small towns in North Carolina, the loss of life from the war had a great effect on the community.

In the years following the Civil War, Asheville began to attract visitors drawn to the beauty, fresh air, and perceived healing powers of the Blue Ridge Mountains. The numbers were small because of Asheville's remoteness, but all of that changed in 1880 with the coming of the railroad. In short order, Asheville became a popular resort destination. These early tourists were people of means, and the hospitality industry grew to meet their needs. Many were drawn to Asheville for their health, and the city became a popular destination for pulmonary patients suffering from the symptoms of tuberculosis. Visits for health reasons brought many "outsiders," as the locals called them, who then decided to stay and make Asheville their home. Outsiders such as George Pack, George Vanderbilt, and E.W. Grove brought even more people to Asheville. By the turn of the 20th century, it had become a playground and investment opportunity for the wealthy and famous.

While Asheville's reputation grew in the years immediately before World War I, it was in the years following the war, during the Roaring Twenties, that it would become a boomtown. From 1920 to 1930, the city's population exploded, from 28,504 to 50,193. A sense of "urban patriotism" overcame the city as Ashevillians came to realize that theirs was on the path to being one of the East Coast's great cities. These urban patriots ignited both a civic and commercial building boom. Much of the face of Asheville today was built at the hands of these leaders in the 1920s. By the time the stock market crashed in October 1929, Asheville's boom had led to an excruciating bust, and the city had the highest debt per capita of any city in the country.

The Great Depression ushered in a period of steady decline for the once great city. Rather than default on its bonds, the city crafted a repayment plan that crippled its ability to grow and support development for much of the 20th century. The county would recover, as it attracted industry drawn to its cheap land, low labor costs, and the modest presence of labor unions. The city tried to rebuild its tourist industry during the Great Depression with the public opening of Biltmore, George Vanderbilt's famous chateau, but, like the rest of the nation, it was World War II that finally revitalized the economy.

Even with the rise of the postwar economy, Asheville continued to decline, still crippled by its Depression-era debts. When the area's first regional mall opened in the 1970s and the department stores moved out of downtown, Asheville was all but a ghost town, much of it boarded up.

Finally, in 1976, as part of its bicentennial celebrations, Asheville paid off the last of its Depression-era debt and burned its bonds on the steps of city hall. To the city's fortune, its financial condition had frozen Asheville much like an insect caught in prehistoric amber, and, unlike many cities, most of its historic structures were still intact.

With a canvas of historical architecture, a new group of rebuilders emerged in the 1980s to revitalize Asheville, not only as a tourist destination but also as a great city in which to live and work. By the 1990s Asheville's renaissance had truly begun, the result of which has been one of the nation's great success stories of downtown revitalization. With its roots deep in the Appalachian soil, contemporary Asheville is an extraordinary city, made so by the women and men who have called and continue to call it home.

CHAPTER ONE

Pioneers of the First Frontier

In the late 1700s, during the early days of the New Republic, long before cowboys and wagon trains, the Appalachian range was the American frontier. The mountains had proven to be a formidable geographic barrier to westward expansion. After the Revolutionary War, however, several soldiers began to stake their claims in Western North Carolina for land promised in return for their service to the new nation. By 1784, the Davidson family had made their way up the mountains and laid claim to ancient Cherokee lands as the area's first settlers.

These earliest pioneers crafted a small but vital community from the wilderness. Businesses emerged to support the locals, as well as weary travelers, and, though they were remote, the women and men of Asheville were involved not only in the leadership of the state, but also in the leadership of the nation. In the years following the Civil War, there were former slaves who built new lives in Asheville and women who asserted formidable leadership in education and medicine. By the latter half of the 19th century, there emerged a group of medical pioneers who made Asheville one of the leading health destinations in the country.

Asheville's pioneering spirit extended well into the 20th century, from the first woman ever elected to a state office in the Southeast, to the extraordinary high school students who formed their own civil rights organization and successfully broke the stranglehold of segregation, to the retired engineer who kicked off the city's nationally recognized craft beer movement. That pioneering spirit has never left Asheville, and it still guides its citizens as the city moves into its third century.

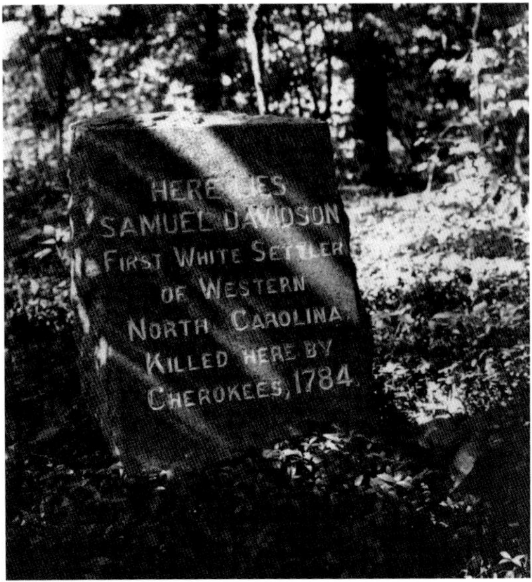

Samuel Davidson
Samuel Davidson and his wife are generally accepted as the first Europeans to settle Western North Carolina, in 1784. A colonel in the Revolutionary War, Davidson received a land grant in the Swannanoa Valley. One night, realizing that the presence of the Davidsons foretold future settlements, a group of Cherokee ambushed and killed Davidson. Members of his family avenged his death and, eventually, made a permanent settlement where Bee Tree Creek joins the Swannanoa River. (Courtesy of the North Carolina Collection, Pack Library.)

"A PLAN OF THE TOWN OF ASHEVILLE"

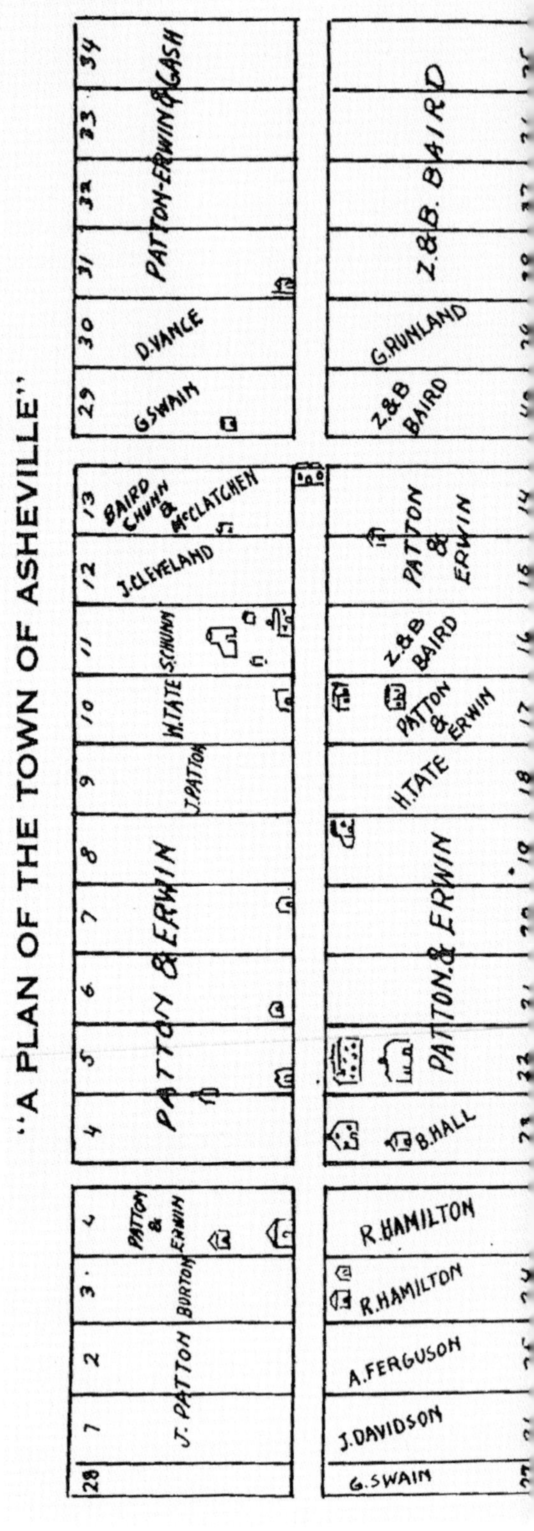

John Burton
Credited as Asheville's founder, John Burton, a farmer and land speculator, received 203 acres as a land grant from the state of North Carolina on a level plateau in the newly established Buncombe County (1791). He recorded his first sale on July 28, 1794. In hopes of making his new village Buncombe's county seat, Burton courted the vote of assemblyman William Morrison and named the new village Morristown. That name lasted only a year until the community instead sought the favor of the new governor, Samuel Ashe. Asheville became the county seat, and it was officially chartered in 1797. (Reprinted from F.A. Sondley's *Asheville and Buncombe County*; courtesy of the North Carolina Collection, Pack Library.)

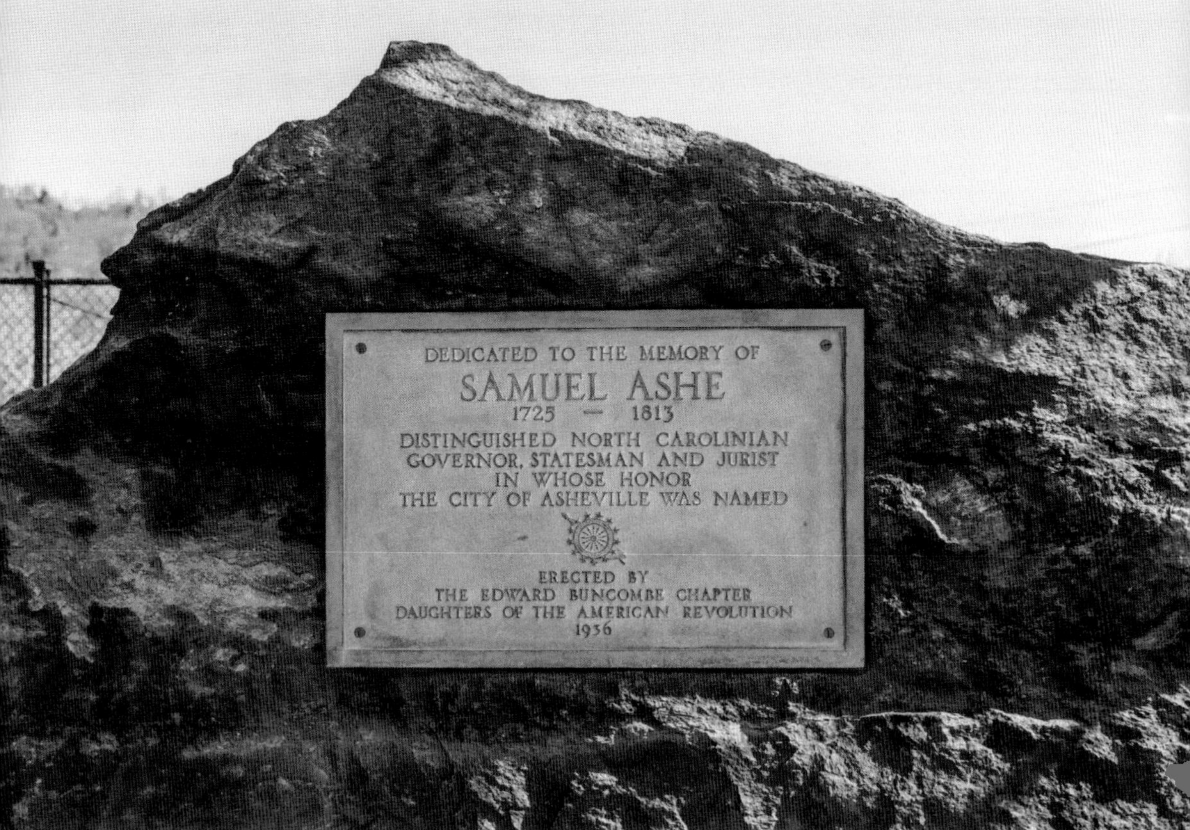

Samuel Ashe

Asheville's namesake, Samuel Ashe, was a noted leader of the patriot cause during the Revolutionary War and served as North Carolina's ninth governor. Ashe was born into affluence in 1725 outside Bath, North Carolina, to John Baptiste Ashe and Elizabeth Swann. At his father's encouragement, he studied law at Harvard and eventually became the assistant attorney for the British crown in Wilmington, North Carolina. Despite his ties to Britain, Ashe was an active patriot, organizing the colony's first revolutionary provincial council in 1774, when the colonial governor refused to call the legislature. Ashe was later on the committee that drafted North Carolina's first constitution and was elected as the first speaker of the new state senate. After the war, he was appointed to a superior court judgeship, but, in 1795, at the age of 70, he resigned his judgeship to become governor, a post he held for three consecutive one-year terms, the most allowed by the constitution at that time. It was during Ashe's service as governor that the citizens of the small western outpost of Morristown began to call their new town Asheville, the name under which it was eventually chartered in 1797. Ashe died in 1813, and there is no evidence that he ever came to the town named in his honor. (Photograph by Aaron Dahlstrom.)

Edward Buncombe

In 1791, David Vance and William Davidson petitioned the North Carolina House of Commons to create a new county out of Burke and Rutherford Counties. Residents of the emerging Western North Carolina communities found it increasingly difficult to reach a county seat, a necessity for conducting legal affairs. The new county was originally to be called Union, but the decision was made instead to name the county in honor of Col. Edward Buncombe, a noted Revolutionary War soldier from Tyrell County, North Carolina. Buncombe was a member of the First Provincial Congress of North Carolina (1774), which was the first assembly in the 13 colonies to meet in defiance of British orders. Later, as colonel of the 5th North Carolina Regiment, Buncombe was wounded and captured in the Battle of Germantown in 1777, eventually dying in custody a year later in Philadelphia. In an unfortunate twist of historic fate, Buncombe's name inadvertently became a derogatory term in American slang thanks to Felix Walker, a member of the US House of Representatives representing Buncombe County. In 1820, after months of debate over whether to admit Missouri as a free or slave state, just hours before the final vote was to be called, Walker rose and insisted that he be able to give a long "speech for Buncombe." Already exhausted by the debate, the House shouted Walker down, despite his calls that he was bound to "make a speech for Buncombe." "Buncombe" was later changed to "bunkum" and became slang for meaningless political chatter. Henry Ford would famously codify the term in the early 20th century with his notorious statement that "History is more or less bunk." (Courtesy of the North Carolina Collection, Pack Library.)

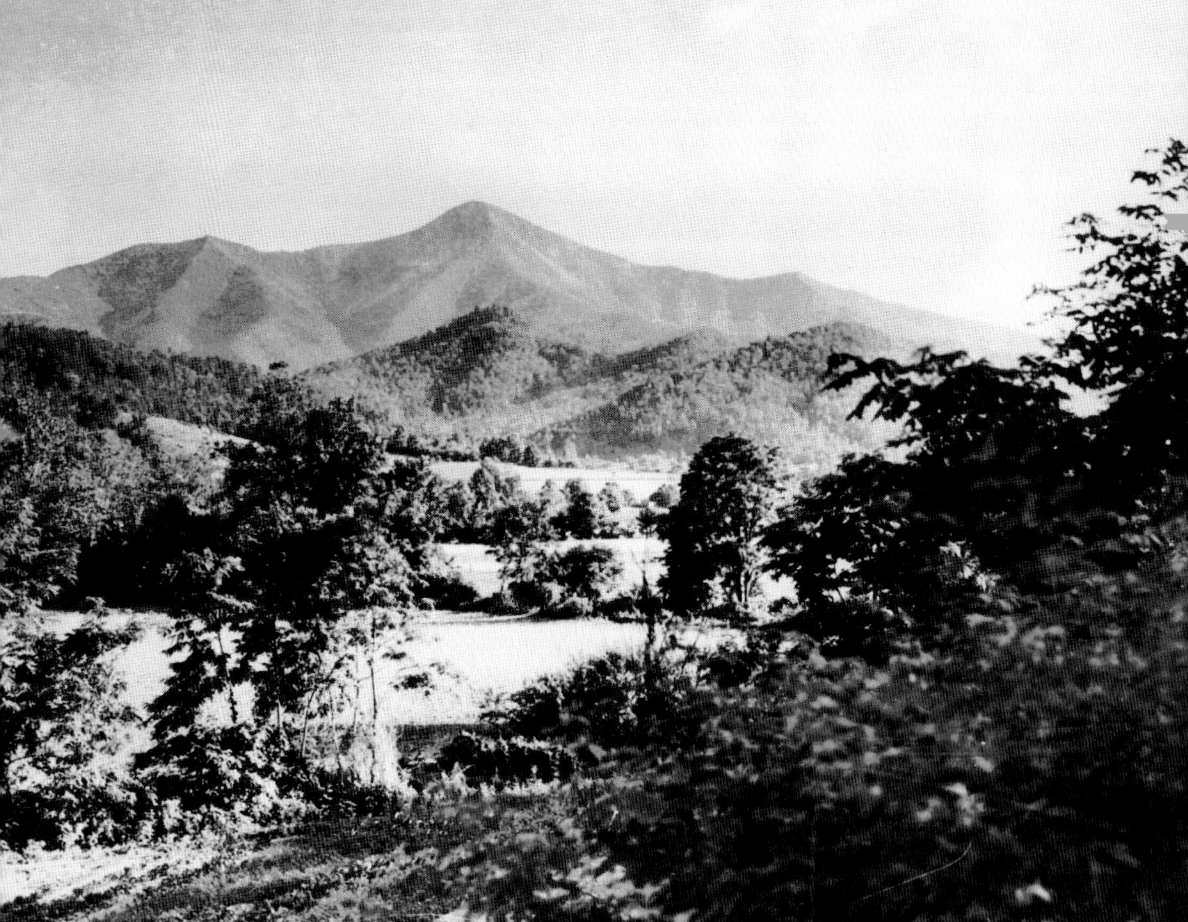

David L. Swain

Born in 1801, David Swain took up law practice in Asheville in 1823. A year later, he was elected to the general assembly for five terms, where he was known for his advocacy of the western counties and for statewide internal improvements such as railroads. He was chosen by the assembly in 1832 to serve as governor, which he did for three one-year terms. Upon leaving office, he was chosen as the president of the University of North Carolina, a post he held for 33 years. (Courtesy of the North Carolina Collection, Pack Library.)

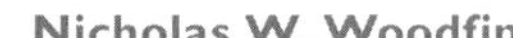

Nicholas W. Woodfin

In 1831, Nicholas Woodfin, after studying law under David L. Swain and others, was admitted to the North Carolina bar. He later served as a state senator. A significant landowner, Woodfin was also the largest slaveholder in the county, with 122 slaves. He opposed secession until Pres. Abraham Lincoln sent troops to the states that had seceded. After the war, he played key roles in the state during reconstruction. Several years after his death, a neighboring town was named in his honor. (Courtesy of the North Carolina Collection, Pack Library.)

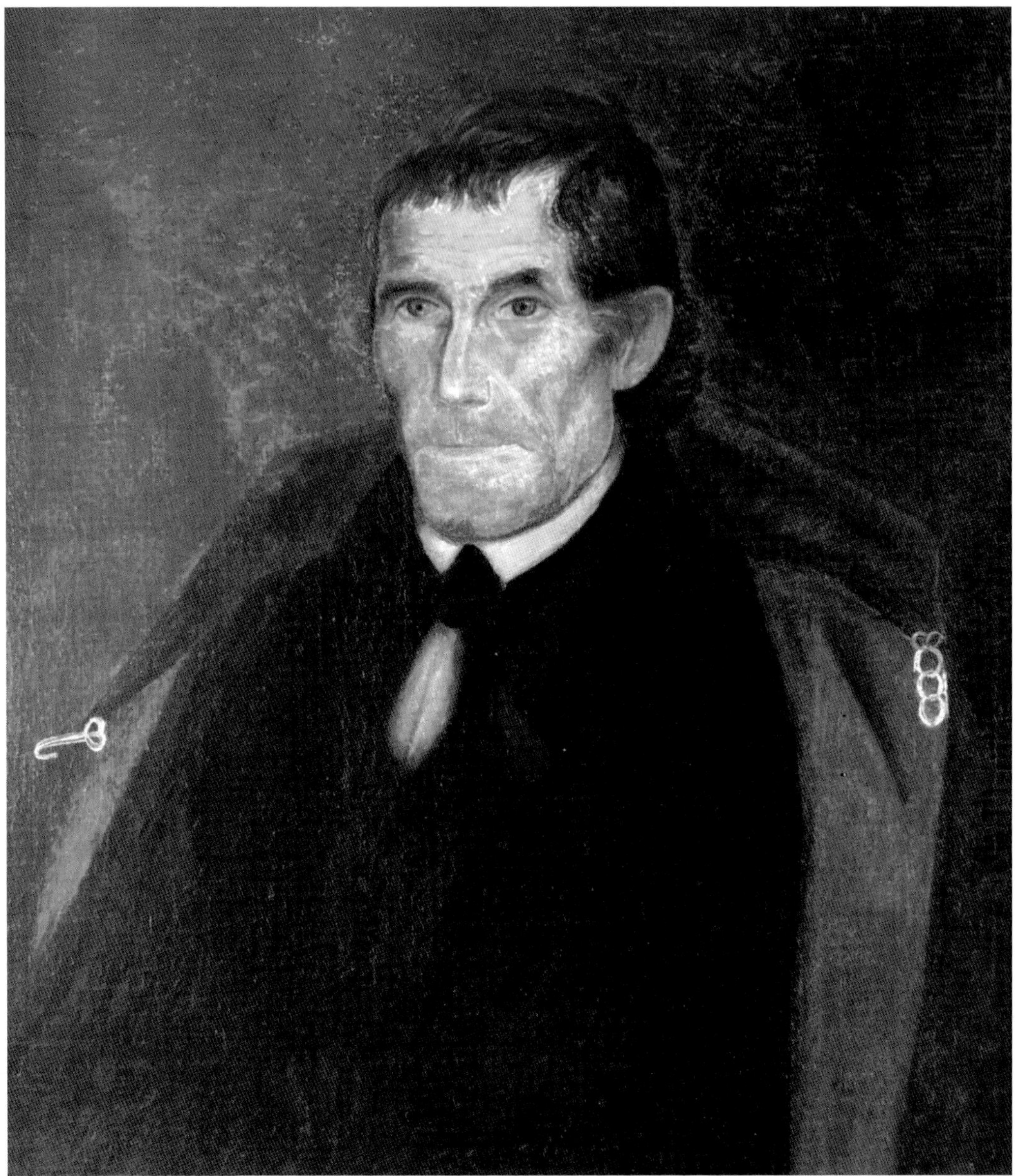

James and James W. Patton

James Patton (pictured) was an immigrant from Ireland who made his way to North Carolina by way of Philadelphia. He and his brother-in-law bought one of the last of John Burton's original lots. By 1814, he had opened up a store, a hotel (the Eagle Hotel), and a tannery in Asheville. Patton's son James W. was born in 1803 and became a prominent merchant in Asheville of his own right. James W. helped complete an east-west thoroughfare through Asheville that still bears the Patton name. The Pattons were instrumental, along with George Swain and Samuel Chunn, in creating the Buncombe Turnpike, which was considered to be the finest road in all of North Carolina at the time. The 75-mile stretch of "improved" road from Tennessee to South Carolina opened Asheville up to livestock drovers, traders, and others, all of which significantly grew the 19th-century Asheville economy. (Courtesy of the North Carolina Collection, Pack Library.)

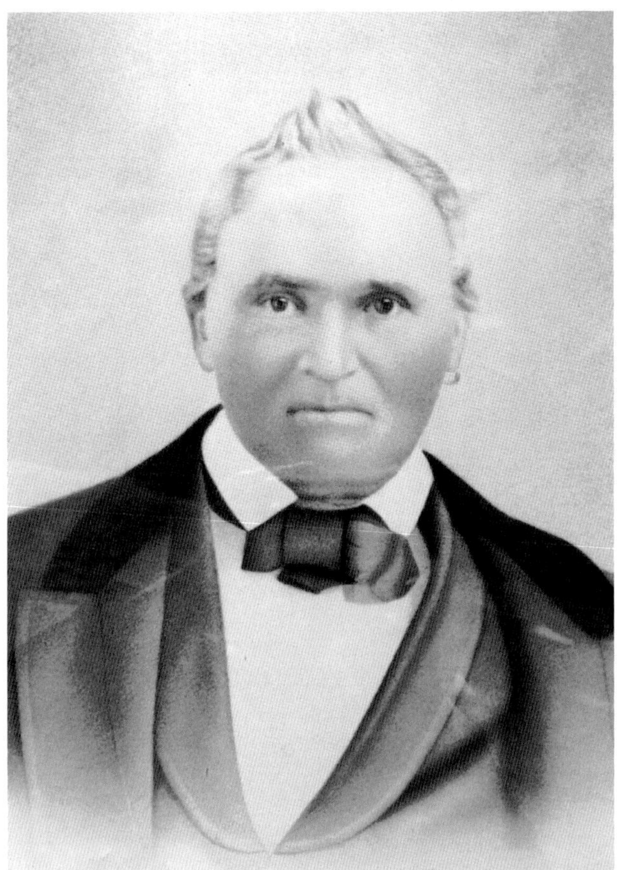

Joshua Roberts
Born in Cleveland County, North Carolina, in 1795, Joshua Roberts practiced law in Asheville and married Lucinda Patton, daughter of Col. John Patton. After settling for a time in Macon County, the Roberts returned to Asheville, where Joshua joined John Christy in founding the *Highland Messenger*, Western North Carolina's first newspaper. In 1848, Roberts served as the founding master of Mt. Hermon Lodge 118 of Ancient Free and Accepted Masons. He died in 1865. (Courtesy of Mt. Hermon Lodge 118.)

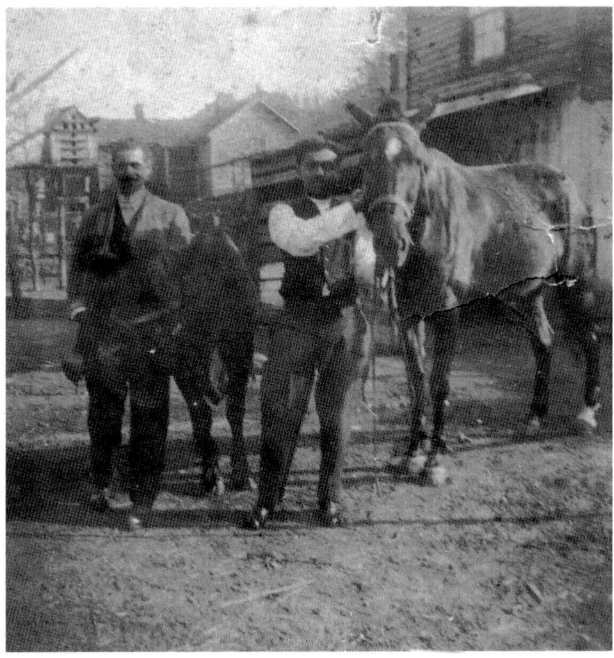

Isaac Dickson
Born in 1839, the son of a slave mother and her Dutch master, Isaac Dickson (left) spent the first 24 years of his life as a slave in Cleveland County. He moved to Asheville after emancipation, took up several jobs, and eventually bought the former slave quarters of the Thomas Patton family, where he built a village for freedmen that came to be called Dicksontown. Dickson was very active in community affairs, hosting the first meeting that led to the establishment of the Young Men's Institute and eventually serving on the city's first school board, where he helped found the first public school for African Americans in Asheville. Dickson died in 1918. (Courtesy of Ramsey Library Special Collections.)

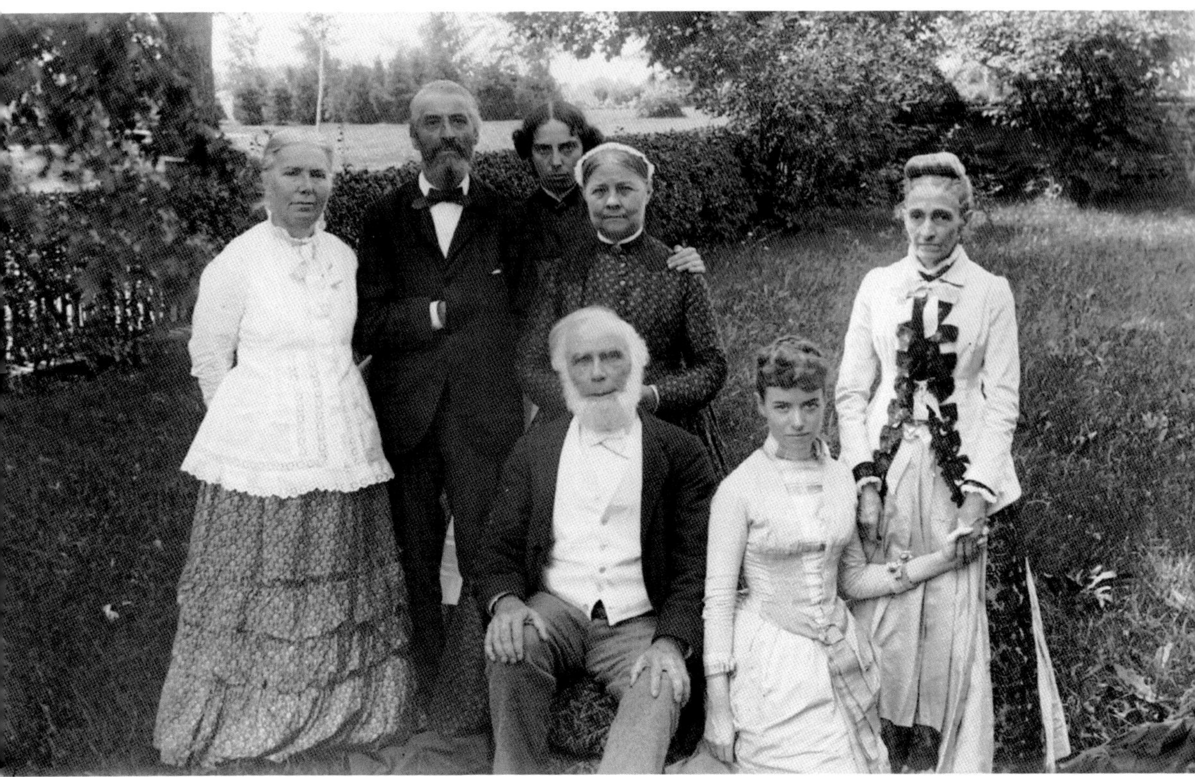

Elizabeth Blackwell

The first woman to earn a medical degree in the United States, Elizabeth Blackwell (left) emigrated from England to the United States in 1832 and came to Asheville in the mid-1840s to work as a music teacher to earn the money needed for medical school. She lodged with Rev. John Dickson, a clergyman and former physician who supported Blackwell in her medical endeavors and loaned her his collection of medical books to help her study. Blackwell was in Asheville for two years; soon after, she gained admission to Geneva Medical College in Western New York, where she earned her medical degree in 1849. She established her first practice in New York and later opened a practice in England. She left medicine in 1877 and was very active in several reform movements, from women's rights to moral reform, until her passing in 1910. (Courtesy of the Library of Congress.)

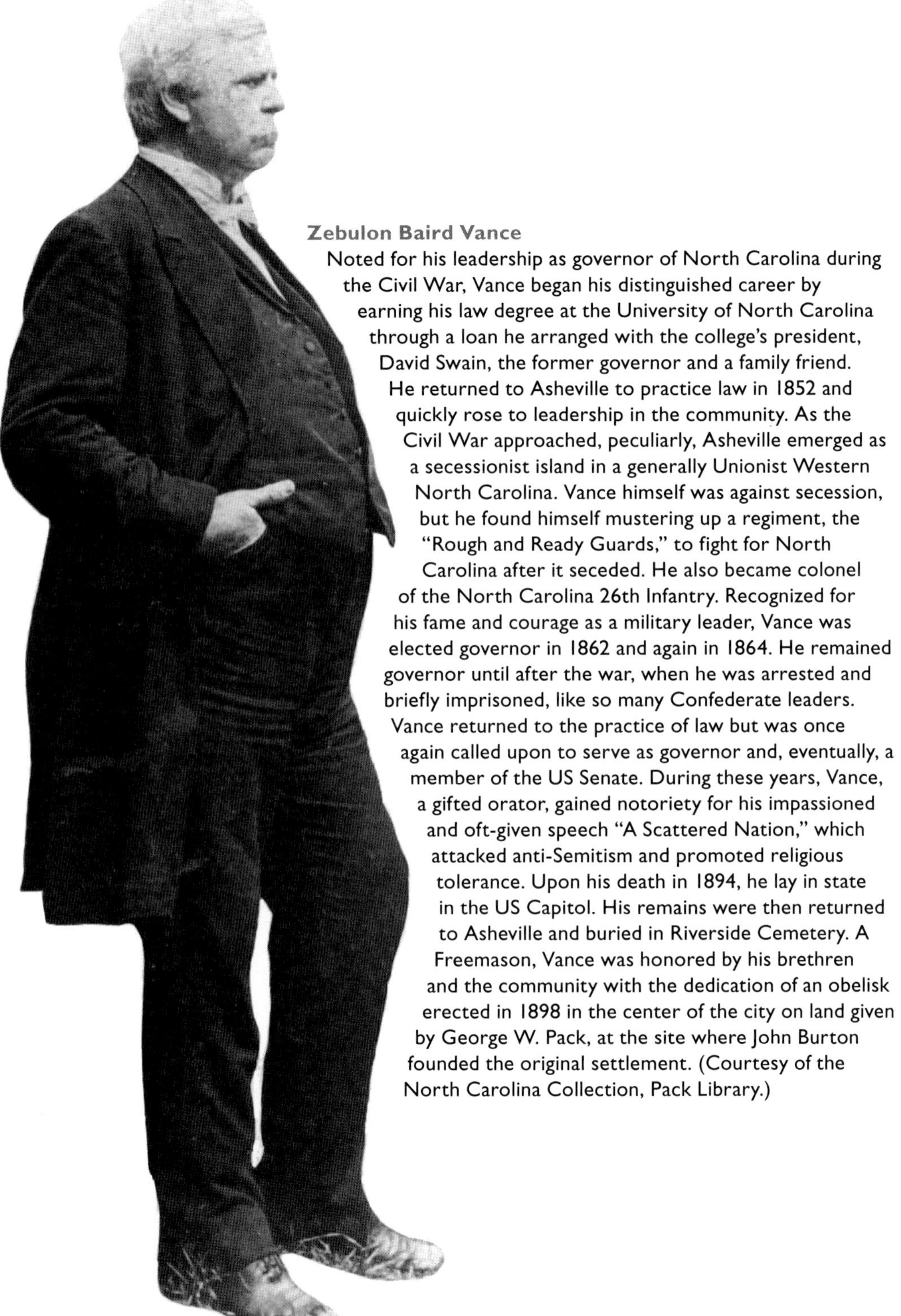

Zebulon Baird Vance

Noted for his leadership as governor of North Carolina during the Civil War, Vance began his distinguished career by earning his law degree at the University of North Carolina through a loan he arranged with the college's president, David Swain, the former governor and a family friend. He returned to Asheville to practice law in 1852 and quickly rose to leadership in the community. As the Civil War approached, peculiarly, Asheville emerged as a secessionist island in a generally Unionist Western North Carolina. Vance himself was against secession, but he found himself mustering up a regiment, the "Rough and Ready Guards," to fight for North Carolina after it seceded. He also became colonel of the North Carolina 26th Infantry. Recognized for his fame and courage as a military leader, Vance was elected governor in 1862 and again in 1864. He remained governor until after the war, when he was arrested and briefly imprisoned, like so many Confederate leaders. Vance returned to the practice of law but was once again called upon to serve as governor and, eventually, a member of the US Senate. During these years, Vance, a gifted orator, gained notoriety for his impassioned and oft-given speech "A Scattered Nation," which attacked anti-Semitism and promoted religious tolerance. Upon his death in 1894, he lay in state in the US Capitol. His remains were then returned to Asheville and buried in Riverside Cemetery. A Freemason, Vance was honored by his brethren and the community with the dedication of an obelisk erected in 1898 in the center of the city on land given by George W. Pack, at the site where John Burton founded the original settlement. (Courtesy of the North Carolina Collection, Pack Library.)

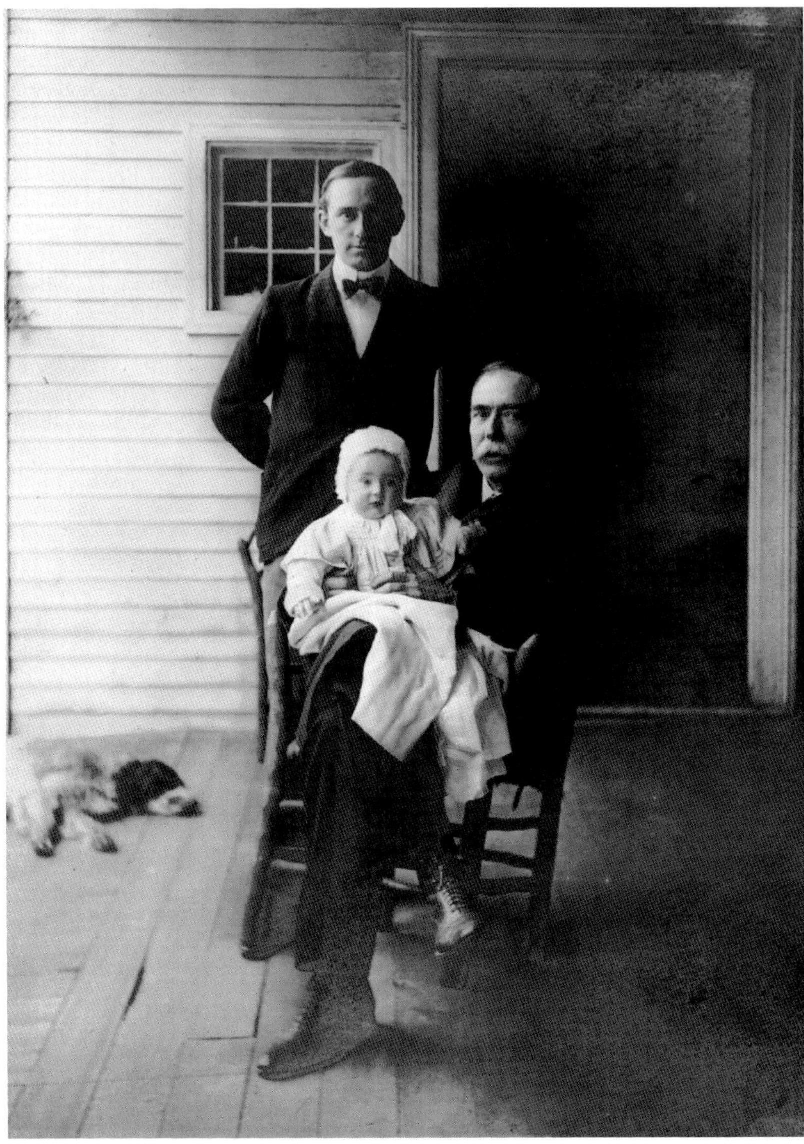

Franklin Coxe

When Col. Franklin Coxe (seated) returned to Western North Carolina after the Civil War, he invested in the Western North Carolina Railroad, which brought the first train to Asheville in 1880. Six years later he built the Battery Park Hotel, the grandeur of which brought the wealthy from throughout the country to Asheville on holiday. Coxe was one of the key leaders in building Asheville's early tourist economy and was close personal friends with William Henry Vanderbilt and his wife, Maria. It was Coxe who welcomed Maria and her son, George, to Asheville in 1888, the trip that inspired George to build Biltmore. At his death, Coxe's holdings were taken over by his son Tench Charles Coxe (standing). Tench constructed a 40-room mansion at the end of Montford Avenue called the Klondyke. He also sold the Battery Park Hotel to E.W. Grove in 1924, the transaction that led to the construction of the New Battery Park Hotel and the Grove Arcade. Tench's son Frank Coxe (child) became a noted Asheville banker, developer, and civic leader for much of the 20th century. (Courtesy of Ramsey Library Special Collections.)

Edward J. Aston

A native of Rogersville, Tennessee, Edward Aston and his wife, Cordelia, moved to Asheville in 1853 and began a varied business career that included a drugstore, a bookstore, and real estate and insurance interests. Aston was the first person to promote Asheville as "the sanatorium of the nation," initiating in 1871 what became a significant industry for Asheville, especially the treatment of patients with tuberculosis. Aston tied the burgeoning health industry with an emerging tourism industry, encouraging physicians and others across the country to come to Asheville to discover its health benefits. Aston is also credited with starting the city's first public library, providing not only the space but also books from his own collection. Aston died in 1893. (Courtesy of the North Carolina Collection, Pack Library.)

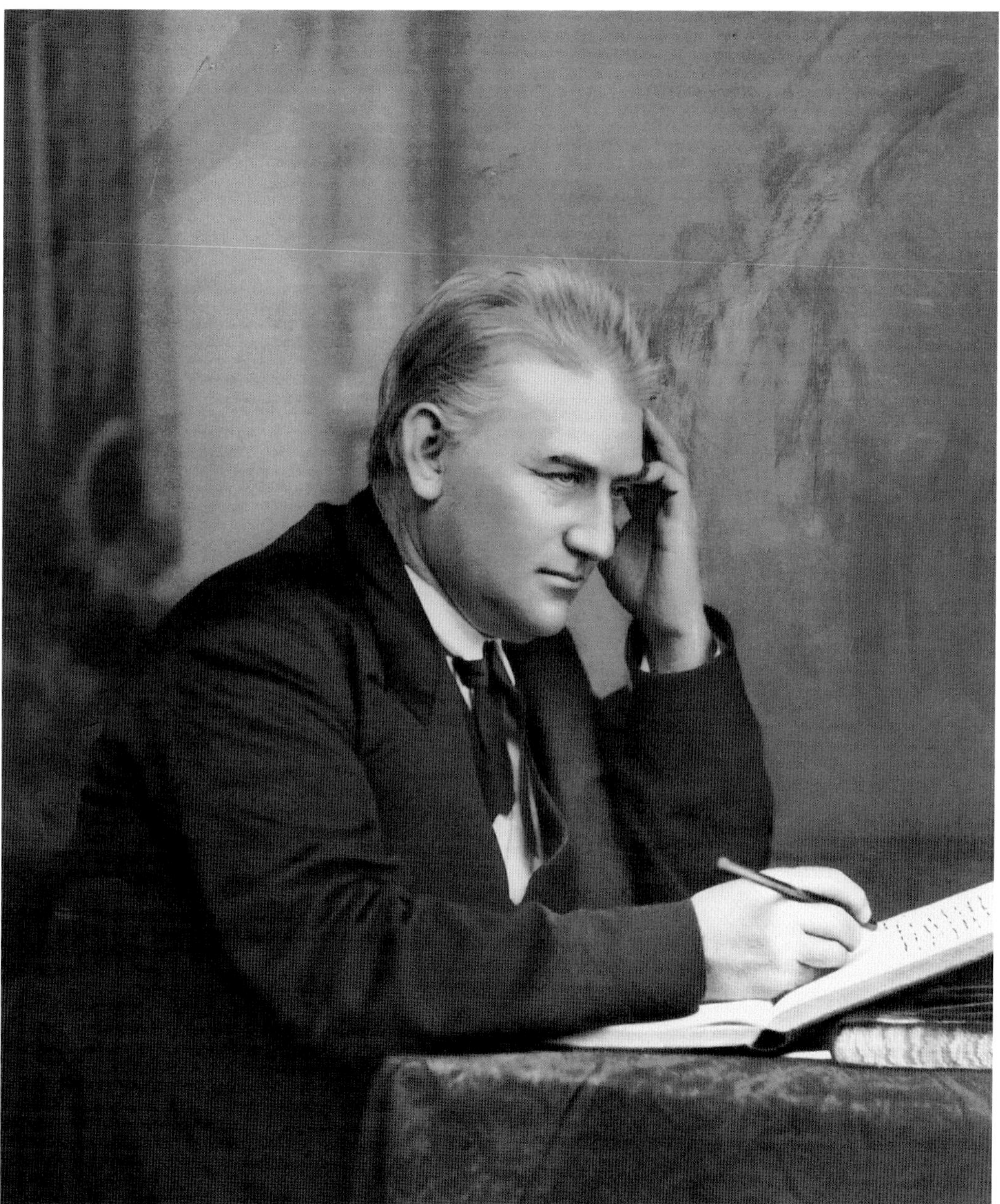

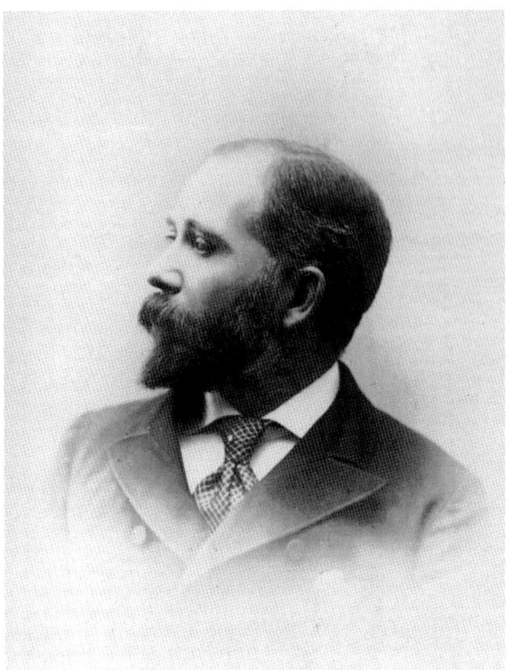

Karl Von Ruck

Dr. Karl Von Ruck is one of the key figures who established Asheville as a health destination in the late 19th century. Von Ruck arrived in Asheville from Ohio in 1886. Two years later he established Winyah Sanitarium, the first private institution for the treatment of tuberculosis. In 1895 he founded the Von Ruck Research Laboratory for Tuberculosis, and later, the *Journal of Tuberculosis*. Von Ruck became one of the global authorities on tuberculosis and was also instrumental in establishing Asheville as a key national treatment center for the disease. (Courtesy of the North Carolina Collection, Pack Library.)

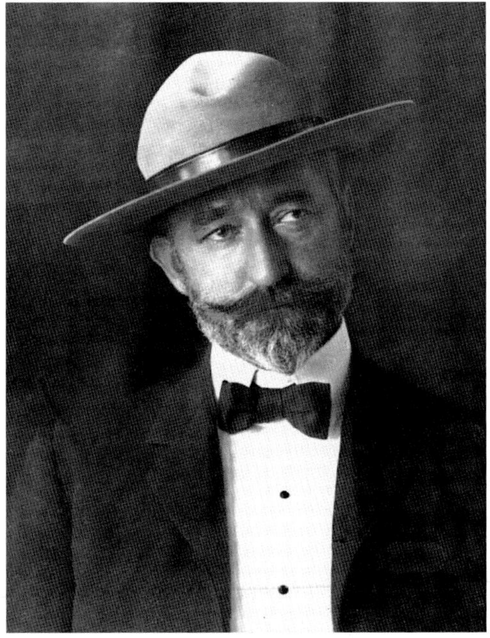

Samuel Westray Battle

Dr. Samuel Westray Battle moved to Asheville in 1885 after a serious injury caused him to retire early from his post as a Navy physician. A nationally reputed physician, Battle became one of the leading promoters of Asheville as a national health destination. His reputation led George Vanderbilt to bring his mother to Asheville in 1888 for her chronic malaria. Battle was also widely known for his gregarious personality, and was often seen wearing a cape with a cane in one hand and a bouquet of flowers in the other. (Courtesy of the North Carolina Collection, Pack Library.)

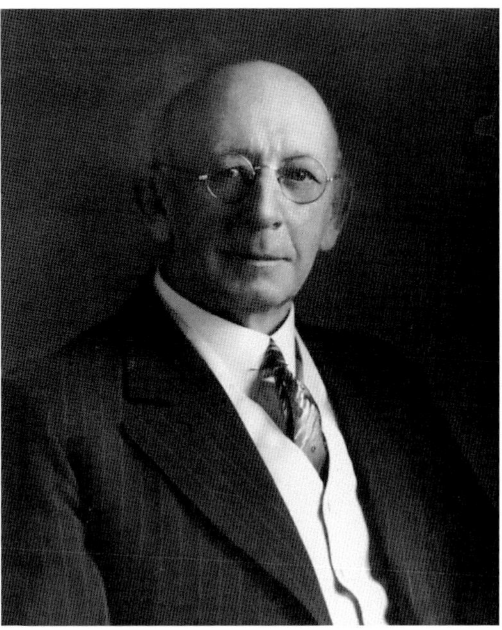

Robert S. Carroll

Drawn by the mountain climate, Dr. Robert S. Carroll established a new psychiatric sanatorium in 1904 in downtown Asheville that became nationally known for its innovative, though today questionable, therapies. In 1909, he moved it to a small campus he built in the Montford neighborhood, where he also built his own home, the castle-like Homewood. There, his wife, Grace, taught music to the likes of students such as Nina Simone. In 1939, Carroll gave Highlands Hospital, as he came to call it, to Duke University, which operated it until 1980. (Courtesy of the North Carolina Collection, Pack Library.)

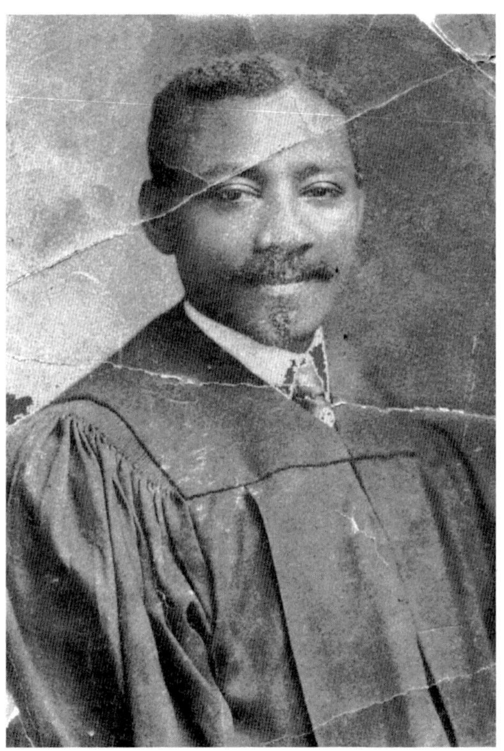

William G. Torrence

A graduate of Shaw University and Dearborn Medical College, Dr. William Torrence founded the first hospital for African Americans in Asheville. It was established in 1910 on Eagle Street. Torrence and his family lived downstairs while maintaining the hospital upstairs. His home and hospital eventually moved to Hill Street, but he also maintained a private practice at the Young Men's Institute building. Torrence died young in 1915. (Courtesy of Ramsey Library Special Collections.)

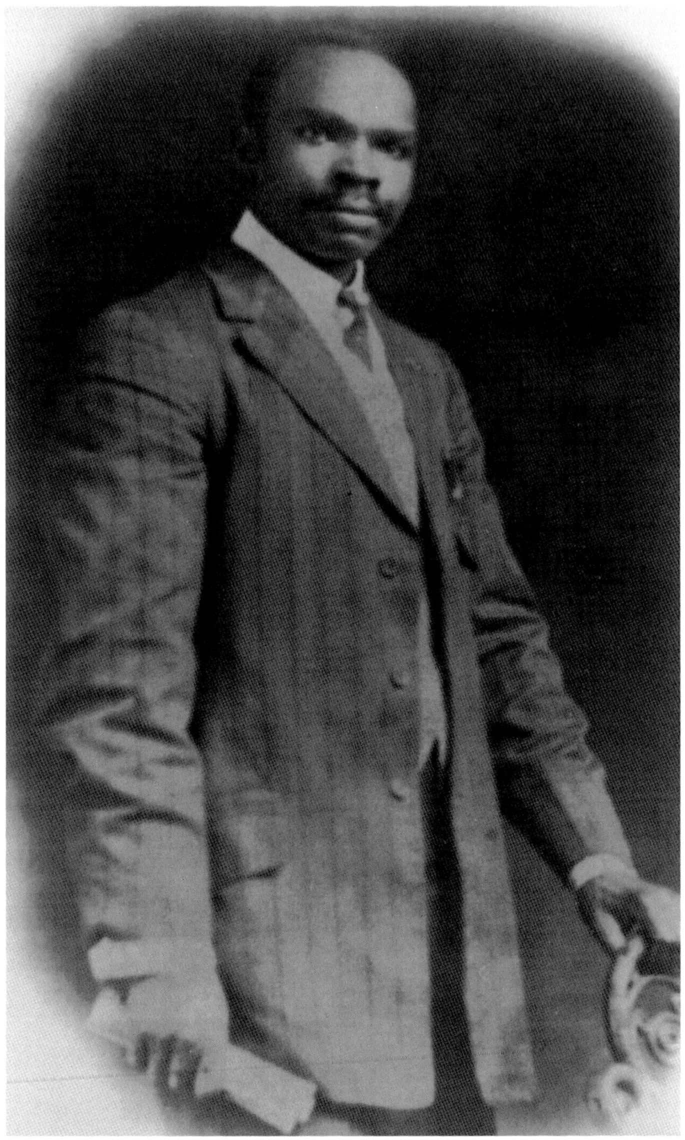

E.W. Pearson Sr.

E.W. Pearson was one of Asheville's most active community leaders. Born in Glen Alpine, North Carolina, Pearson served as a soldier in the Spanish-American War before moving to Asheville in 1906. Despite having only completed the fourth grade, Pearson was a lifelong learner and took many correspondence courses on insurance, business, religion, and law. Widely considered a savvy businessman, his center of operations was a general store in West Asheville, from which he also ran real estate development and general insurance businesses. He developed Park View in West Asheville as a subdivision for African Americans. An active community leader, Pearson founded and was the first president of the Asheville Chapter of the NAACP and served as president of the Asheville chapters of the Universal Negro Improvement Association and the North Carolina Negro Improvement Association. Pearson also founded Asheville's first black baseball team, the Asheville Royal Giants, as well as the Buncombe County Colored Agricultural Fair, held annually in Pearson Park, a park he donated to Asheville. Pearson died in 1946. (Courtesy of the North Carolina Collection, Pack Library.)

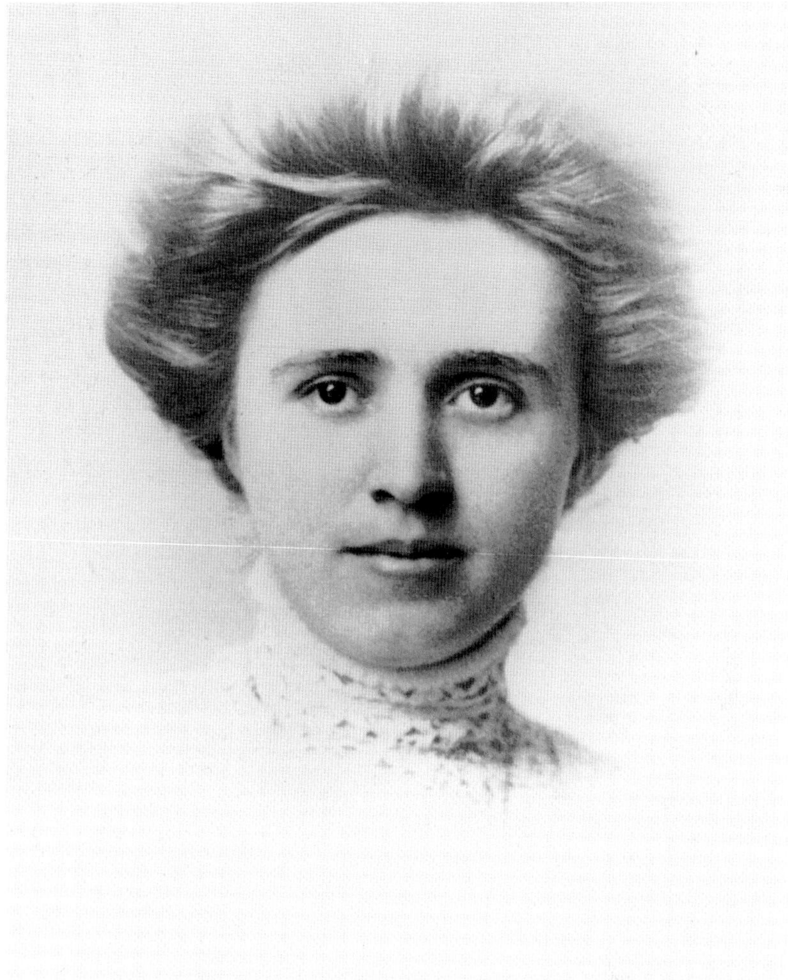

Lillian Exum Clement

At only 26 years old, Lillian Exum Clement was the first woman elected to state office, in North Carolina and in the Southeast. She won her primary by a landslide months before women even had the right to vote. Clement began her journey to the statehouse in Asheville in the early 1900s. After graduating from Asheville Business College, she worked for the Buncombe County Sheriff's Office and studied law by night. In 1916, she passed the state bar with one of the highest scores ever on the exam and became the first woman in North Carolina to open her own law practice. Clement became a highly respected defense attorney and gained the nickname "Brother Exum" from a local judge, a name that stuck with her the rest of her life. In 1920, she was approached by the Democratic Party to run for state office, and she won her primary and the main election handily. Though she served only one term, Senator Clement was an active legislator and saw 16 of her bills passed, a significant number for a freshman legislator. Clement achieved success on issues such as the secret ballot, pure milk, and a state home for unwed mothers and delinquent girls. She was later appointed by Gov. Cameron Morrison to serve as director of the state hospital in Morganton. In 1923, she gave birth to her only child, a daughter, Nancy. Unfortunately, it was a difficult birth, and Clement's health began to deteriorate. She died of pneumonia in 1925 at only 38 years old, yet the impact of her accomplishments resonates to this day. (Courtesy of the North Carolina Collection, Pack Library.)

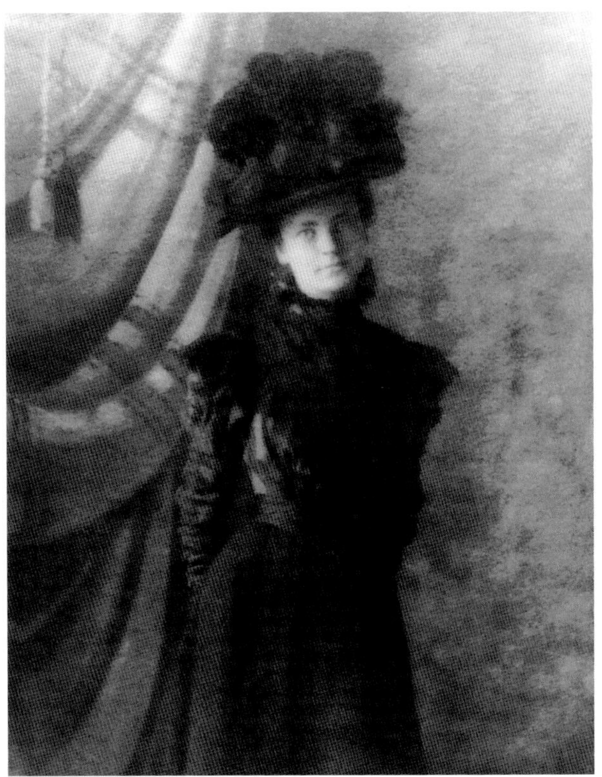

Irene Wortham
Irene Wortham was the first special education teacher in Western North Carolina. In the late 19th century, she was a pioneer in the teaching of children with developmental disabilities. Her method of focusing on what children could achieve, rather than what they could not, had amazing results. Likewise, Wortham was a tireless community advocate, working to ensure that her students did not experience discrimination. (Courtesy of the Irene Wortham Center.)

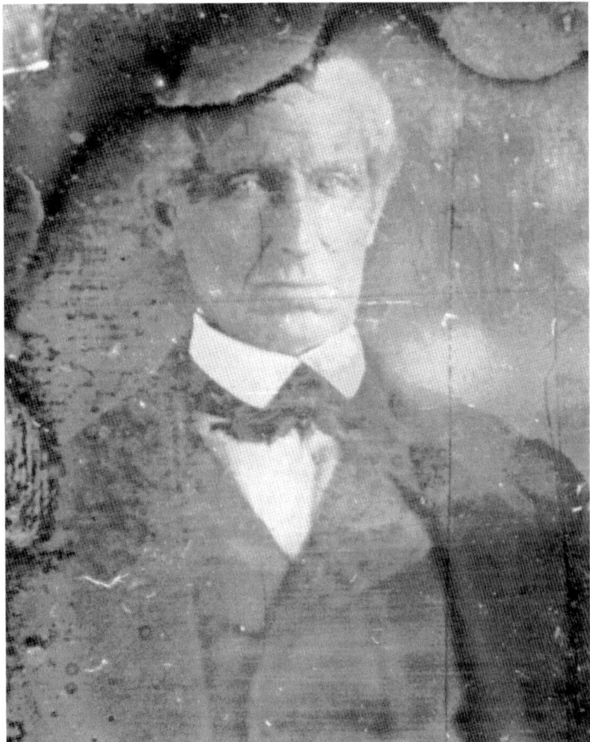

Isaac B. Sawyer
Born in 1810 in what is now Swain County, Isaac Sawyer was the first mayor of Asheville. An attorney, he, James W. Patton, and John Burgin were the three magistrates who composed the Buncombe County court. Sawyer's son Capt. James P. Sawyer was president of the Battery Park Bank. (Courtesy of the North Carolina Collection, Pack Library.)

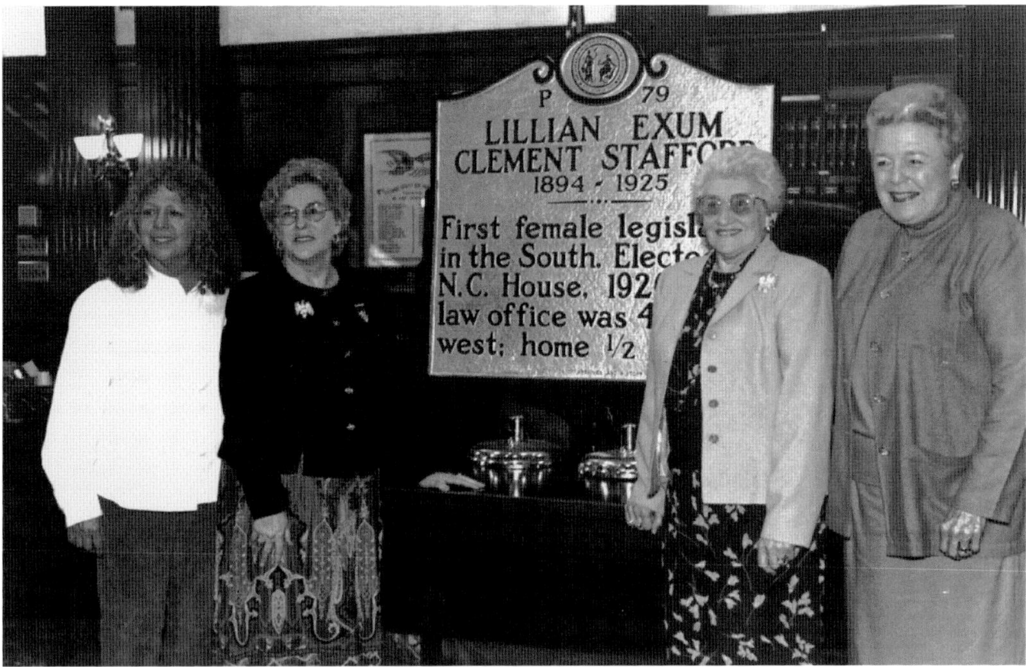

Leni Sitnick

In 1996, Leni Sitnick (left) became Asheville's first female mayor. A longtime community activist, Sitnick ran for city council in 1996 after an unidentified caller said to her, "You've been blabbing your mouth around here for quite awhile, sometimes, you know, good stuff, sometimes stuff I don't agree with. But I think you oughta run for office, and if not you, who? And if not now, when?" As mayor, Sitnick was known for her transparency and accessibility, often answering the mayor's office phone herself and always allowing every constituent to be heard at council meetings. She left office in 2001 and remained in Asheville as a community activist and leader. (Courtesy of the North Carolina Collection, Pack Library.)

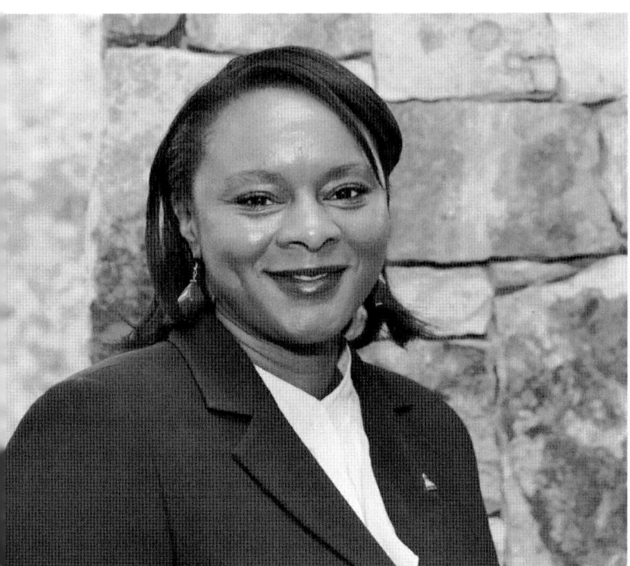

Terry M. Bellamy

Elected to the Asheville City Council in 1999, Terry Bellamy was elected mayor in 2005, making her the first African-American and only the second woman to hold the post. Bellamy served as mayor for eight years, during which time she oversaw a significant expansion of the city's water system, growth in affordable housing, and the development of the city's River Arts District. (Photograph by Perry Hebbard; courtesy of UNC Asheville Communication and Marketing.)

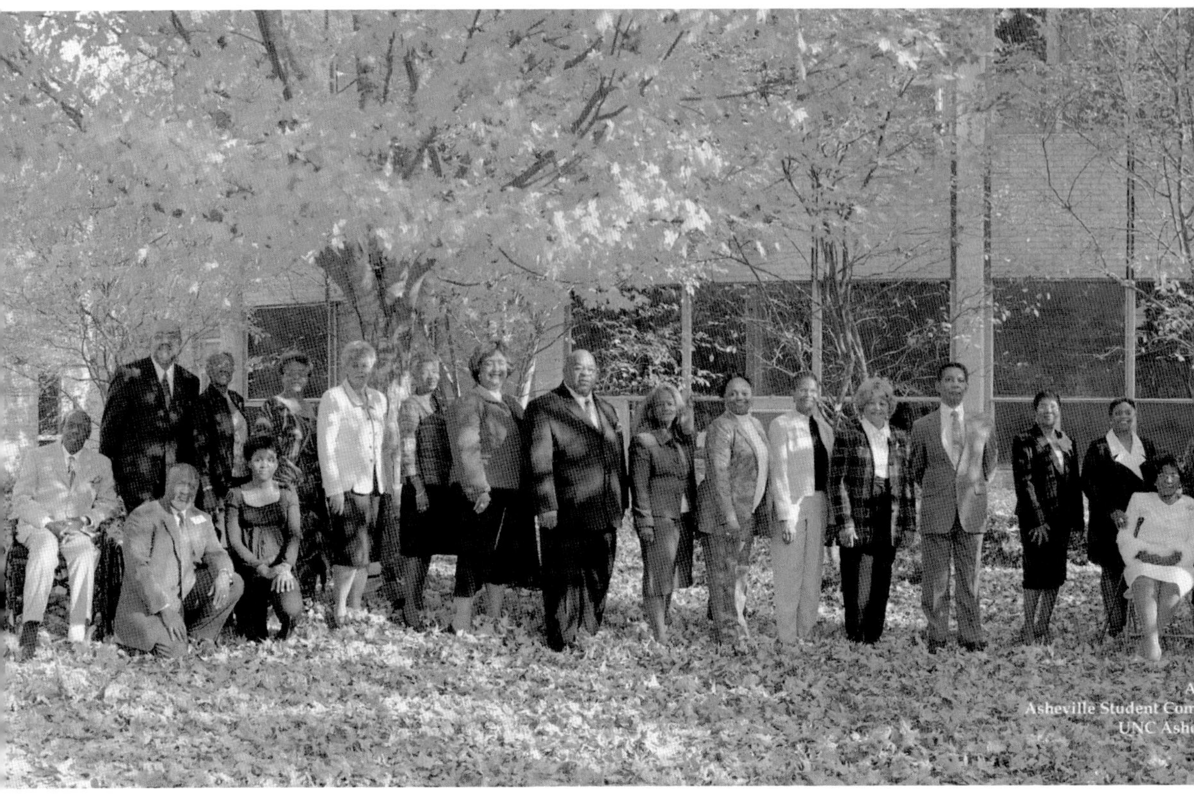

Asheville Student Committee on Racial Equality
The members of the Asheville Student Committee on Racial Equality (ASCORE) gathered for a reunion

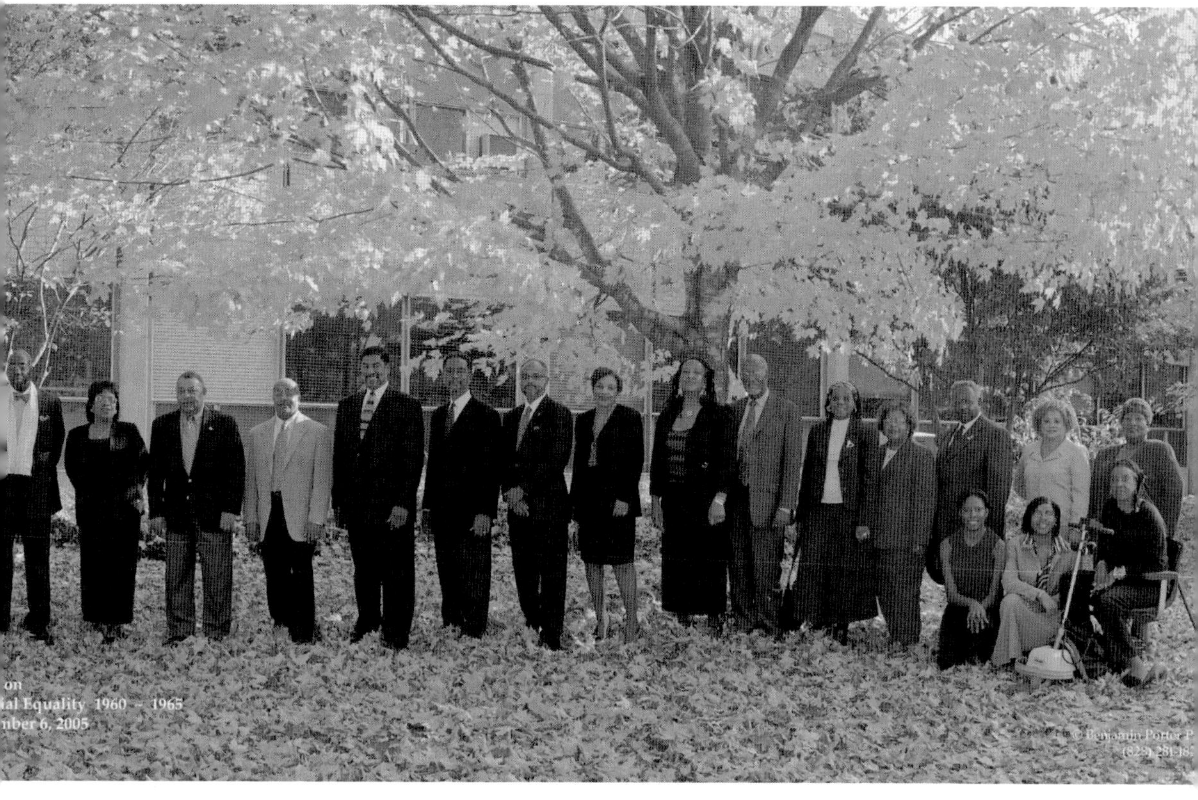

to celebrate the 50th anniversary of ASCORE's founding. (Photograph by Benjamin Porter, courtesy of Benjamin Porter Panoramics.)

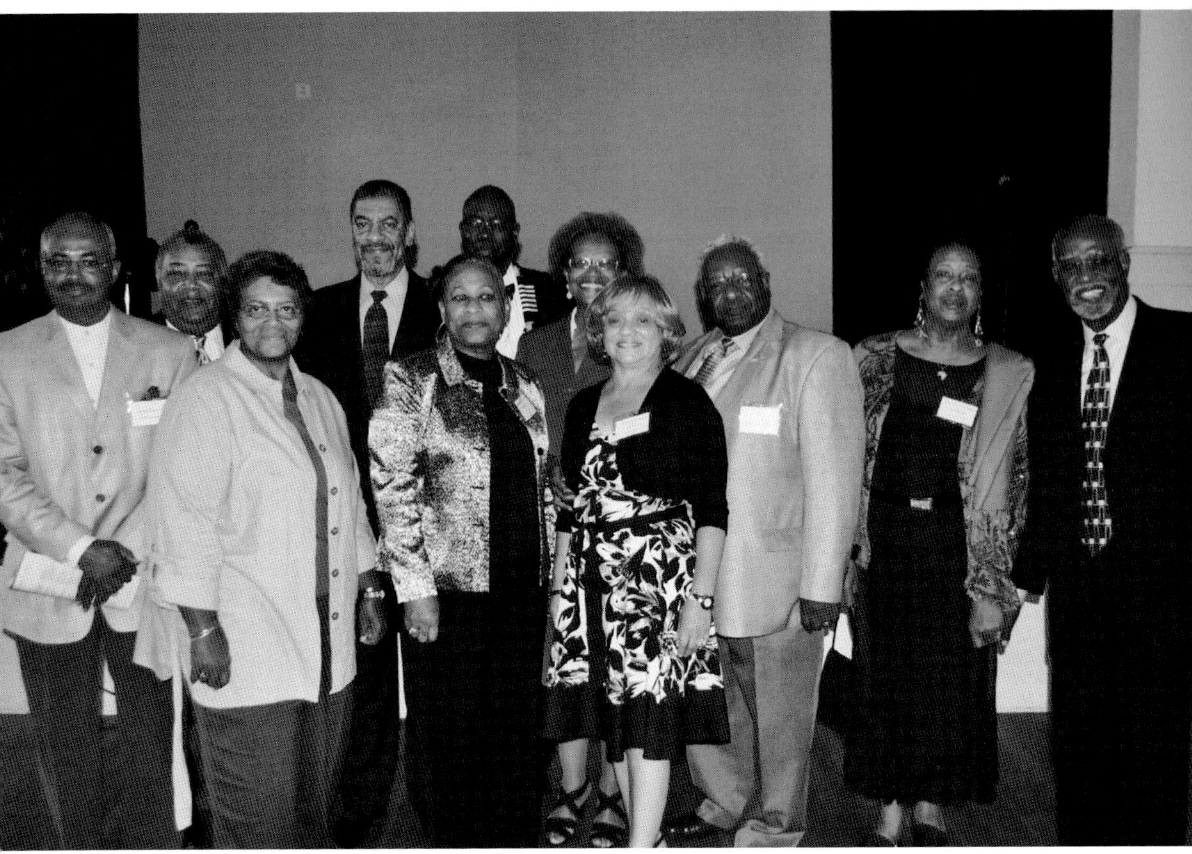

ASCORE

Inspired by the lunch counter sit-ins in Greensboro, an extraordinary group of students from Stephens-Lee High School (the black high school during segregation) formed the Asheville Student Committee on Racial Equality (ASCORE). The founding members included Charles Bates, James Burton, Jayne Burton, Marvin Chambers, Burnell Freeman, Patricia Greer, and James Ferguson, the group's first president. Even before forming ASCORE, these students had already been active in working on getting facilities at Stephens-Lee that were equivalent to the all-white Lee Edwards High School. Rosetta Hill, Niolus Avery, Leah Butler, Lloyd McCoyd, Ruben Dailey, Harold Epps, and, most notably, local jeweler William Roland mentored and supported the group, regularly meeting in the back of Roland's store on Market Street. ASCORE is unique in American civil rights history in that it was comprised exclusively of high school students. Almost all other student civil rights groups at the time were at colleges. ASCORE carefully chose its battles, first tackling segregated lunch counters at Kress, Woolworth's, and Newberry's. The owner of the Kenilworth Drug Store was so against desegregation that he removed all of the stools and booths to prevent the students from ever sitting down. With success at the other drugstores, the group then turned to other public facilities such as Pack Library, the S&W Cafeteria, and Aston Park. Etta May Whitner became ASCOREs second president and was the first African American student admitted to Asheville-Biltmore College, the predecessor of UNC Asheville. Barbara Turman, who later married James Ferguson, succeeded Whitner. As the students graduated, they recruited and trained younger classmates. By the time ASCORE disbanded in 1965, some 100 students had gone through its ranks, the vast majority of whom went on to college and had extraordinary careers around the country, including many who became lifelong leaders in the Asheville community. (Courtesy of the *Urban News*.)

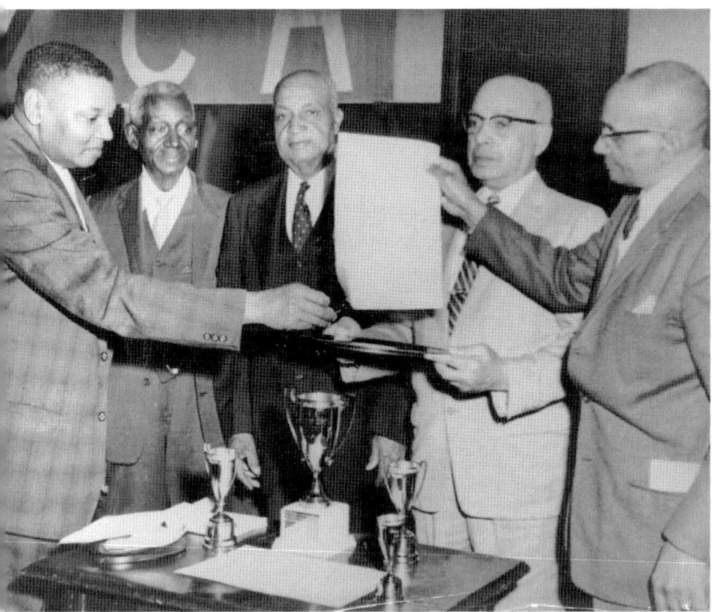

Ruben J. Dailey
Ruben Dailey (far left) was the first African American attorney to practice in Buncombe County. After serving in the Navy in World War II, Dailey became a highly respected trial attorney and spent much of his career ensuring compliance in Western North Carolina with the 1954 *Brown v. Board of Education of Topeka* decision, which ended school segregation. In 1969, Dailey was the first African American elected to the Asheville City Council, and was reelected in 1971. (Courtesy of the North Carolina Collection, Pack Library.)

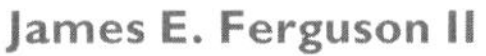

James E. Ferguson II
After serving as the first president of ASCORE, James Ferguson went on to law school and worked with noted attorney Julius Chambers and others on the landmark case *Swann v. Charlotte-Mecklenburg Board of Education*, regarding school busing. Ferguson also served as the defense attorney for the noted "Wilmington 10" civil rights case and as a "private prosecutor" in the racially charged case against Henry Marro's killer in Oxford, North Carolina, made famous in Tim Tyson's book *Blood Done Signed My Name*. Ferguson, a nationally recognized attorney, has been honored as one of the country's top 10 litigators in several categories for many years. (Courtesy of Ferguson, Chambers & Sumter, PA.)

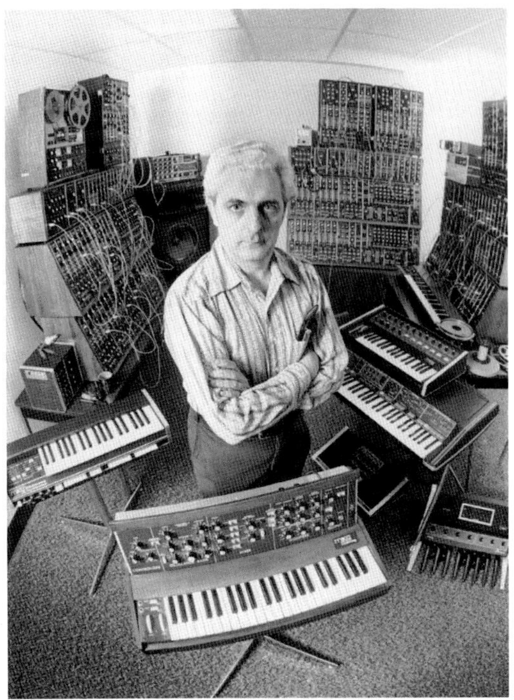

Robert Arthur Moog
In the 1960s, Bob Moog created a revolutionary new electronic synthesizer, the first of its kind to be modular, have a keyboard, and be relatively compact. His instruments transformed rock music and are featured on such noted albums as the groundbreaking *Switched-On Bach* and the Beatles' *Abbey Road*. His later invention, the MiniMoog, was portable, great for live concerts, and made electronic synthesizers a ubiquitous instrument in modern music. He moved to Asheville in 1978 to restart his company and later joined the faculty at UNC Asheville. Moog died in 2005, but Moog Music, based in Asheville, continues his pioneering legacy. (Courtesy of Moog Music Inc.)

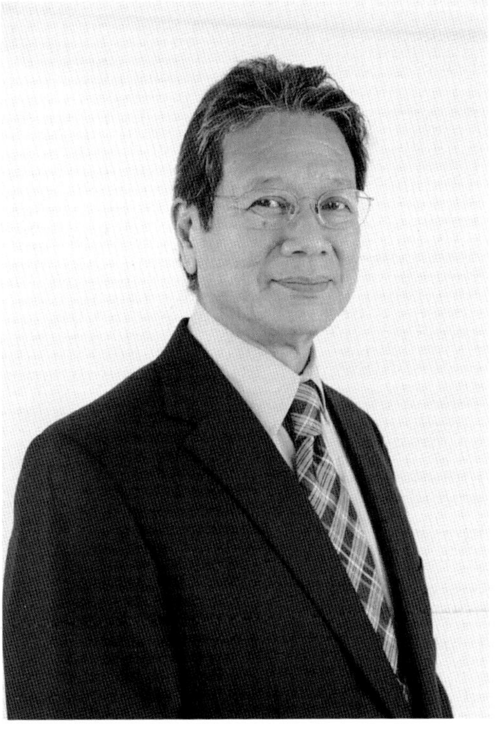

Oscar Wong
Widely regarded as the "godfather" of the modern craft beer movement in Asheville, Oscar Wong was born in Jamaica in 1940 and immigrated to the United States to study engineering at the University of Notre Dame. After a 30-year career in engineering, Wong retired to Asheville in 1994 and began Highland Brewing in the basement of Barley's Taproom "as a hobby." Wong's hobby became the progenitor of Asheville's nationally recognized craft brewing industry. (Courtesy of UNC Asheville Communication and Marketing.)

CHAPTER TWO

Biltmore and its Continuing Legacy

When George Washington Vanderbilt II came to Asheville in 1888, he saw an opportunity, an opportunity not only to build a country estate but also an opportunity to restore the land in these ancient mountains. While Vanderbilt is readily known as a man of letters, he was also an avid outdoorsman and conservationist. Much of Western North Carolina had been over farmed and over timbered in the 19th century. The mountains were bald and the valleys were rutted. Vanderbilt knew it would take centuries to restore the land, but, if not now, when?

Vanderbilt enjoyed nearly 20 years at Biltmore before his untimely passing. His wife, Edith, would carry on the work her husband started and, surprisingly, become a woman of agriculture in her own right. The operations of the estate would come to be managed by a friend and local attorney who helped Biltmore blossom, even in times of hardship. Ownership of the estate eventually passed to the Vanderbilts' only daughter, Cornelia, who, during the Great Depression, opened the house to the public for the first time. Soon thereafter, Cornelia divorced her first husband, John Cecil, a British aristocrat, and left for Europe with their two sons, never to return. John remained and, after World War II, once again welcomed the public back to Biltmore. It was not until his younger son William took over the operations of the house and gardens and his older son George took over the agricultural operations that the Biltmore Estate became a centerpiece of the Asheville economy.

Biltmore's legacy runs even deeper. Many of the architects and craftsmen who came to Biltmore stayed and left their own indelible marks on Asheville. Much of the Asheville skyline is credit to these great artists. Likewise, Vanderbilt's commitment to the land, through thoughtful preservation and cultivation, resulted in the birth of scientific forestry as a discipline in the United States. Modern American forestry traces its roots directly to Biltmore. For locals and tourists alike, Biltmore's legacy remains strong.

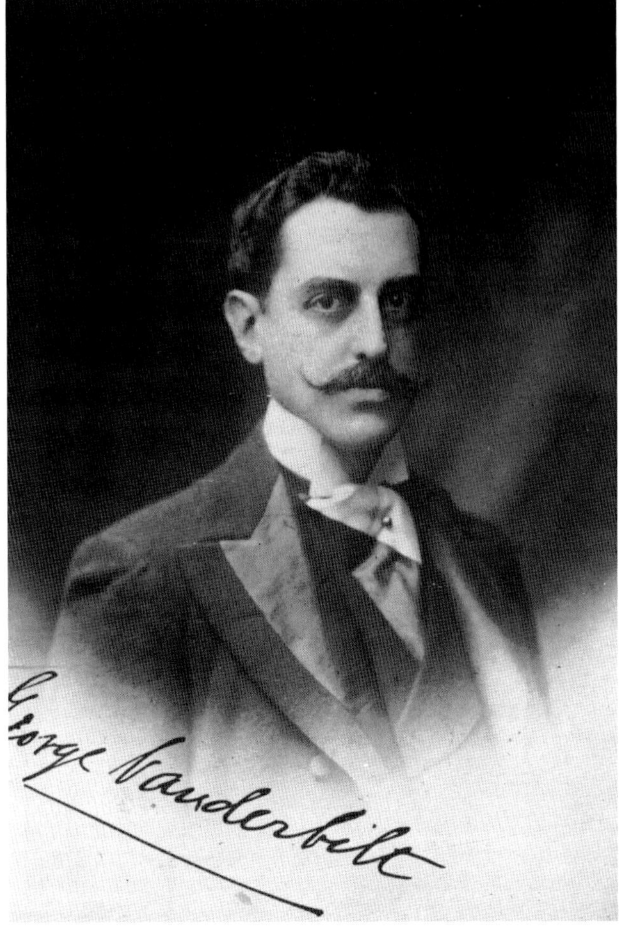

George Washington Vanderbilt II

The youngest grandson of railroad magnate Cornelius Vanderbilt, George W. Vanderbilt came to Asheville for the first time in 1888 with his mother, Maria. Drawn to Asheville because of its reputation as a health destination, George brought his mother to the mountains in hopes of helping her to find relief for her chronic malaria. During their visit, Vanderbilt fell in love with Western North Carolina and began to think about building a country estate outside of Asheville. In a matter of months, Vanderbilt acquired some 2,000 acres for his new estate, which eventually grew to a mammoth 125,000 acres by the time of his death. Vanderbilt retained Richard Morris Hunt to design the house and Frederick Law Olmstead to design the grounds. After six years of construction, Vanderbilt welcomed his first guests on Christmas Eve 1895 to the 250-room chateau, the largest house ever built in America. Three years later, at age 35, Vanderbilt married Edith Stuyvesant Dresser, and they had one daughter, Cornelia, in 1900. Thanks to his inherited wealth, Vanderbilt was never really part of the family business, and became a man of letters. He traveled extensively and read and spoke several languages fluently. While the Vanderbilts had several homes throughout the East Coast and in Europe, Asheville was their primary residence. George and Edith were active members of the community, supporting such endeavors as the Young Men's Institute, a YMCA-like facility built by the African American business community with Vanderbilt's financial support. Likewise, George invested heavily in Biltmore to make it a self-sustaining and profitable estate. George died unexpectedly in March 1914 from latent complications from an appendectomy. With Biltmore being the state's most visited tourist attraction, Vanderbilt's legacy in Asheville remains great. (Courtesy of the National Archives and Ramsey Library Special Collections.)

Edith Stuyvesant Dresser Vanderbilt Gerry

A descendent of Peter Stuyvesant, the first governor of Dutch Colonial New York, Edith Stuyvesant Dresser married George W. Vanderbilt in June 1898 in a small ceremony in Paris. Upon their arrival at Biltmore after their European honeymoon, the Vanderbilts were welcomed by the Biltmore community with great fanfare and festivities. Much to the surprise of many, Edith was very down-to-earth and immediately began to build close relationships with the staff at Biltmore. She was known to often visit families throughout the estate with maternity baskets for new mothers, as well as food and supplies for the sick. She gave Christmas gifts to every employee and their children at the annual estate Christmas party. Within the larger community, she developed a particular interest in preserving and advancing Appalachian handcrafts as part of Biltmore Estate Industries. Edith was shocked and devastated by her husband's unexpected death in 1914. Nonetheless, she persevered and continued to run Biltmore as an active working estate. She turned to local attorney Junius G. Adams to help her reorganize the estate's finances, including the sale of much of the land to the federal government to create Pisgah National Forest and the creation of the residential development Biltmore Forest. She had a surprising interest in agriculture and served as the first female president of the North Carolina State Fair and the North Carolina Agricultural Society. In 1925 she married Sen. Peter Gerry of Rhode Island, whose famous contribution to American politics was "gerrymandering," the reorganization of political districts to favor a particular party. Edith died in 1958. (Courtesy of The Biltmore Company.)

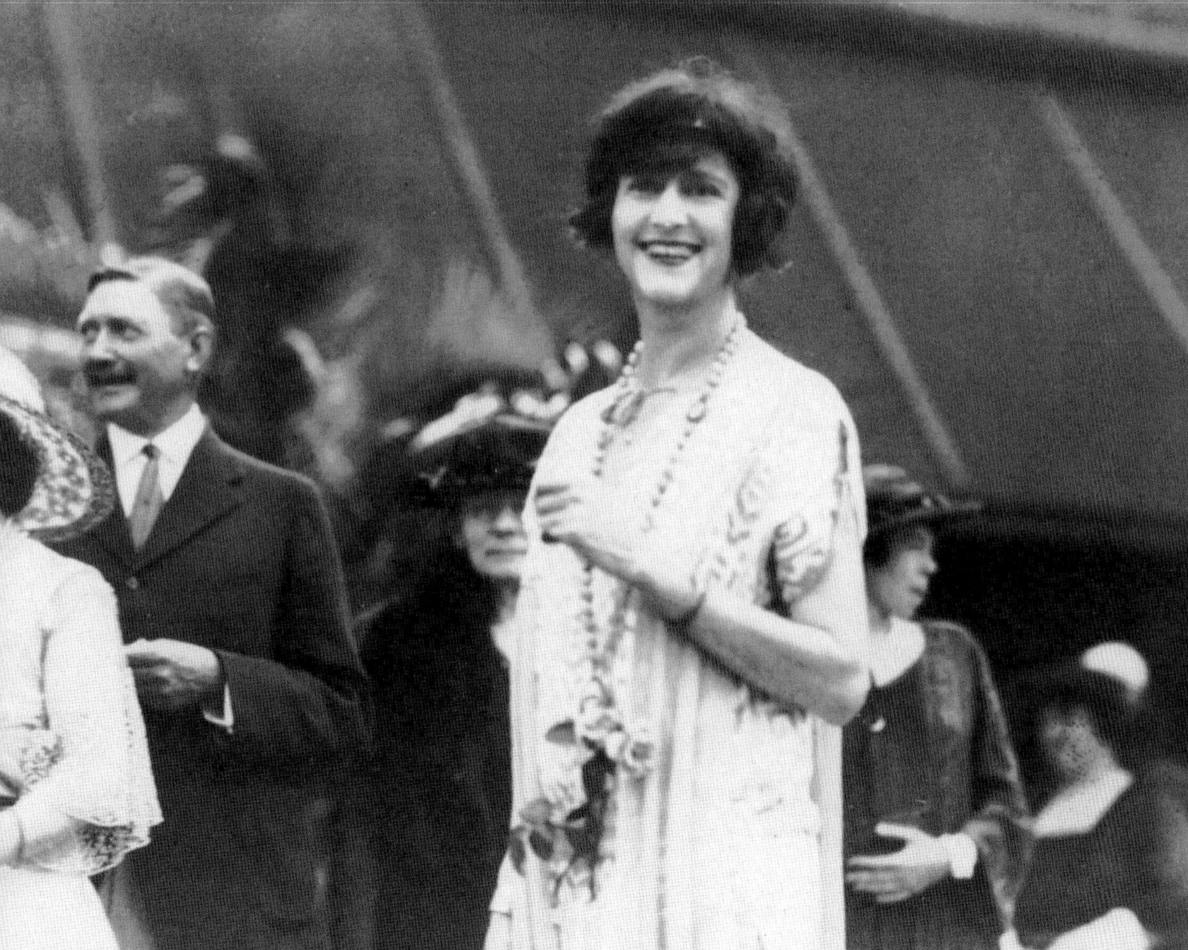

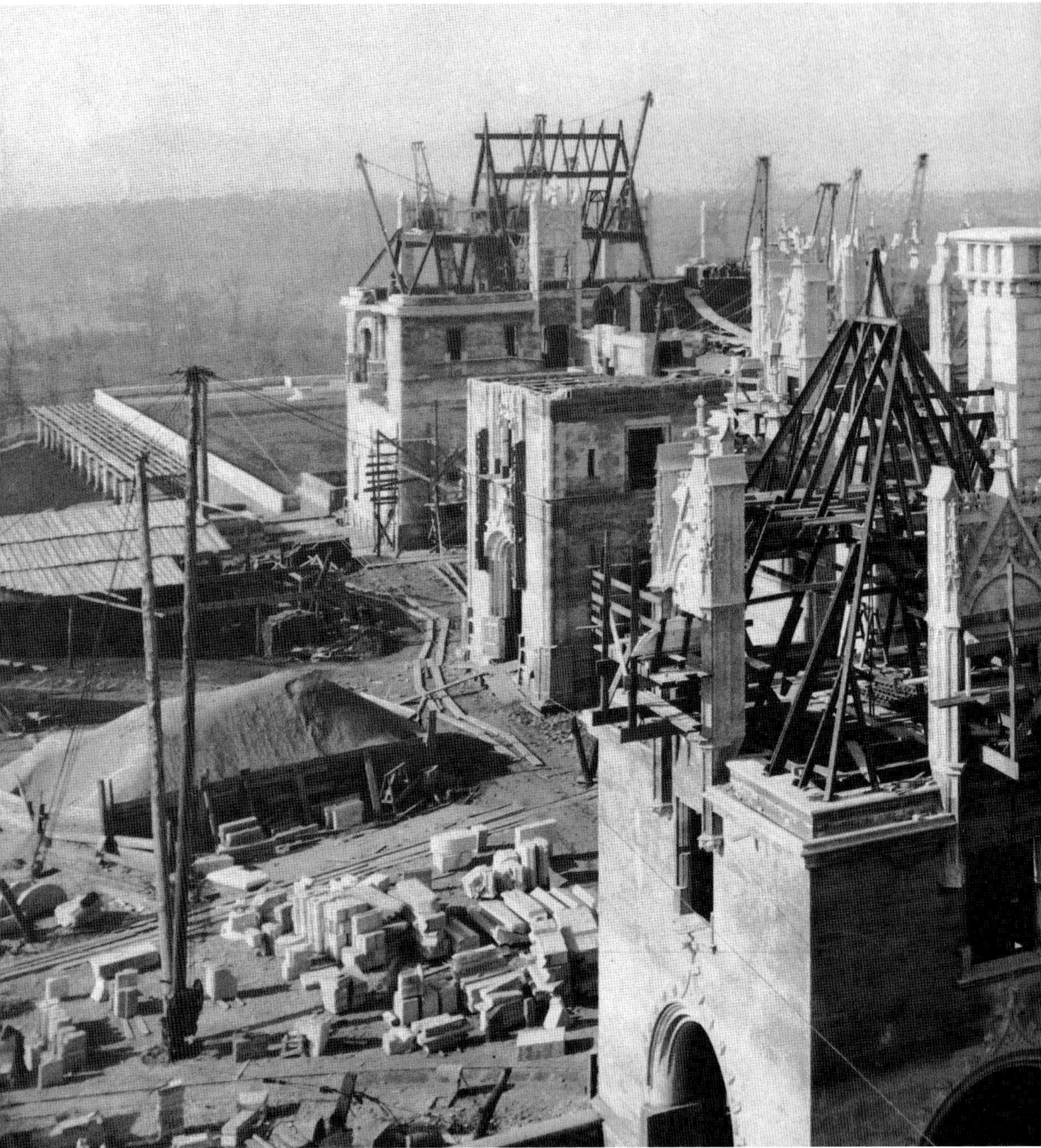

Biltmore House
Construction began on Biltmore in 1889. To accommodate the delivery of materials, such as the nearly 10 million pounds of Indiana limestone, George Vanderbilt had a railroad spur built onto the estate from the main line in Asheville. Hundreds of craftsmen, masons, trades workers, and artists worked

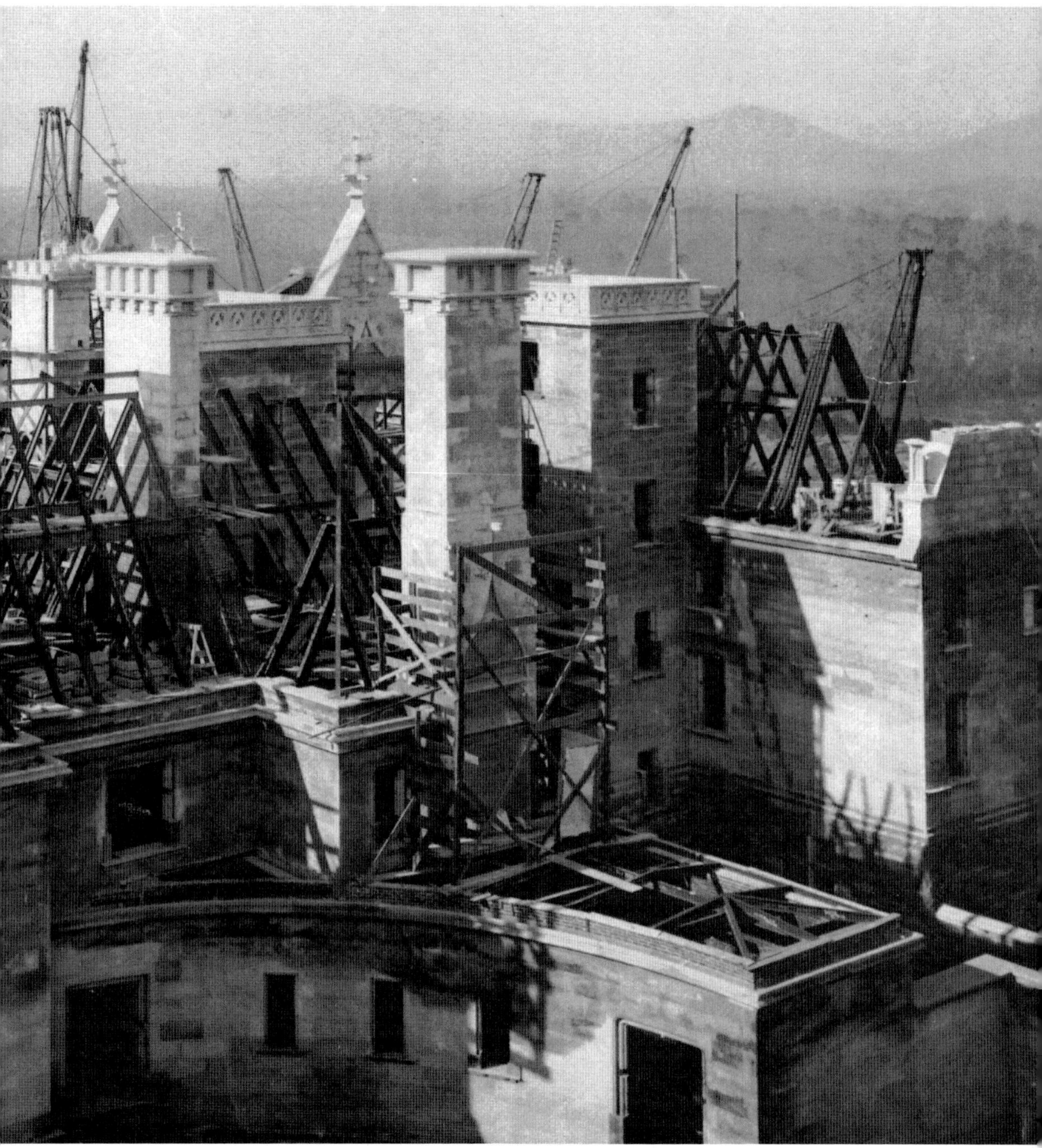

for the better part of six years to build the massive chateau and landscape the enormous estate. The finished home contains more than four acres of floor space, including 35 bedrooms, 43 bathrooms, and 65 fireplaces. (Courtesy of The Biltmore Company.)

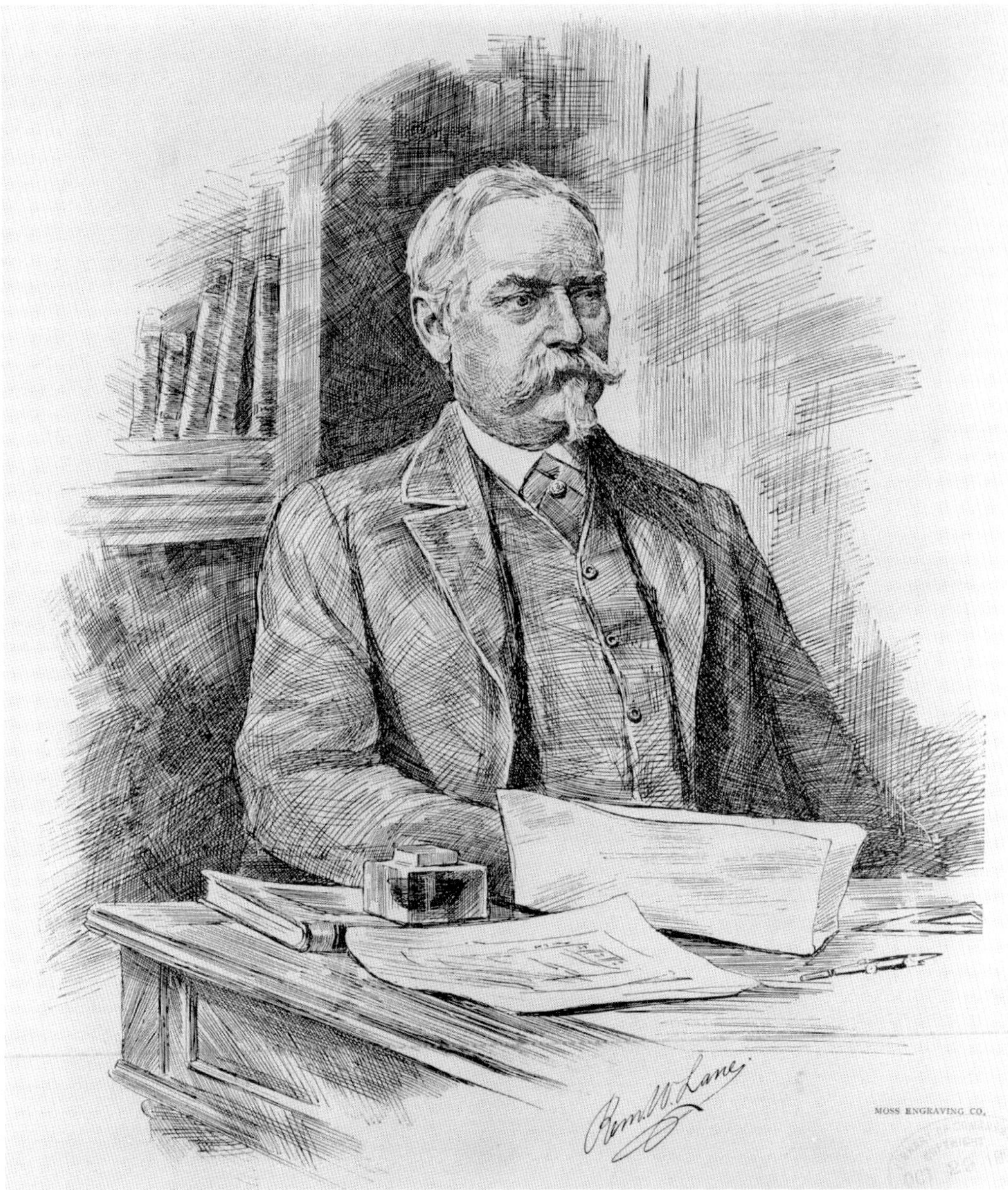

Richard Morris Hunt
One of America's most important architects, Richard Morris Hunt, noted for such significant structures as the New York Tribune Building and the base of the Statue of Liberty, came to Asheville in the late 1880s at the behest of George W. Vanderbilt. Vanderbilt wanted Hunt to design a country estate for him. What emerged was the largest house ever built in the United States, at 175,000 square feet, and a structure that is now considered a masterpiece in American architecture. Biltmore became Hunt's last and most beloved project. He died a few months before its completion. The work was finished by his son, Richard H. Hunt, and the on-site architect, Richard Sharp Smith. (Courtesy of the Library of Congress.)

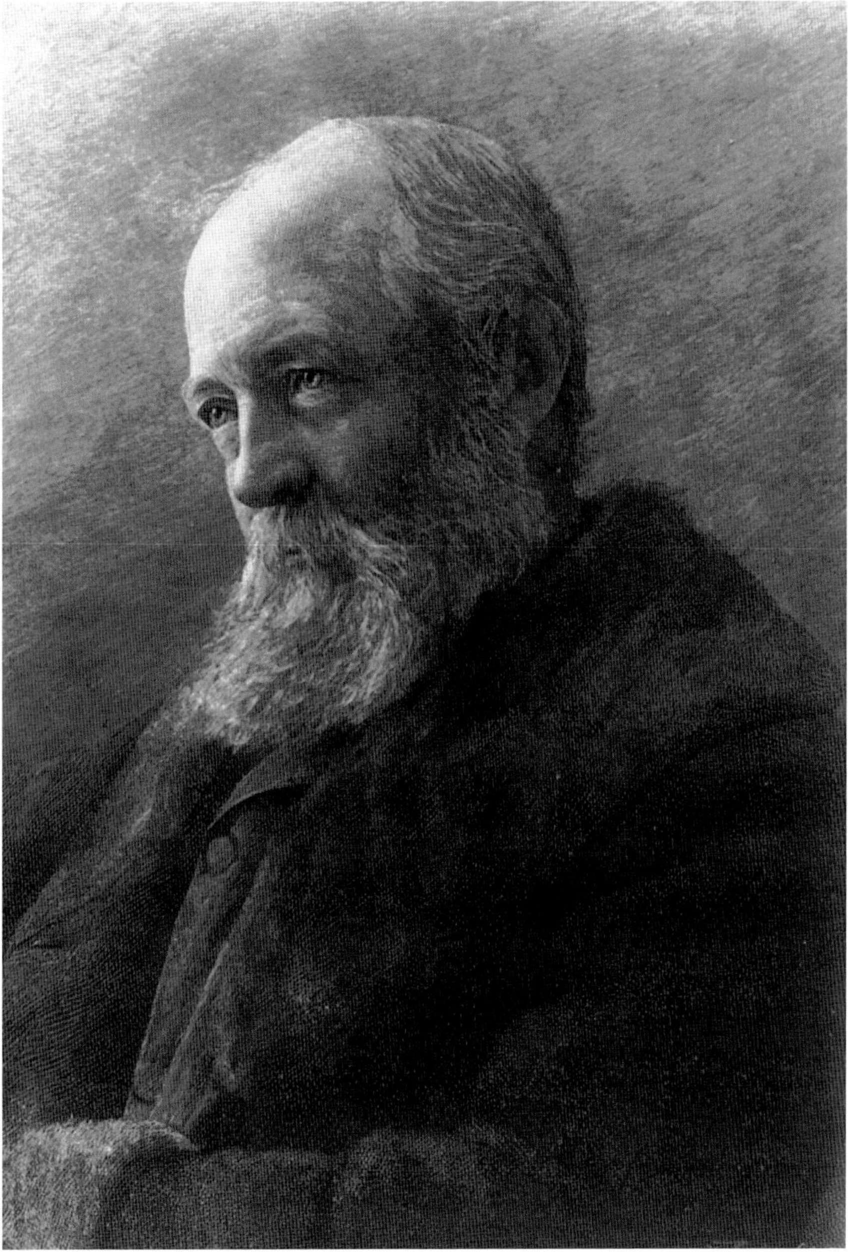

Frederick Law Olmstead

Often regarded as the founder of American landscape architecture, Frederick Law Olmstead had already left a significant mark on the national landscape when George W. Vanderbilt brought him to Asheville in 1888. By this time Olmstead had designed numerous parks, such as New York's Central Park, Boston's Emerald Necklace, and the grounds of the US Capitol. Olmstead designed for Vanderbilt an astonishing series of formal gardens and a 25-acre natural park surrounding Biltmore House, and replanted much of the forests on other parts of the property. Scholars consider the three-mile approach road to Biltmore House to be one of Olmstead's greatest masterpieces. (Courtesy of the Library of Congress.)

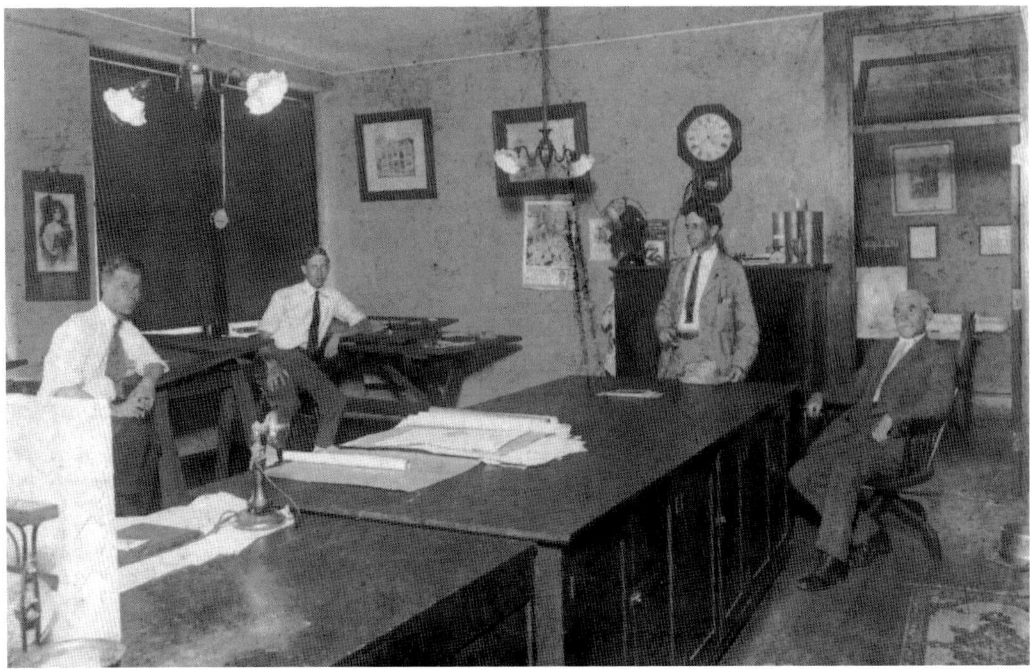

Richard Sharp Smith

English-born architect Richard Sharp Smith (right) came to Asheville in 1889 under assignment from Richard Morris Hunt to serve as the supervising architect during the construction of Biltmore. Even before the completion of Biltmore, Vanderbilt hired Smith to design a number of other structures around the estate, and in 1896, Smith took up permanent residence in Asheville and opened his own firm. In his first five years of business, Smith had more than 60 commissions, including numerous structures in Biltmore Village, the Young Men's Institute, several homes in Montford and Chestnut Hill, and the Vance Monument, an Egyptian obelisk to honor former governor Zebulon Vance on Pack Square. Smith's commissions became so numerous that he brought on Albert Heath Carrier as a partner in 1906. The Smith & Carrier firm had more than 700 commissions before Smith's passing in 1924. Though he worked in a variety of styles, including Tudor Revival, Colonial Revival, Classical Revival, and Craftsman, Smith took a unique approach to each project such that his "signature" remains strongly evident in the Asheville vernacular. From churches and civic buildings to commercial structures and residences, Smith left an indelible mark on the face of Asheville. (Above, courtesy of the North Carolina Collection, Pack Library; right, Courtesy of The Biltmore Company.)

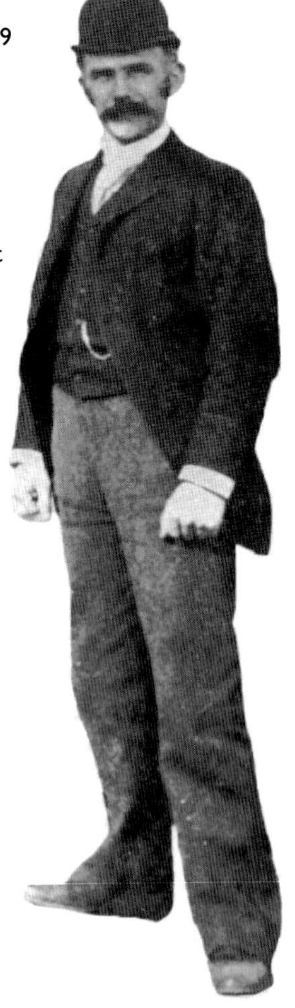

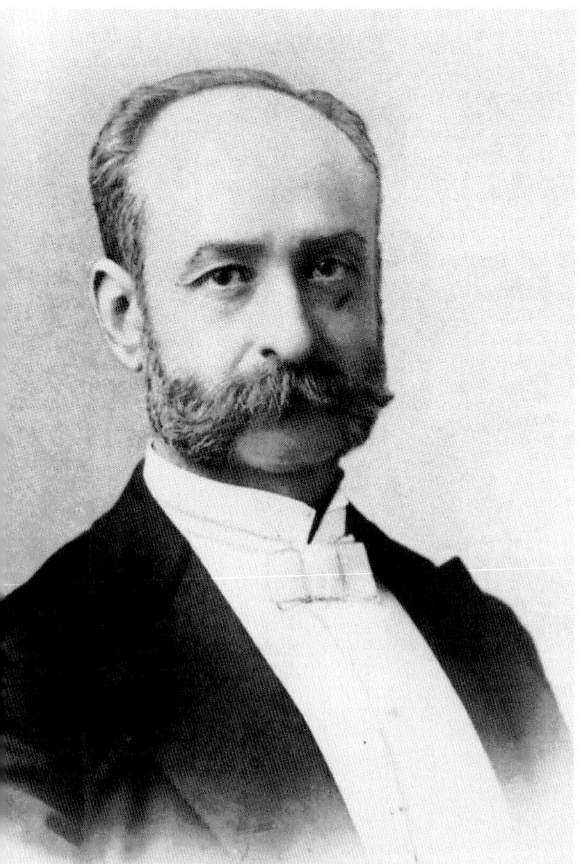

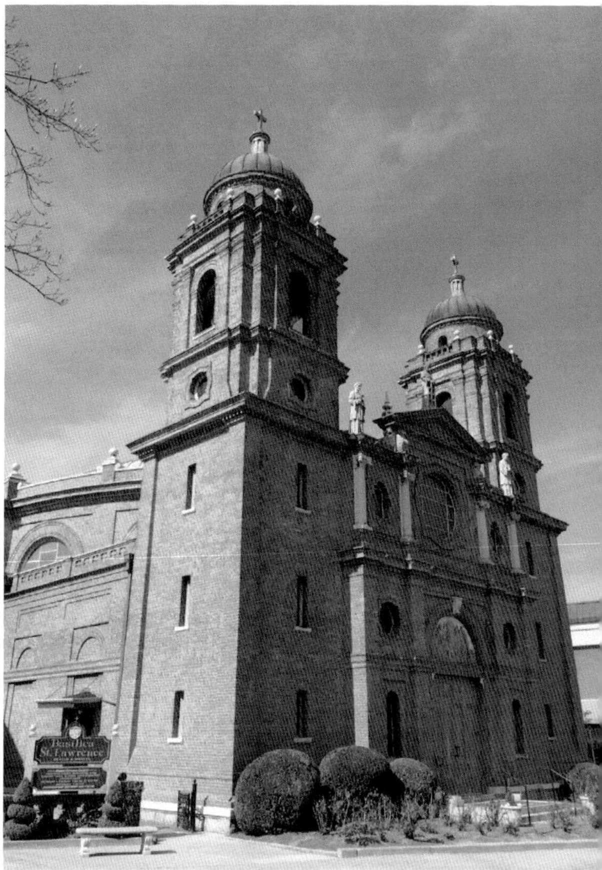

Rafael Guastavino

Spanish-born architect Rafael Guastavino immigrated with his son Rafael Jr. in 1881 to the United States, where they founded the Guastavino Fireproof Construction Company. Guastavino had developed a system, based on ancient techniques, for constructing self-supporting arches and architectural vaults made of interlocking terra-cotta tiles. Over the next 20 years, the Guastavinos were involved in more than 1,000 major construction projects. Many were quite prominent, including Grand Central Terminal, Carnegie Hall, and George Vanderbilt's Biltmore chateau. Work on this project led Guastavino to move permanently to Black Mountain, just outside of Asheville. After the completion of Biltmore, Guastavino turned his attention to building a larger Catholic church for Asheville and asked colleague Richard Sharp Smith to help him design and build St. Lawrence Catholic Church (now Basilica) downtown. The central feature of the Spanish-revival church is an enormous elliptical dome, built with Guastavino's technique, which is believed to be the largest freestanding elliptical dome in North America. Guastavino died in 1908, and his son completed the church shortly thereafter. Guastavino is interred in a crypt in one of the chapels. (Left, courtesy of the North Carolina State Historic Preservation Office; right, photograph by Aaron Dahlstrom.)

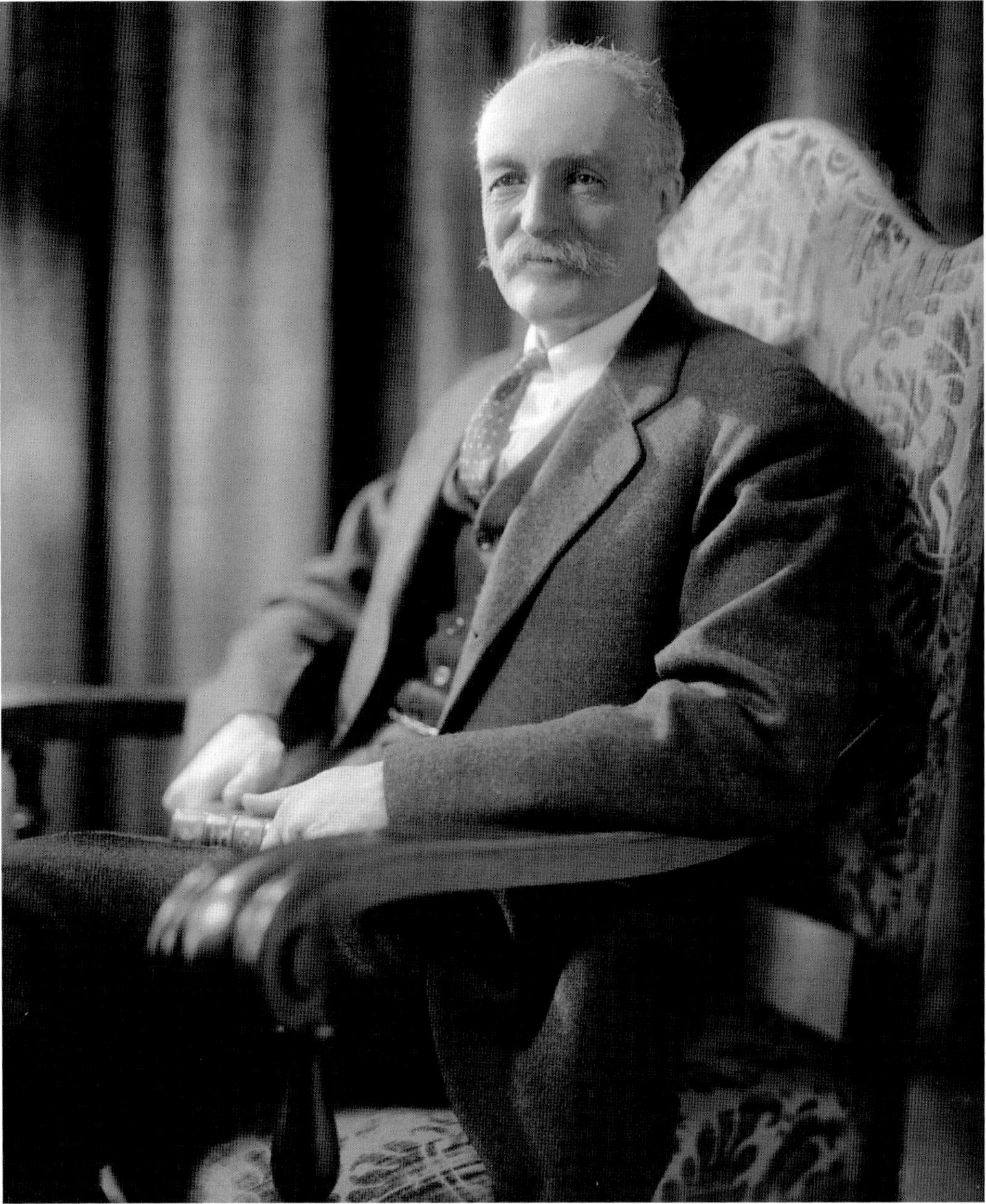

Gifford Pinchot

Gifford Pinchot was the first American-born forester. Born in 1865 to a wealthy family in Connecticut, Pinchot was encouraged by his father to study the burgeoning field of forestry. Noted German forester Sir Dietrich Brandis guided him to enroll in the Ecole Nationale Forestiere in France. Upon his return, Pinchot was recommended by Frederick Law Olmstead to serve as the forester for George Vanderbilt's estate, Biltmore. Pinchot served in that role from 1892 until 1895, when Carl Schenck succeeded him. Pinchot would then go on to become chief of the US Division of Forestry in 1898, the first chief of the US Forest Service in 1905, the founder of the National Conservation Association, and, later, governor of Pennsylvania. (Courtesy of the Library of Congress.)

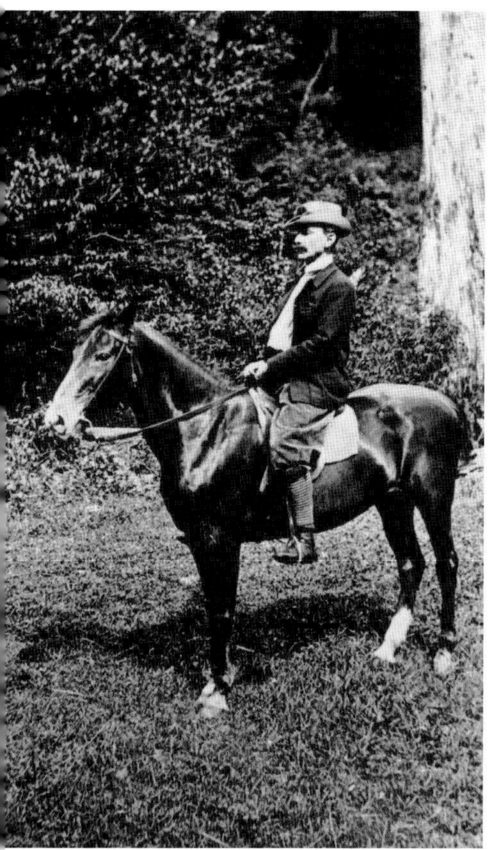

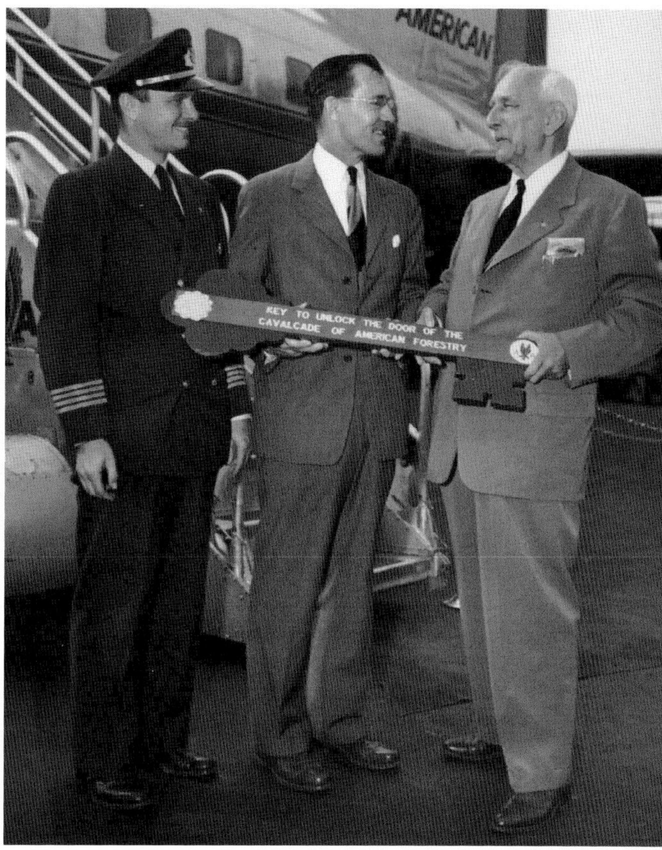

Carl A. Schenck

Carl Schenck (left, and far right) was one of the pioneers of the discipline of professional forestry in North America. German-born and educated in forestry at the Universities of Tubingen and Giessen, he came under the tutelage of Sir Dietrich Brandis, the foremost forester at the time. Upon earning his doctorate in 1895, Schenck was recommended by Brandis and Gifford Pinchot, the first forester of George Vanderbilt's Biltmore Estate, to take over Pinchot's role as forester. Schenck was now one of only three professional foresters in the United States (Pinchot and German Bernard Fernow were the other two). Schenck's charge was to manage the forest on Vanderbilt's more than 125,000-acre estate as a profitable and sustainable operation using techniques heretofore unused in the United States. With Vanderbilt's permission and financial support, Schenck established the Biltmore Forest School, the first of its kind in the country. During its 15 years of operation, the school graduated more than 300 students and helped establish scientific forestry in America. Unfortunately, Schenck's and Vanderbilt's relationship did not end amicably. In an effort to reign in the enormous expense of operating Biltmore, Vanderbilt informed Schenck in 1909 that he could no longer fund the school. Schenck left Biltmore and returned to Germany in 1914 to serve as an officer on the Russian front in World War I. In the years after the war, Schenck traveled the world lecturing and giving forest tours. He returned to Germany in 1939 with the onset of World War II. After the war, the United States Military Government appointed him chief forester over the new German state of Hesse. Schenck returned to the United States in 1951 for a reunion of the Biltmore Forest School and the dedication of several forests in his honor. North Carolina State University also presented him an honorary doctorate of forest science in recognition of his pioneering accomplishments. Schenck died a few years later, in 1955, at the age of 87. (Left, courtesy of Ramsey Library Special Collections; right, courtesy of the North Carolina Collection, Pack Library.)

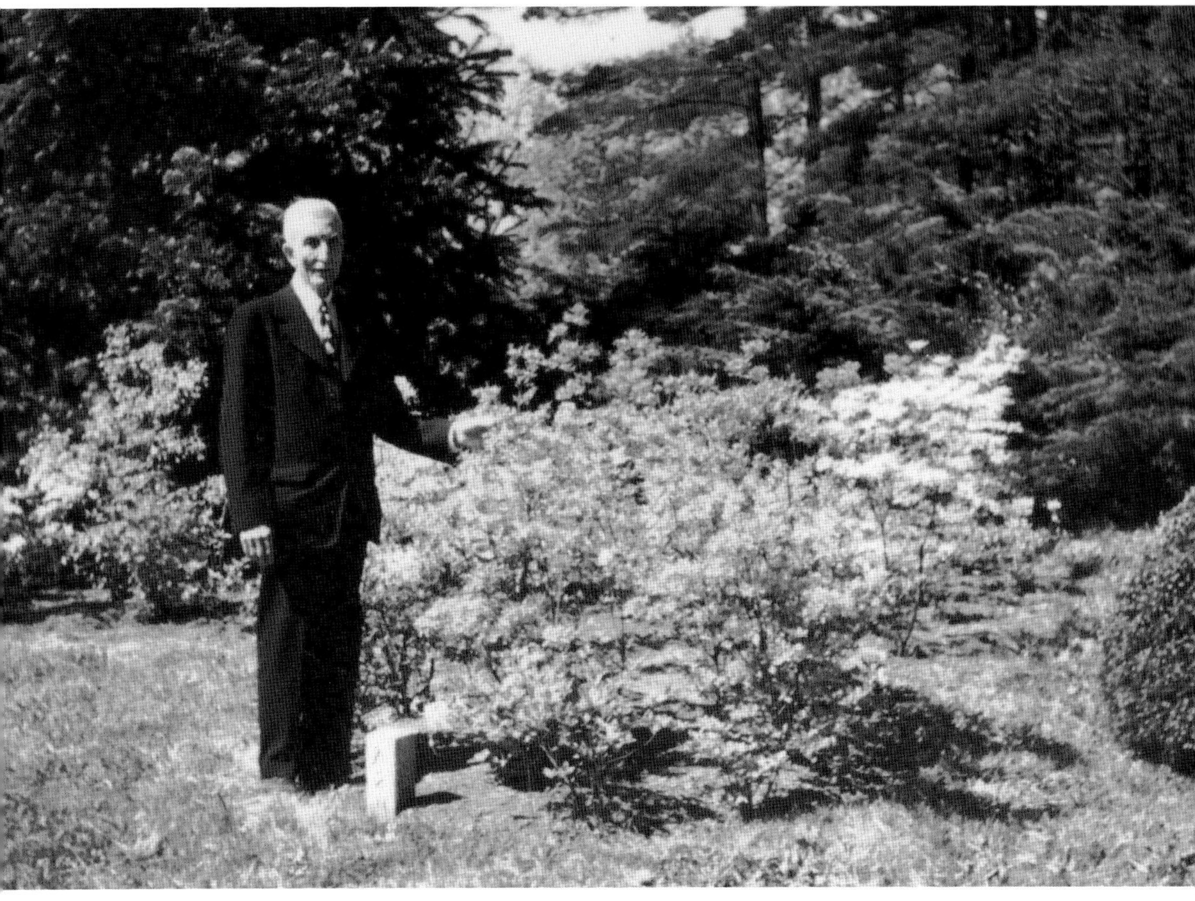

Chauncey D. Beadle

The Canadian-born Chauncey Beadle was hired in 1890 by Frederick Law Olmstead as a botanist to propagate plans for Biltmore's landscapes. Beadle, 23 at the time, had already gained a reputation for his "encyclopedic knowledge" of plants. What was intended to be a temporary post became a 60-year career at Biltmore. In addition to his work on the estate, Beadle also worked with E.W. Grove to design the original Grove Park neighborhood and its later expansion in 1914. He also laid out the grounds for St. Mary's Episcopal Church and helped design the plan for Biltmore Forest, the affluent subdivision developed by Edith Vanderbilt after her husband's death. Beadle lived on Biltmore Estate for six decades until his passing in 1950. (Courtesy of The Biltmore Company.)

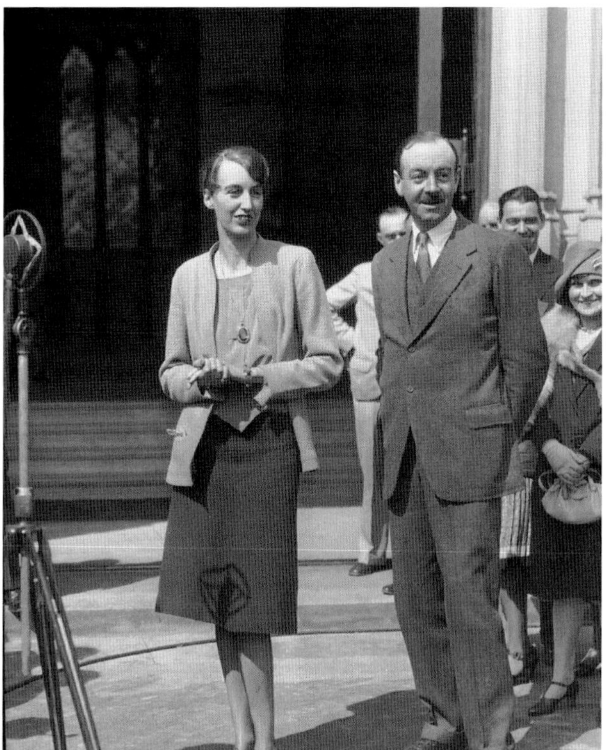

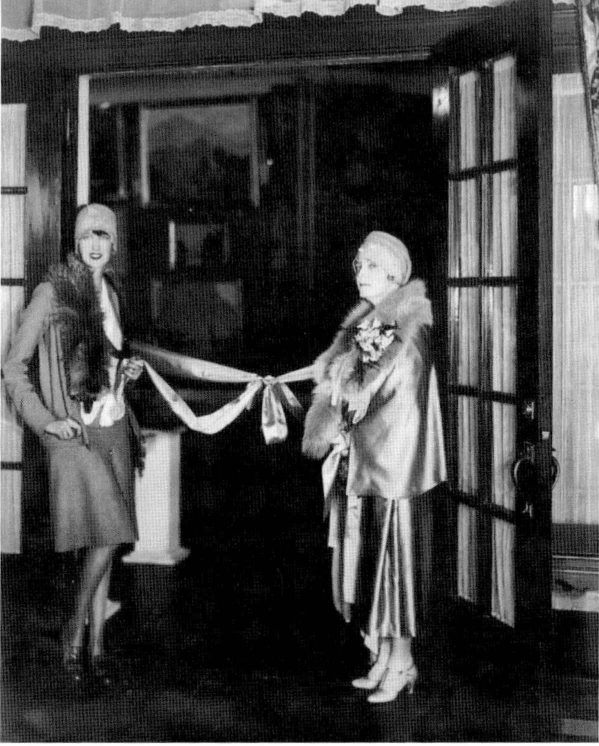

Cornelia and John Cecil
Cornelia Stuyvesant Vanderbilt (left in both images) and the Hon. John Francis Amherst Cecil (top right) were married in 1924 at All Souls Episcopal Church in Biltmore Village. Cornelia was the only daughter of Edith and George Vanderbilt. John was a British diplomat and a descendant of Lord Burghley, Queen Elizabeth I's closest advisor. In 1930, Cornelia and John, now the residents of Biltmore, opened the house to the public in an effort to spur tourism and help pay the bills. They had two sons, George and William, but then divorced in 1934. Cornelia remarried twice and spent the rest of her life in Europe until her passing in 1976. John lived the rest of his life at Biltmore until his death in 1954. (Top, courtesy of Ramsey Library Special Collections; bottom, courtesy of the North Carolina Collection, Pack Library.)

George Henry Vanderbilt Cecil

George Cecil, the oldest son of Cornelia and John Cecil, was born in 1925. After living abroad, he returned to Asheville in 1947 and worked for the Biltmore Company, which included the Biltmore House as a tourist destination and Biltmore Dairy Farms. Cecil married Nancy Owen, and they had six children. In 1978, the Biltmore Company was split into two entities, with George serving as president of Biltmore Dairy Farms, which included the dairy processing and distribution company and a prized herd of jersey cattle. In 1985, George sold the dairy operations to Pet Inc., and he and his son Jack transformed Biltmore Farms into a community development company, investing in commercial real estate, residential communities, and hotel operations. (Courtesy of Biltmore Farms.)

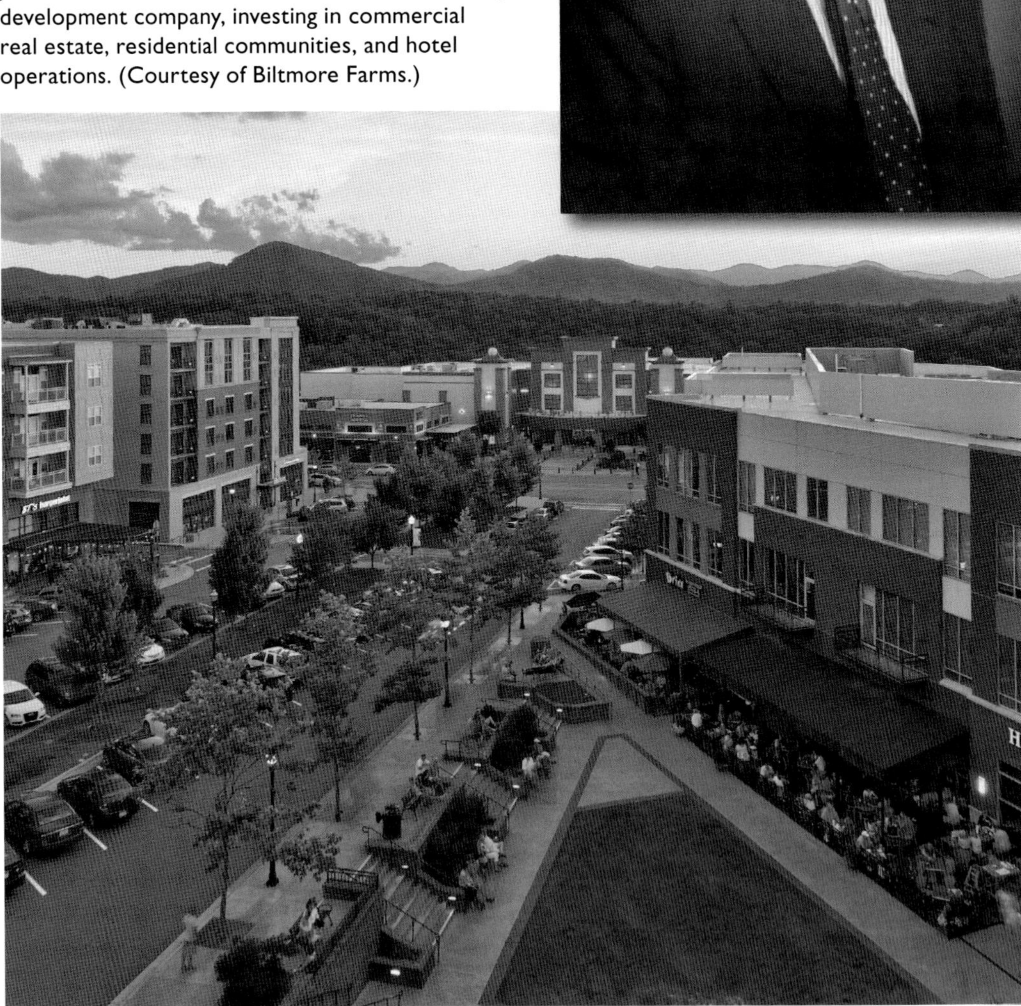

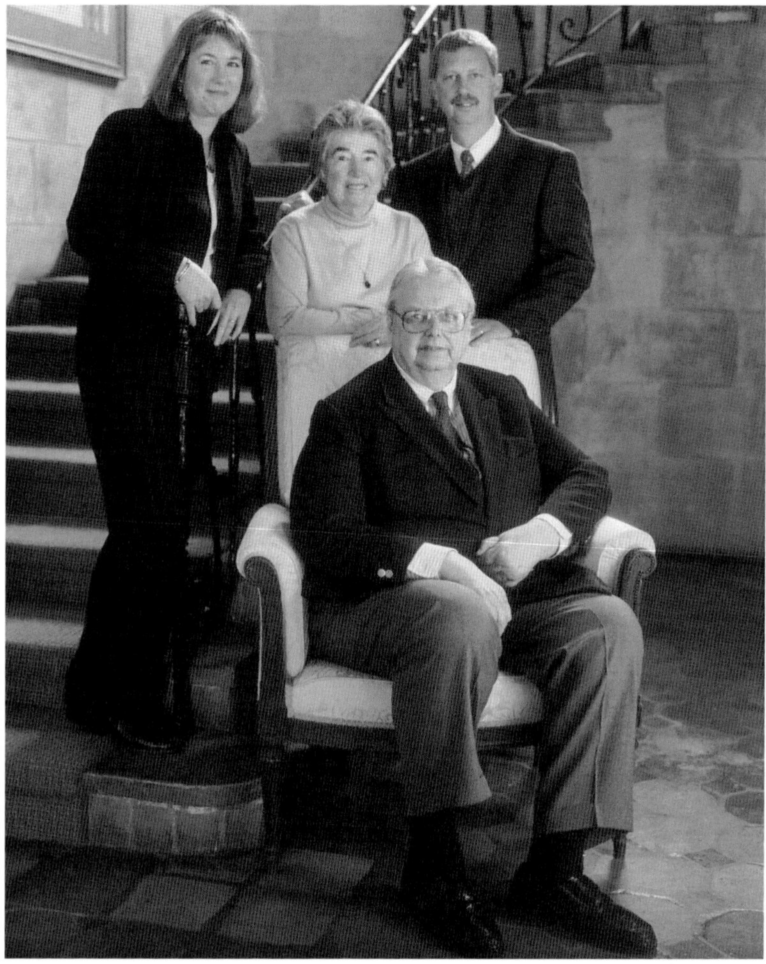

William Amherst Vanderbilt Cecil

The second son of Cornelia and John Cecil, William Cecil (seated) was born in 1928. Educated in prep schools in Europe, William joined the British Navy as a signalman in the final days of World War II. He returned to the United States in 1949 to study at Harvard, where he graduated a year early. His first post after college was with Chase National Bank in New York, where he eventually became an officer in the foreign department. Cecil married Mary Lee "Mimi" Ryan of New York (center), the first cousin of Jacqueline Kennedy. They had two children, William A.V. "Bill" Cecil Jr. (right) and Diana "Dini" Cecil Pickering (left). In the late 1950s, Cecil visited his family's Biltmore Estate to see what could be done about its struggling business model as a tourist attraction. In a chance encounter with David Rockefeller on the return trip, Rockefeller's doubts that Biltmore could be made profitable served to make Cecil more determined than ever. In 1959, he and his family moved to Asheville to continue to preserve Biltmore and make it a commercially viable historic estate. Upon moving to Asheville, Mrs. Cecil became actively involved in the community. She served on the boards of numerous local nonprofit institutions dedicated to the arts, the environment, and education. Mr. Cecil dug in at Biltmore, and, though it took nearly a decade, Biltmore turned its first profit in 1968, a mere $16.34. In the years that followed, Cecil transformed Biltmore into one of the nation's most visited historic attractions, and he was especially proud of the addition of the estate's winery in the 1980s. Cecil played a key leadership role in developing the region's multibillion-dollar tourist economy. He passed the leadership of Biltmore over to Bill Cecil Jr. in 1995 during the estate's centennial. (Courtesy of The Biltmore Company.)

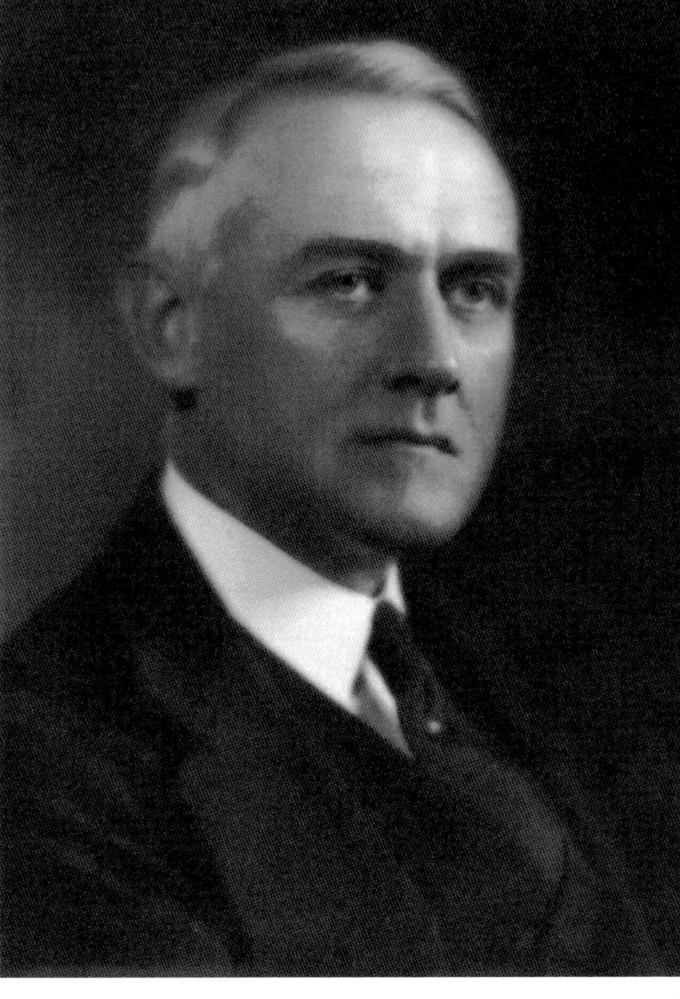

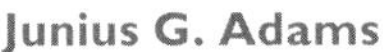

Junius G. Adams

One of Asheville's most prominent community leaders in the early 20th century, Junius Adams (or Judge Adams, as he was called locally) was one of the city's leading attorneys when, upon the untimely death of George Vanderbilt in 1914, he was chosen as the local attorney for the trustees of the Vanderbilt estate. Adams, his father, Joseph, and his brother John "Sneed" had built a successful law practice in the early 1900s representing such prominent clients as E.W. Grove in the development of Grove Park and the Grove Park Inn. After their father's death, the brothers eventually went into practice with James G. Merrimon and A. Hall Johnston, forming Merrimon, Adams & Johnston, which several years later became known as Adams, Hendon, Carson, Crow & Saenger. As the attorney for the estate of George Vanderbilt, Adams led a dramatic reorganization of Biltmore Estate's operations. This included the sale of more than 87,000 acres to the US government to create Pisgah National Forest, a project Vanderbilt had begun before his death. Adams also guided Vanderbilt's widow, Edith, to sell the entirety of Biltmore Village to George Stephens in 1920, and he recommended the development of 1,500 acres of estate lands into the Town of Biltmore Forest, which remains one of North Carolina's most exclusive communities. Adams became one of its first residents and its first mayor, which he remained from 1923 to 1929. During the Great Depression, which hit Asheville extremely hard, Adams was appointed president of the Biltmore Company and crafted a new plan for operations at Biltmore Estate, which included working with Vanderbilt's daughter Cornelia Cecil and her husband, John, to open the chateau for public tours for the first time. In the 1950s, he was instrumental in preventing a new municipal airport from being built on the estate, which would have crippled it as a tourist destination. Likewise, Adams also significantly expanded Biltmore's public dairy operations to make it the largest dairy in the Southeast. Adams's interest in dairy operations gained him state and national recognition, including an honorary doctorate of agriculture from North Carolina State University, induction in the American Jersey Cattlemen Hall of Fame, and having his portrait hung at the National Dairy Shrine. Adams remained an active community leader until his passing in 1962. (Courtesy of The Biltmore Company.)

CHAPTER THREE

Urban Patriots

Asheville emerged out of the Civil War physically unscathed. It was too remote for General Sherman to march through, and, beyond one battle and a few skirmishes, the city was relatively untouched by the war. Its people, however, suffered greatly, as many never returned home to their families. Asheville would struggle, like much of the South, throughout Reconstruction, but by the last quarter of the 19th century, the city emerged as one of the great resort communities in the United States. The coming of the railroad in 1880 made Asheville accessible. Drawn to the temperate climate and fresh mountain air, thousands came for their health, a holiday, or both. Many became so enamored with the city and its mountains that they stayed and made Asheville their home.

Most of Asheville's tourists were people of significant means. The middle class was still small, and the paid vacation was a concept still in the future. This wealth, and the prospect of more, made Asheville a boomtown in the early decades of the 20th century. Double-digit population growth marked each year. Commercial buildings and private homes sprung up everywhere. To manage (not stifle) this rampant growth, the city and the chamber of commerce initiated the "Program for Progress" in the mid-1920s. What emerged was a sort of "urban patriotism." To be for the plan was to be for Asheville. Simply put, Asheville thought it was on the path of civic greatness, and it had the numbers to back it up.

Even after the onset of the Great Depression and the catastrophic consequences suffered by the city, Ashevillians remained optimistic. They continued to support and advance their community, all with a sense of better things yet to come.

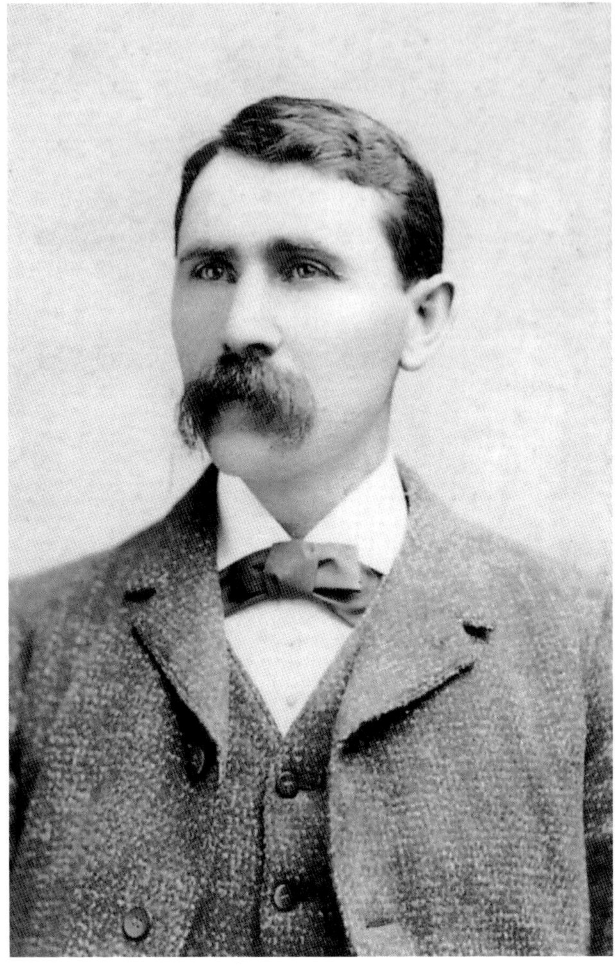

Edwin G. Carrier

Edwin Carrier (above and opposite bottom, right) and his family moved to Asheville after a happenstance visit when traveling between Michigan and Florida. Like so many, Carrier fell in love with not only the beauty of the region but also the financial opportunities available. Carrier had made his fortune in lumber in Michigan, but once in Asheville, he bought some 1,200 acres on the west side of the French Broad River opposite downtown Asheville for real estate development. Included in the purchase was the site of Col. Rueben Deaver's famed Deaver Springs Hotel, which had been destroyed by fire in 1862. Carrier was particularly drawn to the sulphur springs on the property, which were purported to have significant health benefits. In 1887, Carrier constructed a very modern brick hotel, which included such new conveniences as an elevator and electricity—powered by Carrier's own hydroelectric dam, the first in Western North Carolina. He also used the dam to power an electric streetcar system he had built to entice visitors in Asheville to visit his Carrier Springs Hotel (also known as the Sulphur Springs Hotel and the Belmont Hotel). At the same time, Carrier founded the West Asheville Improvement Company and began to develop Haywood Road as well as a nearby horse-racing track and park. West Asheville was incorporated as its own independent township with its own mayor and town council until it merged with Asheville in 1917. Despite being such an influential developer in Asheville, Carrier seemed to lose interest in the area after his hotel burned down in the 1890s, after which he returned to the lumber business. He died in 1927 and is buried in Asheville's Riverside Cemetery. (Courtesy of the North Carolina Collection, Pack Library.)

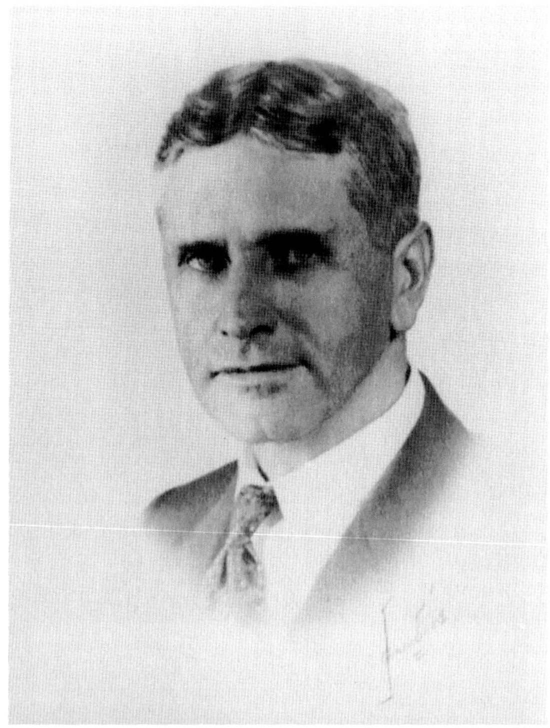

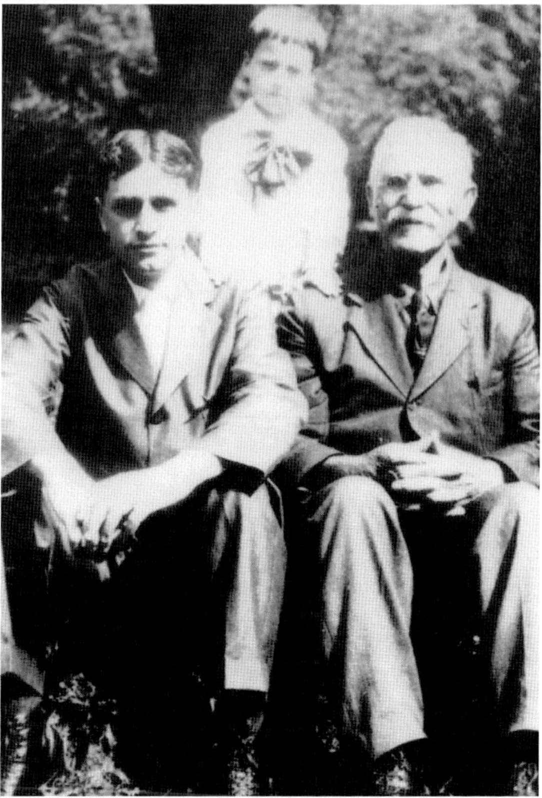

Albert Heath Carrier
Albert Heath Carrier (top and bottom left) is most known in Asheville for his long association with architect Richard Sharp Smith. The two went into practice together in 1906, and their firm, Smith & Carrier, went on to execute some 700 projects before Smith's death in 1924. It is unclear how Smith and Carrier became acquainted, but it is clear that Smith asked Carrier to be an equal partner in his established firm because of Smith's enormous workload. Carrier, who was 26 years Smith's junior, surprisingly did not carry on the work of the firm after Smith's death. He turned his attentions to real estate development in Asheville and Florida, as well as his longtime love of inventions. Carrier held several lucrative patents, including the now-common Carrier Quadrant Casement Adjuster, which allows the outsides of windows to be cleaned from the inside. (Both, courtesy of the North Carolina Collection, Pack Library.)

George Willis Pack

Born in New York state in 1831, George Pack came to Asheville in 1884 by way of Cleveland, where he had managed a highly successful lumber empire. He was drawn to Asheville because of its reputation as a health destination, due to his wife having suffered for many years from respiratory ailments. It is believed that Edward Aston encouraged Pack to move to Western North Carolina. Pack and his wife, Frances, became civically active, as they had done in every community in which they lived, and Pack became one of the city's most beloved philanthropists. During his years in Asheville he established the city's first free kindergarten, donated a permanent home to the Asheville Public Library, gave the city Aston Park and Montford Park, and donated generously to Mission Hospital, the YMCA, and numerous widows', orphans', and veterans' charities. Pack is often remembered for initiating the construction of an Egyptian obelisk in the center of town to honor his friend, former governor and US senator Zebulon Vance, just a few years after Vance's passing. Pack contributed $2,000 to the monument and led a campaign in the city to raise the additional $1,300. Vance was a Freemason, a member of Mt. Hermon Lodge 118 in Asheville, as was the monument architect, Richard Sharp Smith. The monument's ties to Freemasonry, and Pack's lead role in its construction, have often made it a monument of great mystery. Pack is most remembered for a generous but complicated land deal with Buncombe County that resulted in a new park adjacent to the Vance Monument and a new site for the county courthouse. In 1903, as a result of a public referendum, the people of Asheville renamed this historic center of the city Pack Square in honor of one of Asheville's greatest benefactors. Pack died only three years later on Long Island, New York. (Courtesy of the North Carolina Collection, Pack Library.)

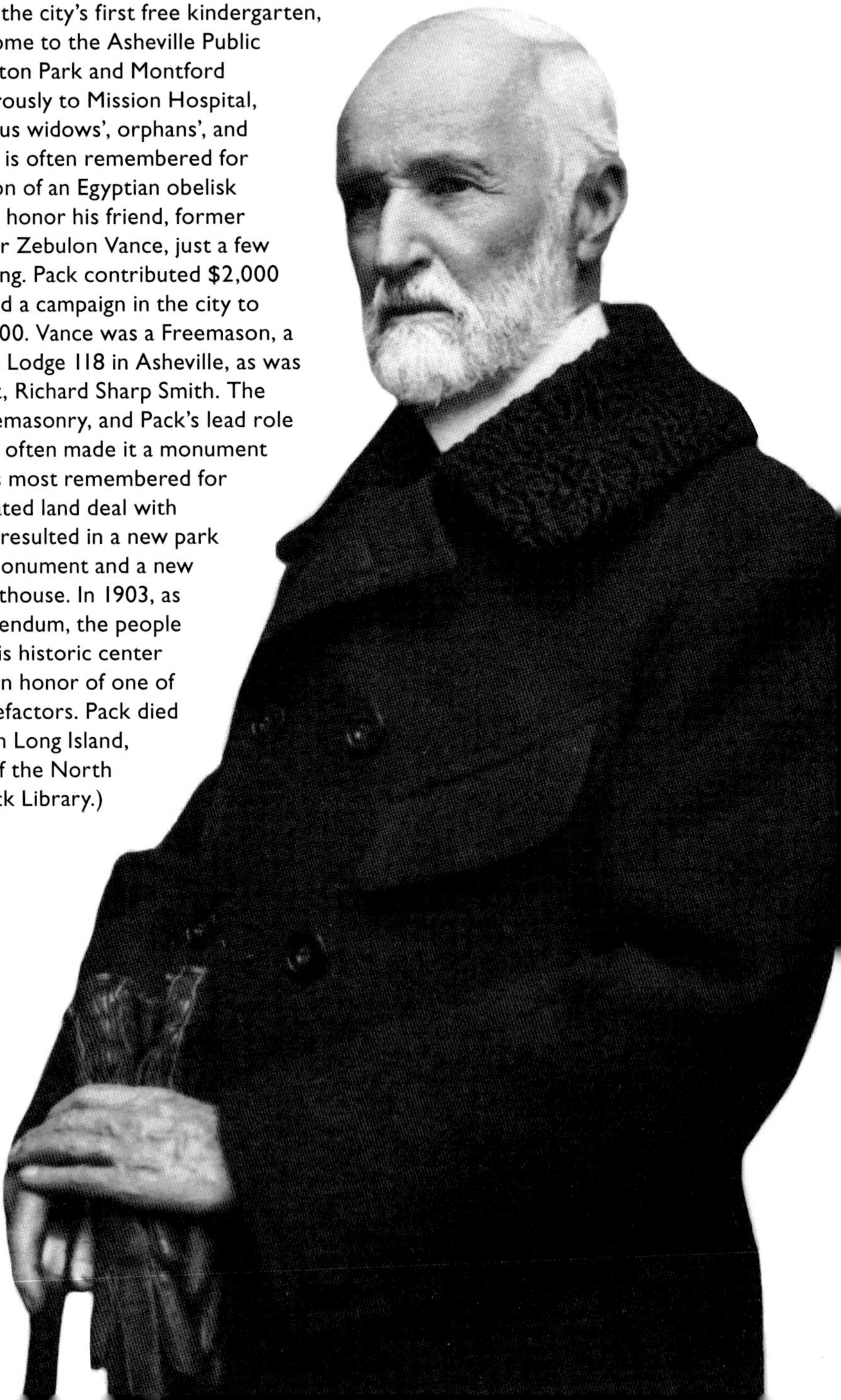

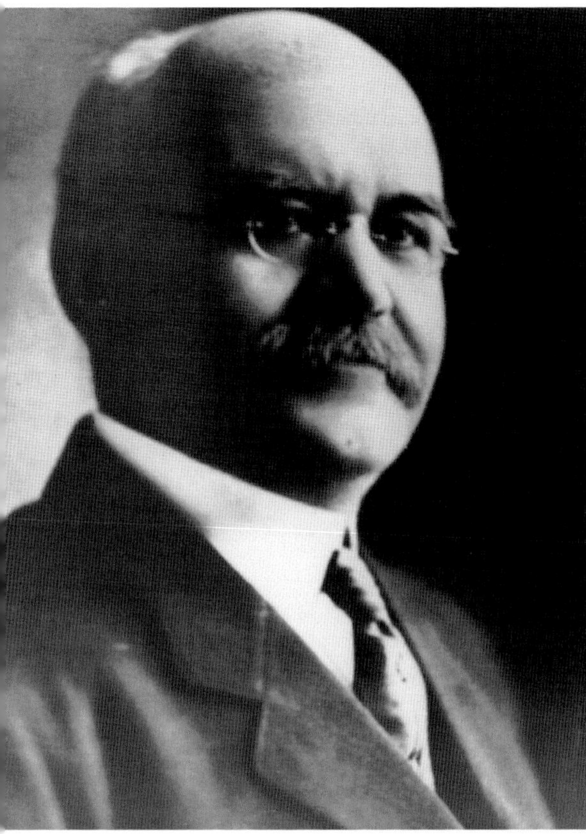

Edwin Wiley Grove

As one of Asheville's most important land developers, E.W. Grove left a significant mark on the city's landscape. Originally from Tennessee, Grove was a self-made millionaire who built his fortune manufacturing Grove's Tasteless Chill Tonic. Grove and his wife became enamored with the city during a visit in 1898. He considered building a factory in the area but instead decided to build the Grove Park Inn (below), which opened in 1913. He also developed an adjacent residential neighborhood called Grove Park. In the years that followed, he developed a community in Swannanoa called Grovemont, a second hotel downtown (the Battery Park Hotel), and, across from it, the Grove Arcade, an elegant shopping and office building. In addition to the hotel and arcade, Grove developed the surrounding Battery Park neighborhood as a key commercial hub in downtown Asheville, which included the city's principal retail district and first car dealerships. (Both, courtesy of the Omni Grove Park Inn and Ramsey Library Special Collections.)

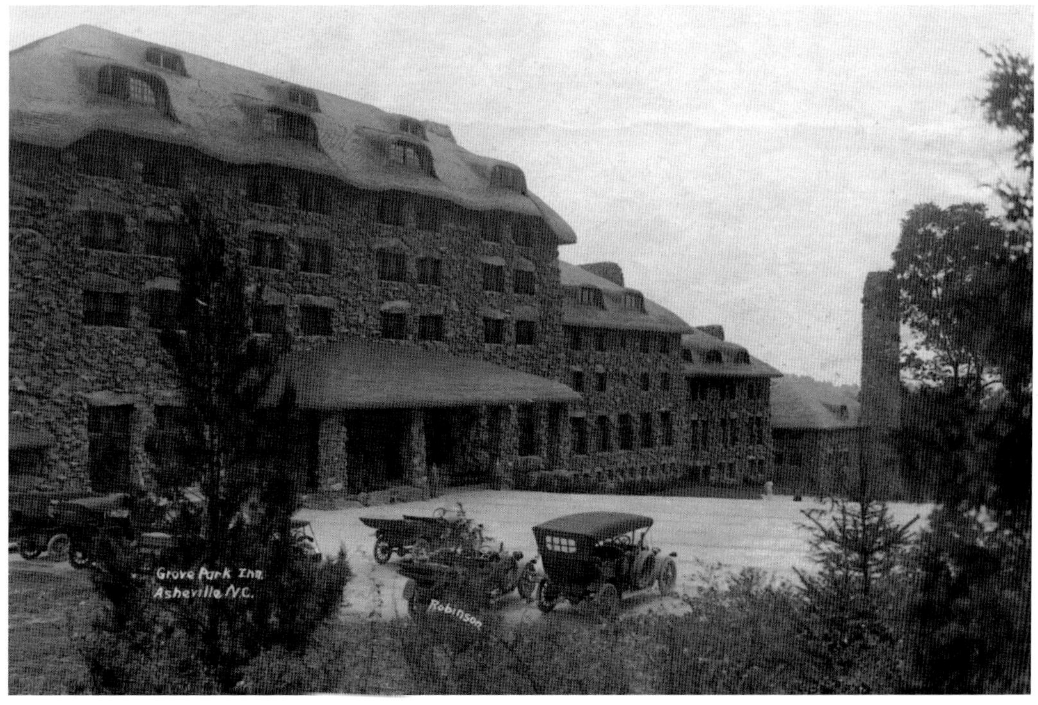

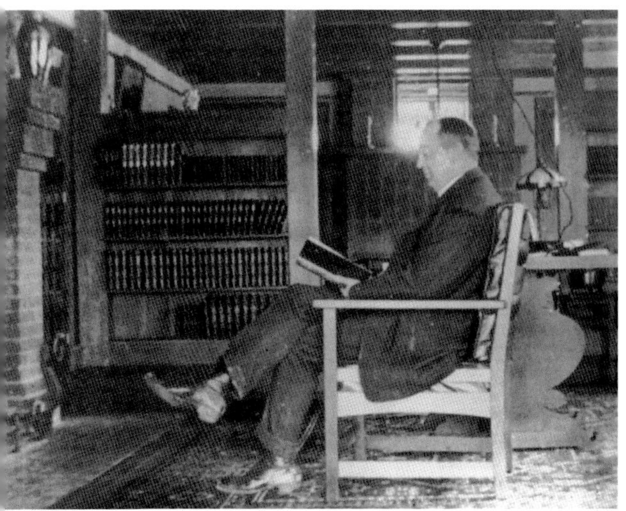

James Madison Chiles
In 1912, developer James Chiles bought the burned-out remains of the famed Kenilworth Inn and the surrounding acreage to develop the town of Kenilworth. Many were surprised by the plan to build a neighborhood in this area because of its rough terrain. The land was so hilly that Chiles rode a horse with loose reigns to let it find the paths of least resistance and thus lay out the neighborhood's streets. Nostalgic for the old hotel, Chiles rebuilt the Kenilworth Inn. The inn's heyday lasted only a few years until it was sold at auction. The Town of Kenilworth was annexed into Asheville as a result of the Great Depression. (Courtesy of the North Carolina Collection, Pack Library.)

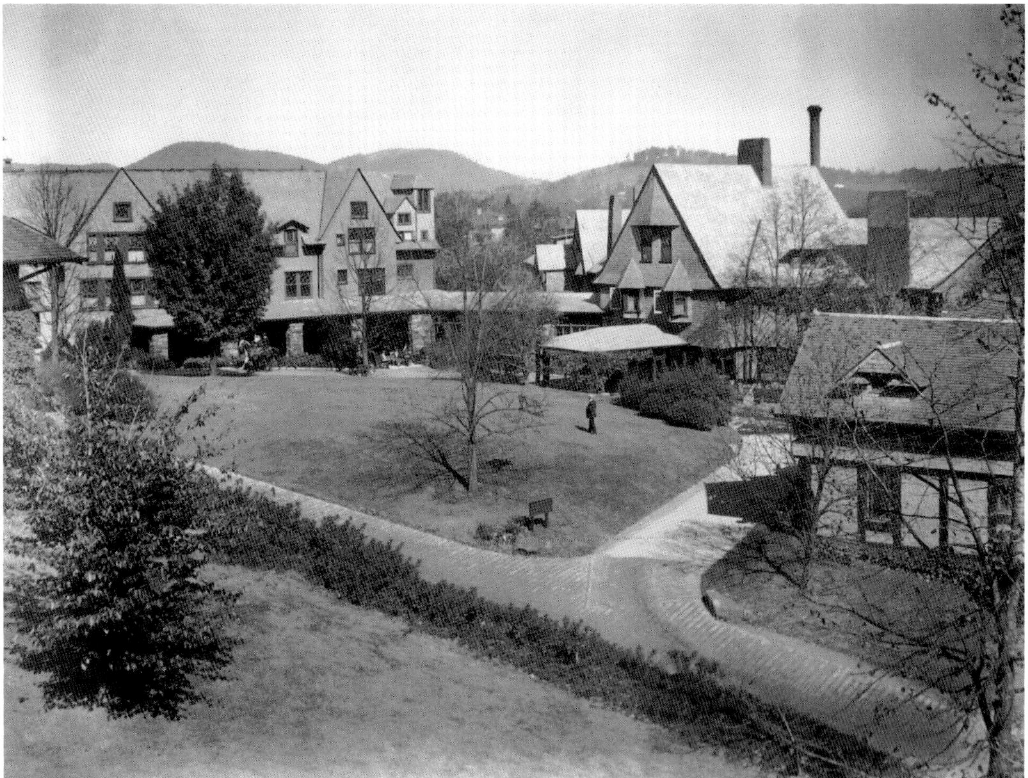

Thomas Wadley Raoul
Thomas Raoul came to Asheville from Georgia in 1897 to help his father develop a farm the family owned in Asheville into a hotel and residential neighborhood. Only 21 at the time, Raoul had contracted tuberculosis, and moving to Asheville proved fortuitous. Raoul led the development of the Manor Inn (shown) and Albemarle Park, adjacent to E.W. Grove's Grove Park neighborhood. Raoul sold Albemarle Park to Grove in 1920 to turn his attention to developing Edith Vanderbilt's Biltmore Forest neighborhood. (Courtesy of Ramsey Library Special Collections.)

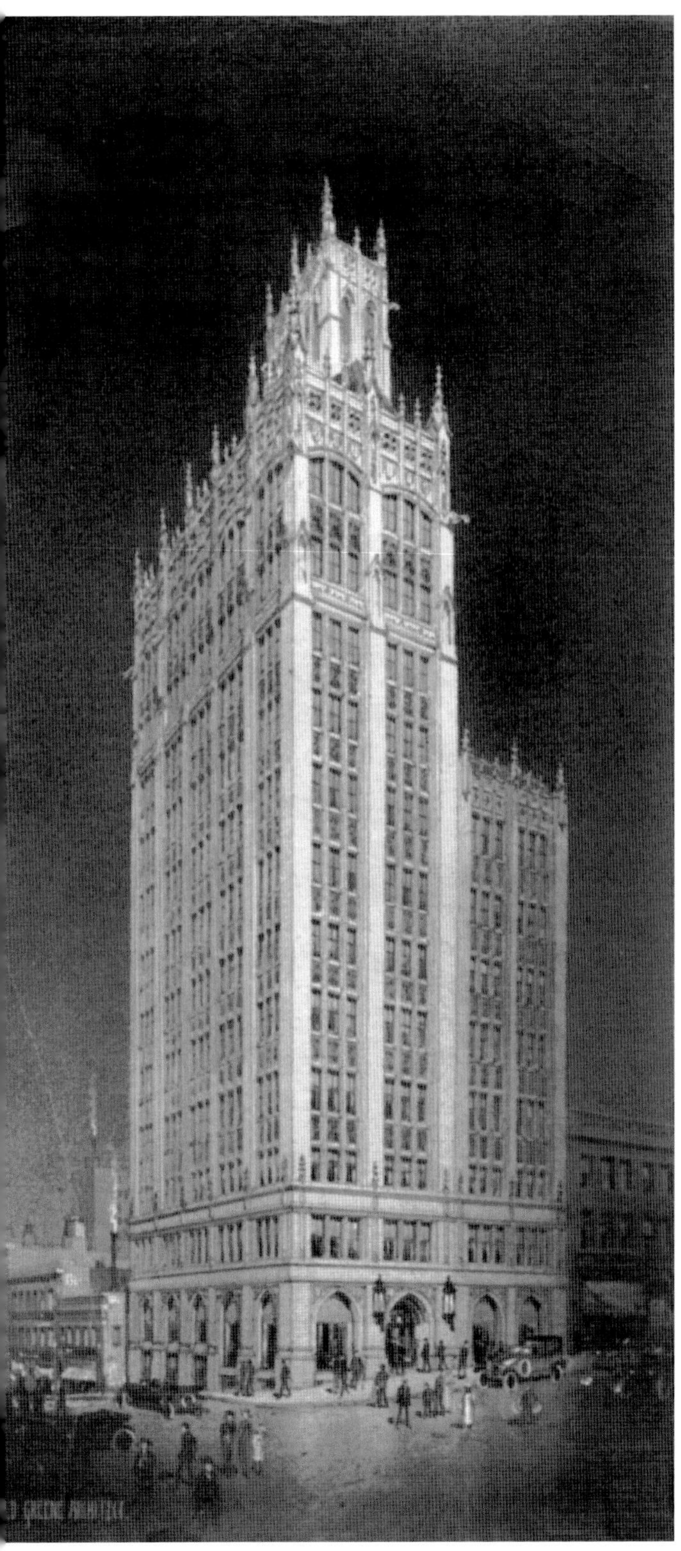

Linwood Baldwin Jackson
Linwood Jackson, or "L.B.," as he was known around town, was one of Asheville's most dynamic developers of the early 20th century. Jackson had moved to Asheville with his family as a young man in 1914. A master salesman, by age 16 he already had enough money to loan his father $5,000 to open a Chero-Cola factory in Asheville. Jackson took the proceeds from the factory and from two of his inventions, a drink bottle tester and a countertop lottery machine, to build Western North Carolina's first skyscraper, the Jackson Building (shown), a narrow Gothic Revival edifice built on the site of W.O. Wolfe's (the father of author Thomas Wolfe) former monument shop. Jackson also invested heavily in the development of the Royal Pines, Beverly Hills, and Kimberly Avenue neighborhoods, as well as other commercial projects, including the Asheville-Biltmore Hotel, the Grove Arcade, and the Flatiron Building. L.B. lost everything in the Great Depression but rebuilt his fortune soon thereafter. He lived until 1974. (Courtesy of the North Carolina Collection, Pack Library.)

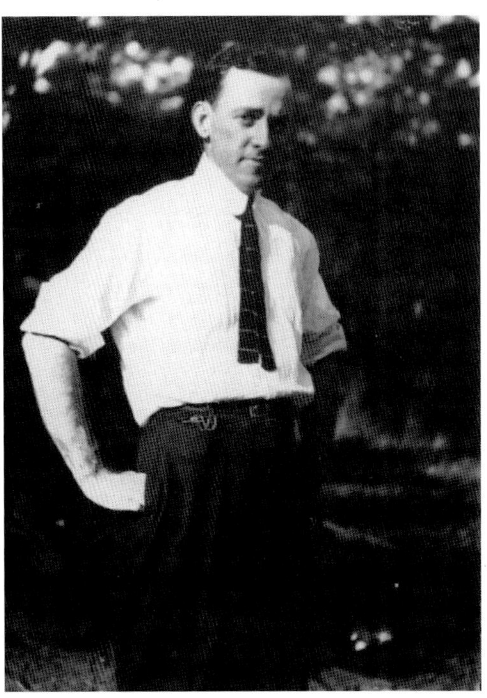

Charles N. Parker
Charles Parker became a leading architect in Asheville under the tutelage of Richard Sharp Smith and Heath Carrier. Parker, who never received formal training as an architect, worked as a draftsman for Smith & Carrier before going out on his own in 1913. While Parker designed numerous notable houses in the Grove Park and Biltmore Forest neighborhoods, he is best known for designing E.W. Grove's enormous Grove Arcade shopping and office complex. (Left, courtesy of the North Carolina Collection, Pack Library; below, photograph by Aaron Dahlstrom.)

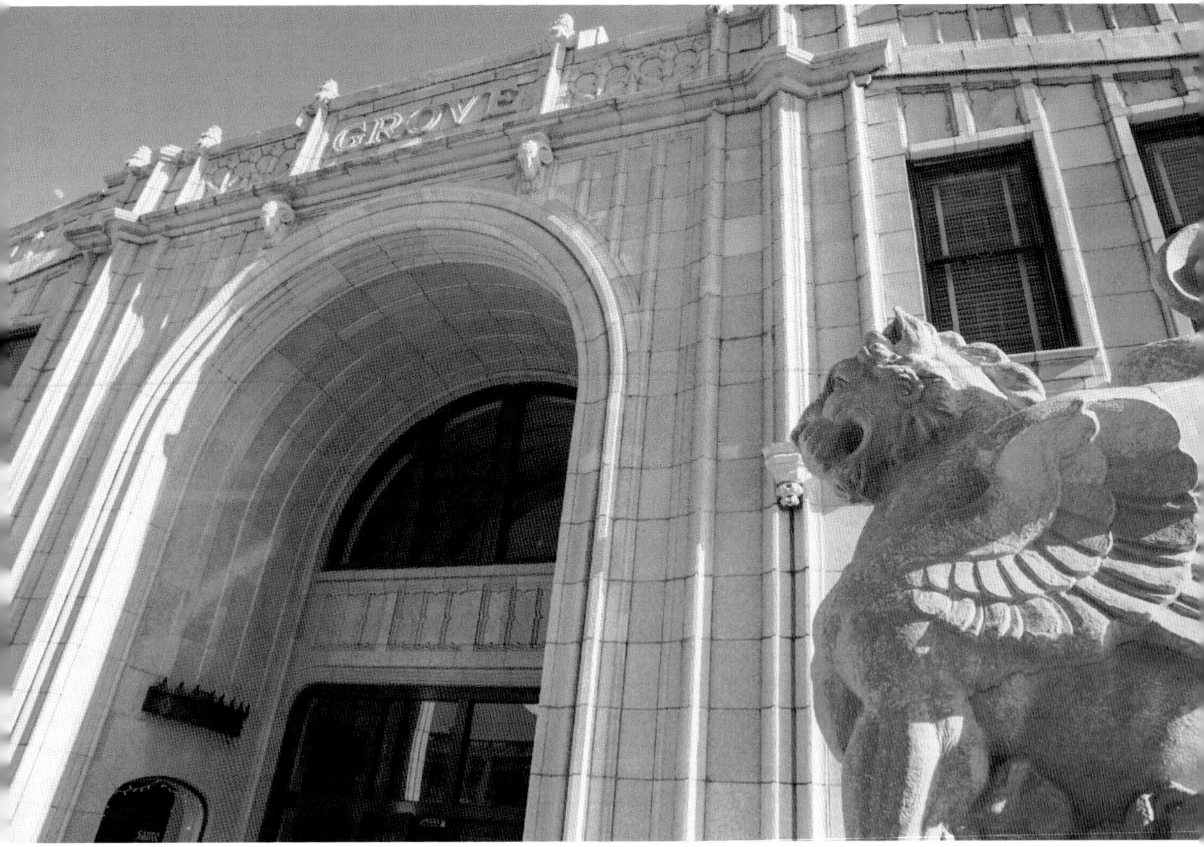

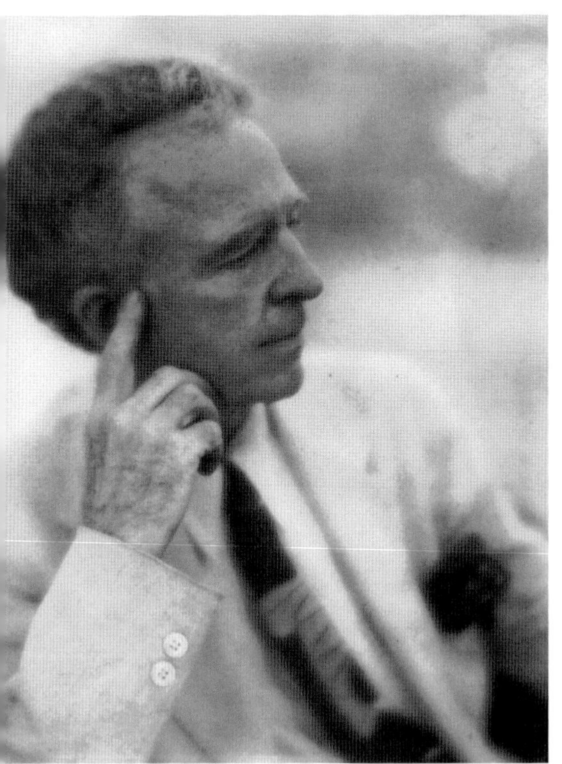

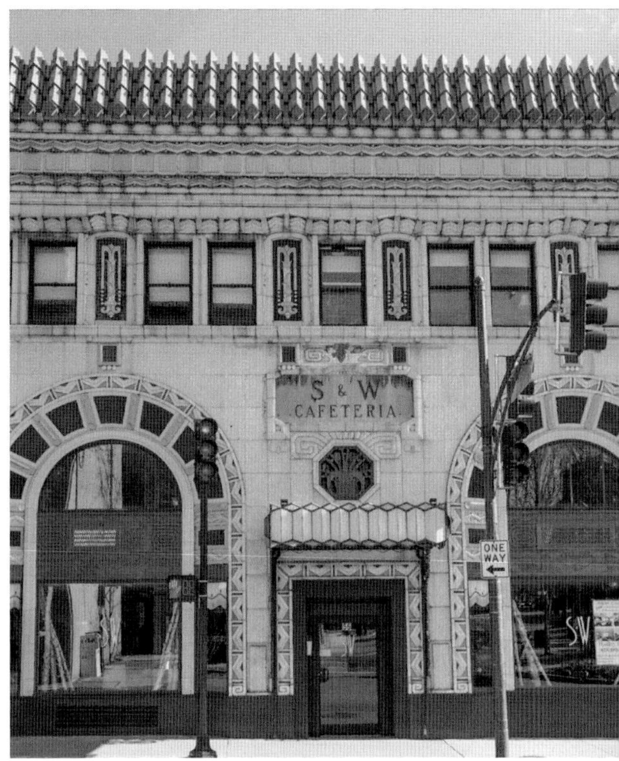

Douglas Ellington

Douglas Ellington returned to his native North Carolina from Pittsburgh in 1926, when he received the commission for the First Baptist Church of Asheville. Originally from rural Johnston County, Ellington's studies eventually took him to the famed École des Beaux Arts in Paris, where he was the first American to win the internationally prestigious Prix de Rougevin award. His work in Paris greatly influenced his blending of the Beaux Arts and Art Deco styles, which would become the hallmark of his work in Asheville and which led to Asheville having one of the most significant surviving collections of Art Deco edifices in the United States, including Asheville City Hall, Asheville High School, and the S&W Cafeteria (right), all Ellington designs. Though he would later live in Washington, DC, and Charleston, South Carolina, Ellington returned to Asheville, where he passed away in 1960. (Left, courtesy of the North Carolina Collection, Pack Library; right, photograph by Aaron Dahlstrom.)

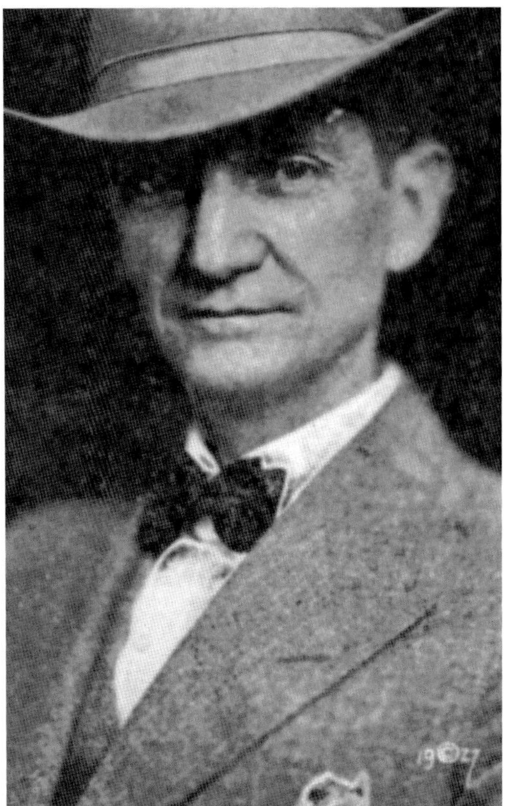

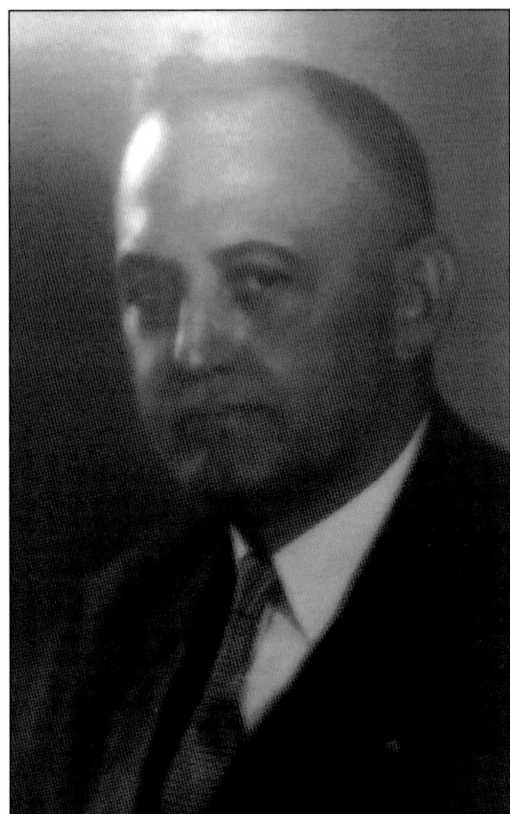

John H. Cathey & Edgar M. Lyda

John Cathey (left) served as mayor of Asheville from 1923 to 1927, one of its most explosive periods of growth. Under his administration, the city began many of its largest bond-funded projects, including the building of a new city hall. The new municipal building was to be part of a two-structure complex that would also include a new county courthouse. In an unexpected gesture of cooperation, the city council and county commission hired architect Douglas Ellington to design a matching pair of towers to form a new "civic center" in the heart of the city. The design was an elaborate execution of the Art Deco style. Cathey and his colleagues were wholeheartedly in favor of the design. E.M. Lyda (right), the chair of the county commission, was not convinced. Lyda, a former police officer and former auditor for Buncombe County, thought the design was ostentatious and preferred a more traditional approach. A chamber of commerce committee asked Cathey to slow down and work to get Lyda on board. In a public response, Cathey called the members of the committee "kickers and soreheads" and vowed that this "city hall is going up, going up if we have to lay the foundations so deep that they will hinge on hell. I intend to see it go up if I loose [sic] every friend I have in the city and forfeit forever the chance of making any more." Cathey was convinced that the county would come along, but, much to his surprise, Lyda announced that the county had hired another architect, Milburn, Heister & Company of Washington, DC, who designed a neoclassical structure not in keeping with the city hall's ornate Art Deco stylings. Cathey was able to secure some changes from Lyda and the commissioners, but, in the end, the matched towers never matched. It was believed at the time that the city hall and county courthouse were the largest erected anywhere in the Southeast. So large were the structures that both the city and county governments rented out office space. As much as these were signs of Asheville's and Buncombe County's prowess in the 1920s, they also become signs of the community's great excess, as both governments went bankrupt during the Great Depression. (Above left, courtesy of Ramsey Library Special Collections; above right, courtesy of the author and Buncombe County; opposite, both courtesy of the North Carolina Collection, Pack Library.)

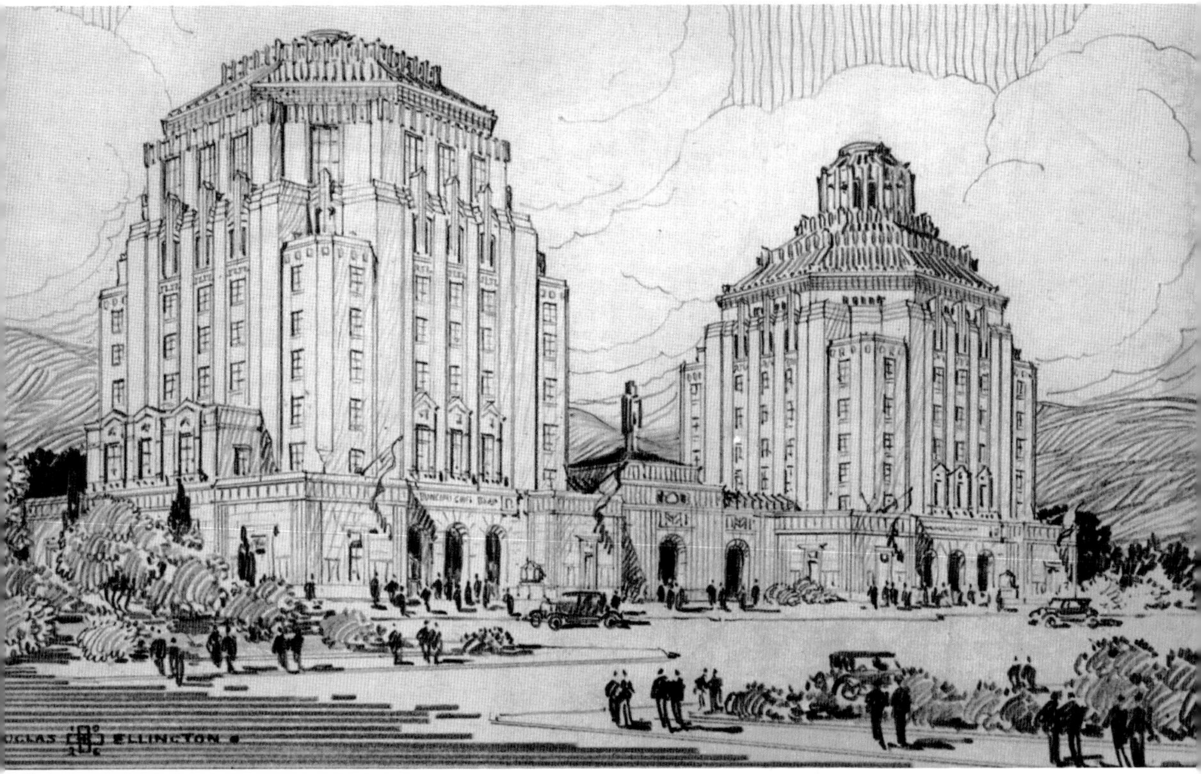

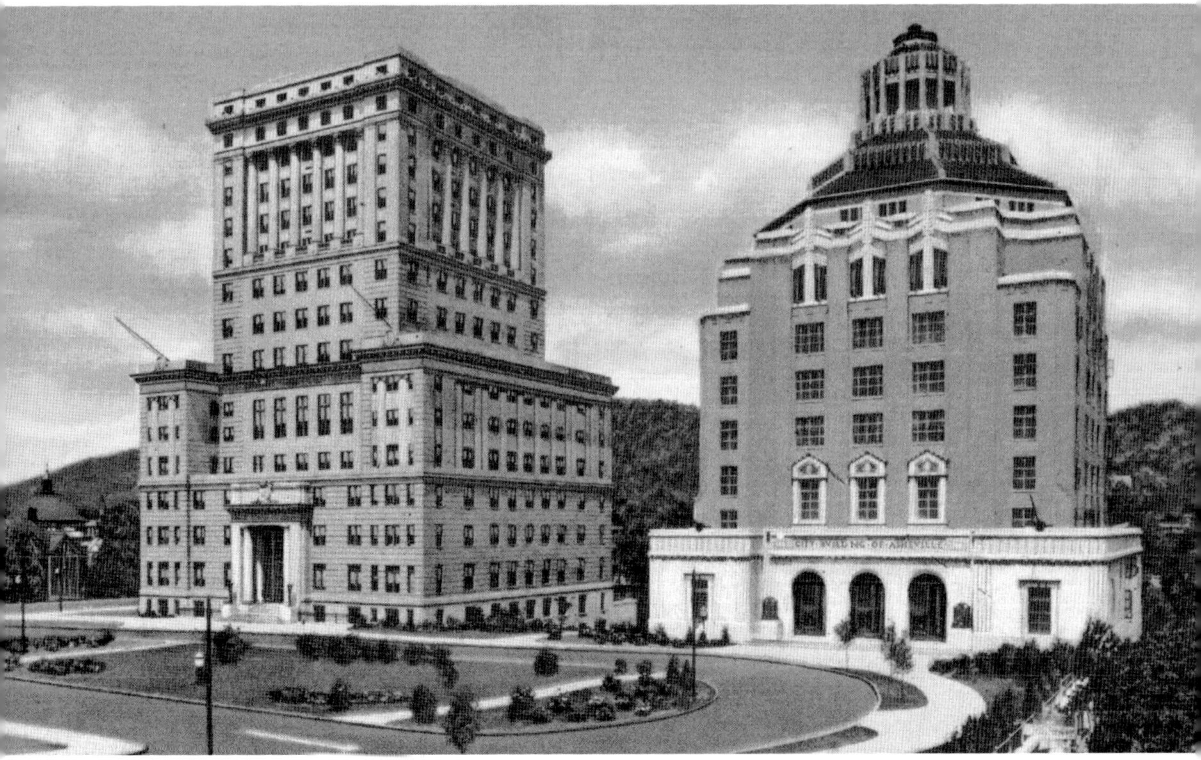

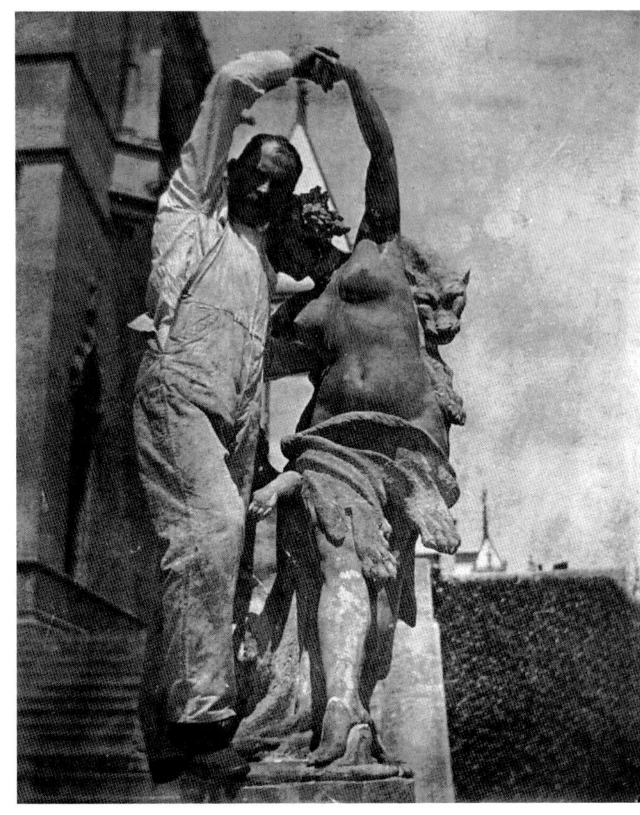

Samuel I. Bean
Originally from Knoxville, Tennessee, Samuel Bean came to Asheville in 1891 to work on the construction of Biltmore House as a stonecutter. After seven years at Biltmore, he opened his own shop in Asheville doing stone and tile work and, later, overall construction. Bean's imprint is on many of the city's finest buildings, including the Drhumor Building, Central United Methodist Church, the Masonic Temple, and the Flatiron, Public Service, and Jackson Buildings. (Courtesy of the North Carolina Collection, Pack Library.)

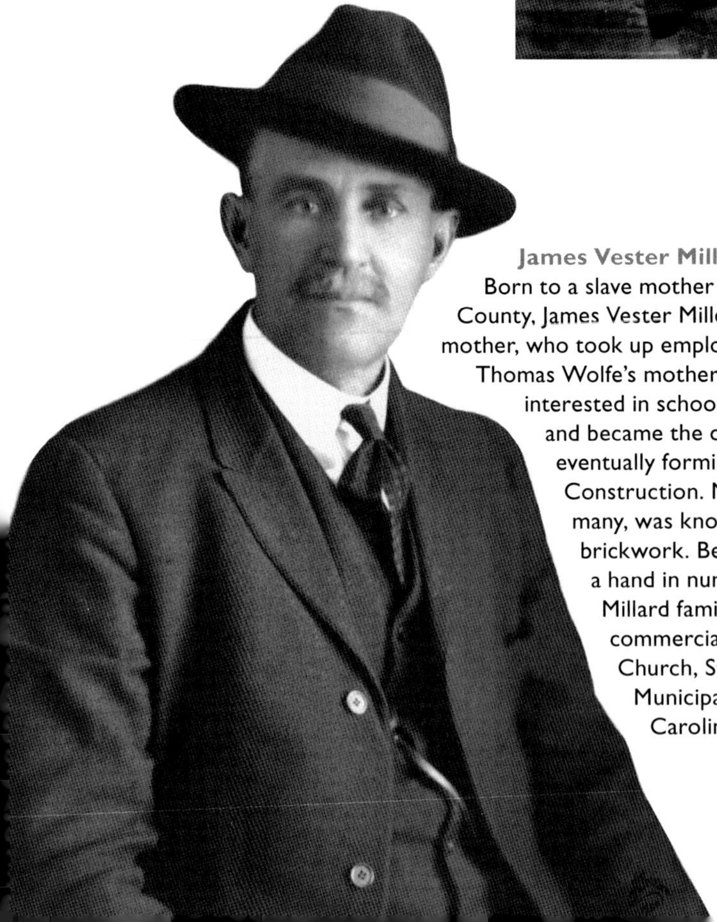

James Vester Miller
Born to a slave mother and a white father in 1858 in Rutherford County, James Vester Miller came to Asheville as a child with his mother, who took up employment as a cook in Julia Wolfe's (author Thomas Wolfe's mother) boardinghouse. Not particularly interested in school, Miller began to work in construction and became the city's most respected brick mason, eventually forming his own company, Miller & Sons Construction. Miller, considered an artist in brick by many, was known for his elaborate and even whimsical brickwork. Before his passing in 1940, Miller had a hand in numerous projects for the Coxe and Millard families, as well as an array of churches and commercial buildings, including Mt. Zion Baptist Church, St. Matthias Episcopal Church, and the Municipal Building. (Courtesy of the North Carolina Collection, Pack Library.)

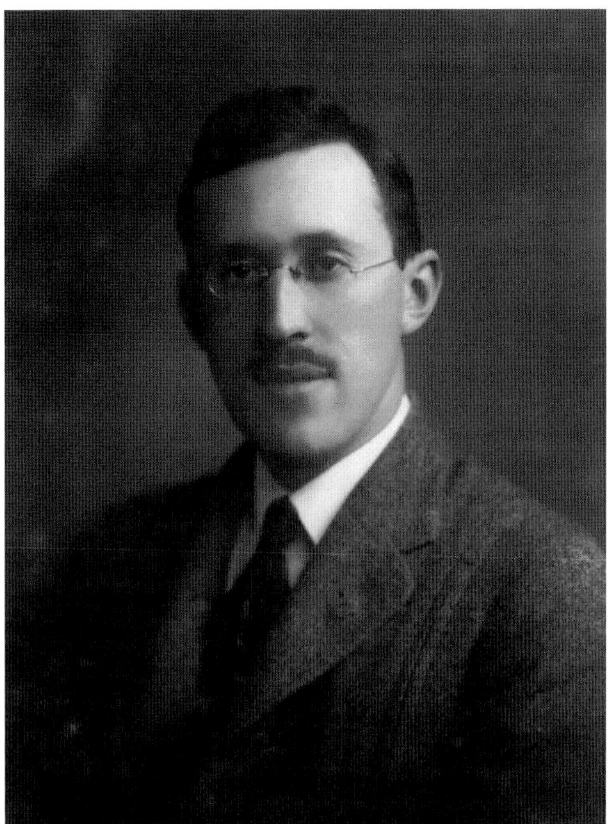

Louis Lipinsky
The youngest son of Solomon Lipinsky, Louis entered the family retail business in 1919, first in Charlotte and then in Asheville. Like his father, Solomon, the younger Lipinsky was very active in community affairs and was one of the key figures in helping Asheville-Biltmore College (the predecessor of UNC Asheville) move to its present campus. He also helped the college join the University of North Carolina system, which it did in 1969. (Courtesy of Ramsey Library Special Collections.)

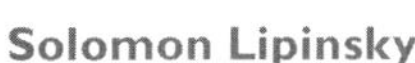

Solomon Lipinsky
Solomon Lipinsky opened his first Bon Marché department store with his sister Eva Ellick in 1890. The store, modeled after the famous Parisian department store of the same name, grew to serve four cities and was one of the largest department store operations in North Carolina for nearly a century. Lipinsky was an active member of the community, serving on several boards and as a founding member of the Congregation Beth HaTephila. (Courtesy of Ramsey Library Special Collections.)

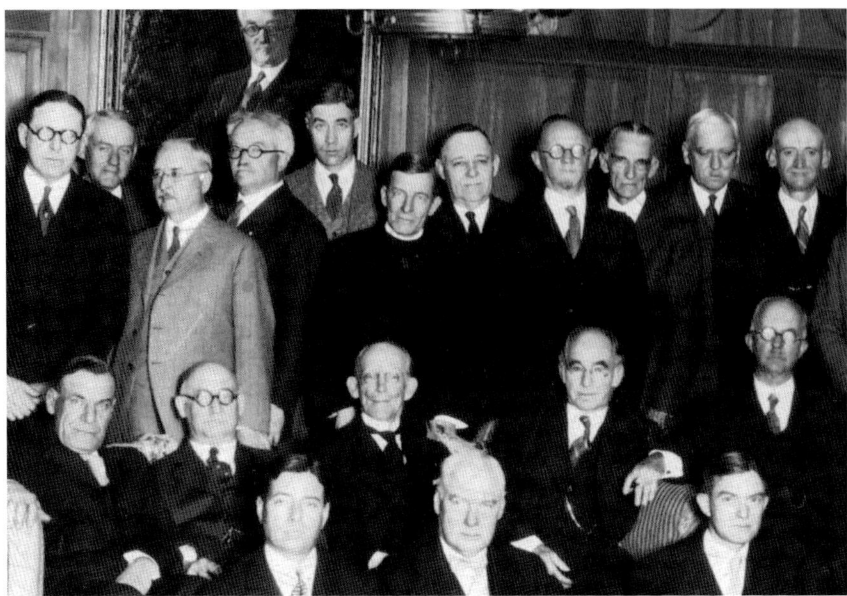

George Stephens

George Stephens (top row, fifth from right) moved to Asheville in 1919 for health reasons after successful careers in banking and real estate development in Charlotte. Stephens bought a half interest with his friend Charles Web in the *Asheville Citizen* newspaper. In developing the Myers Park neighborhood in Charlotte, Stephens had become convinced of the value of city planning, and led a successful campaign for the City of Asheville to hire John Nolen of Boston, one of the nation's first planners, to design a comprehensive city plan for Asheville. The plan became the basis for the 1920s "Program for Progress," which both transformed Asheville and led to its enormous Depression-era debt. Stephens engaged in a great deal of real estate development, including Beverly Hills and Biltmore Village, which he purchased in its entirety from Edith Vanderbilt. (Above, courtesy of the North Carolina Collection, Pack Library; below, author's collection.)

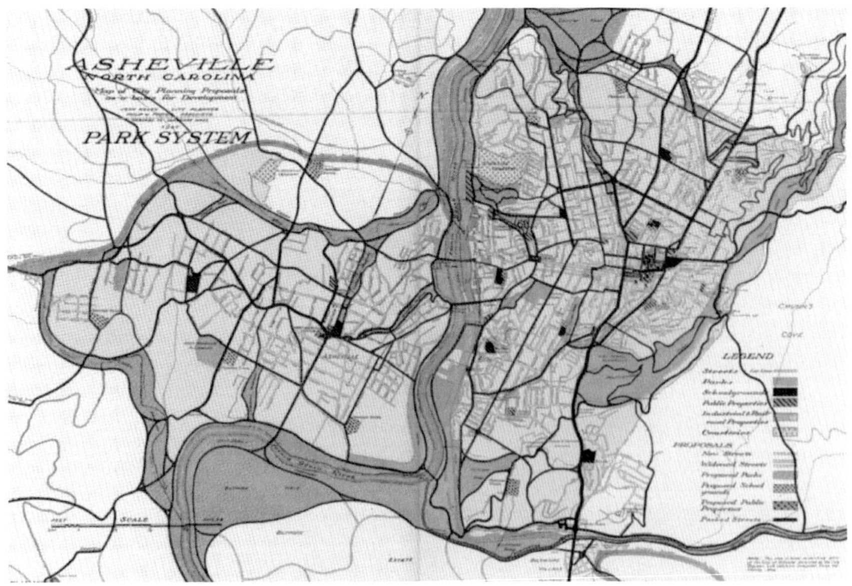

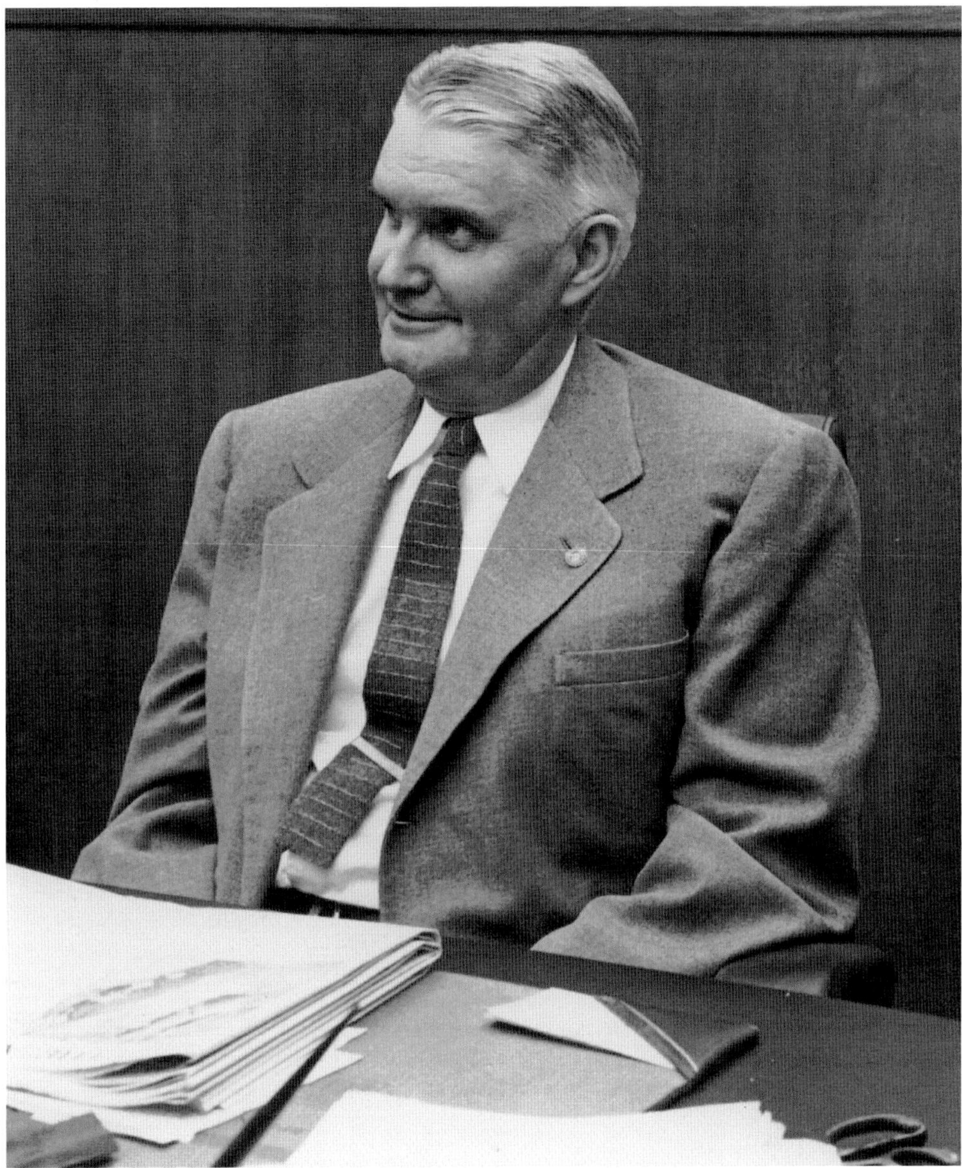

D. Hiden Ramsey

D.H. Ramsey was a highly respected public servant and newspaperman for much of the first half of the 20th century. He served as the commissioner of public safety until 1919 and soon thereafter became the associate editor of the *Asheville Citizen* and two other papers, but he is most noted for serving as the general manager of the consolidated *Asheville Citizen-Times*, which stabilized Asheville's formerly volatile newspaper industry. When Asheville went bankrupt during the Great Depression, it was Ramsey who led the reorganization of the city's enormous debt—the highest municipal debt per capita in the country at the time. Ramsey was also a consummate supporter of education and served as the chair of the state's first board of higher education in the 1950s, whereby he proposed a dramatic reorganization of the state's systems of higher education, which, while not implemented at the time, became the basis for the restructuring of the state's community college and university systems years later. (Courtesy of Ramsey Library Special Collections.)

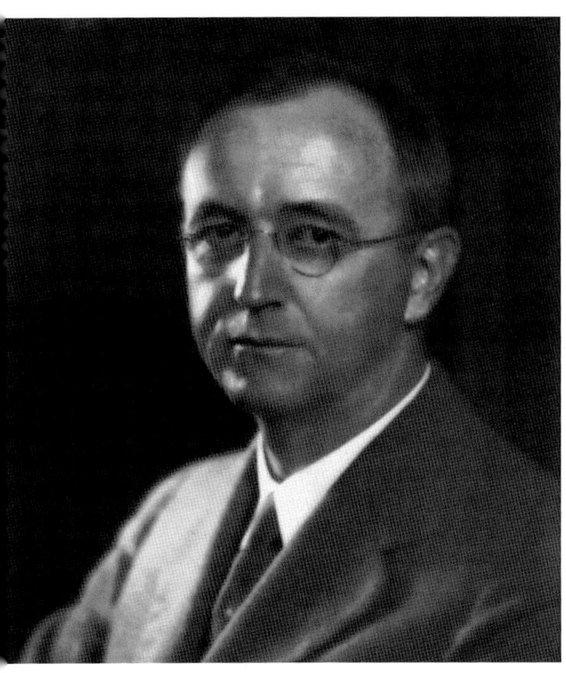

Fred Loring Seely
Fred Seely came to Asheville in 1913 to lead the construction of the Grove Park Inn, developed by his father-in-law, E.W. Grove. A pharmaceutical manufacturer himself, Seely had joined Grove's Paris Medicine Company in 1897 and married Grove's daughter, Evelyn, a year later. Seely and Grove made a great deal of money together, but their relationship was always strained, and eventually Seely sued his father-in-law. Later, Seely bought Biltmore Industries, a weaving and woodworking operation, from Edith Vanderbilt and moved it beside the hotel. He also played a key role in recruiting Eerste Nederlandsche Kunzyd-fabriek Arnhem (ENKA) to build a new rayon fiber factory, which became one of Buncombe County's largest employers, providing well over 5,000 jobs. Seely remained active in business and philanthropy until his death in 1942. (Both, courtesy of Grovewood Galleries and Ramsey Library Special Collections.)

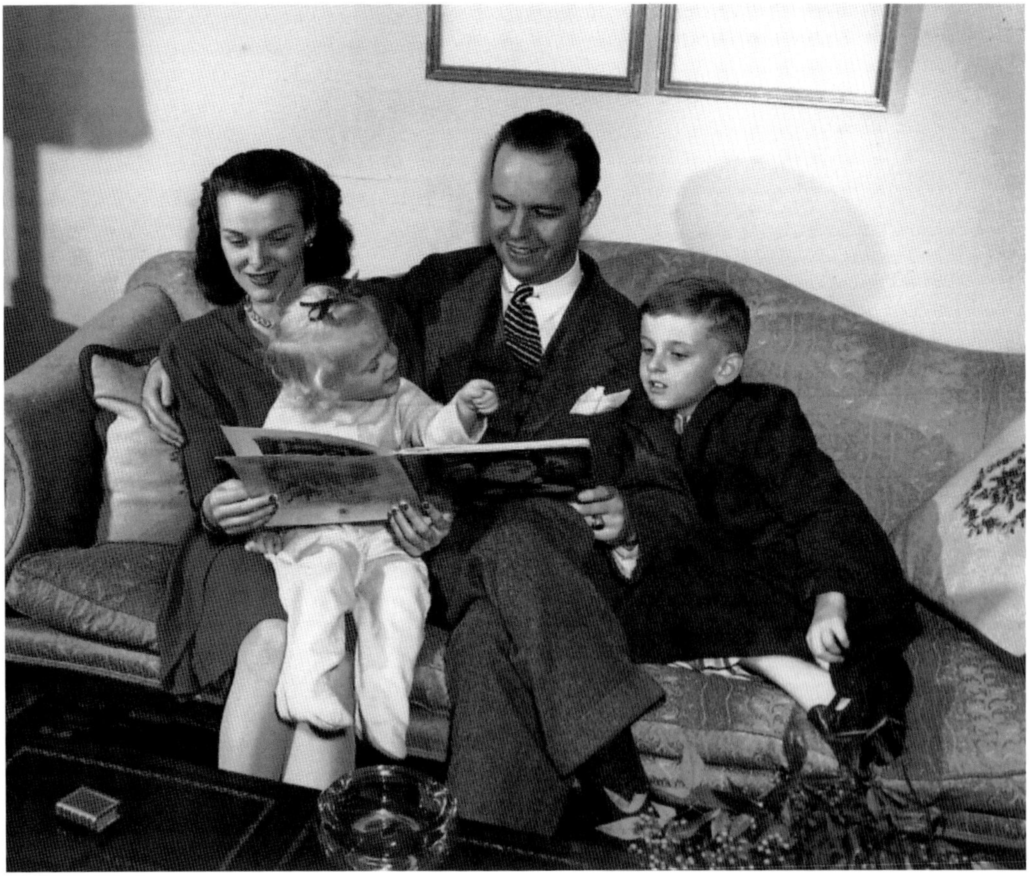

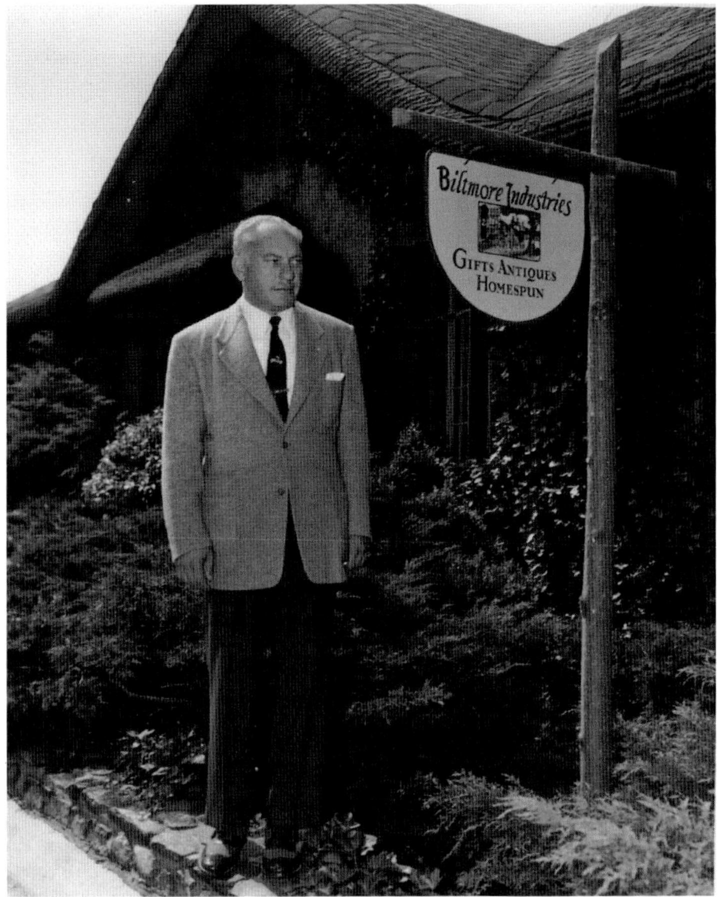

Harry Blomberg

Much to his father, Lewis's, chagrin, Harry Blomberg was captivated by automobiles from an early age. Lewis told Harry he had "wheels in his head" and would "never amount to anything." The younger Blomberg began his business career by opening a service station downtown in 1923. His automobile interests would later include two motor inns and a very profitable Cadillac and Pontiac dealership. An active community leader, Blomberg bought and saved Julia Wolfe's boardinghouse, which was eventually turned into a memorial to her son, famed author Thomas Wolfe. Blomberg also saved Biltmore Industries, an operation originally backed by Edith Vanderbilt to preserve and promote local Appalachian crafts, especially textiles. Fred Seely, the son-in-law of E.W. Grove, had bought Biltmore Industries from Vanderbilt as she reorganized her estate after her husband's death in 1914. Seely relocated it from Biltmore to north Asheville, beside the new Grove Park Inn, which he managed for his father-in-law. After Seely died in 1942, his son Fred Jr. showed little interest in the business, and the nationally acclaimed operation began to fall apart. One day in 1953, Blomberg had come by the shop to get a table for a vacation cabin and was taken by an old still in the corner. After inquiring about its purchase, the manager told Blomberg the only way he could buy the still was to buy Biltmore Industries, and, after less than 30 minutes of negotiations, Blomberg did just that. He helped bring it back to profitability, but as the American textile business waned, so did Biltmore Industries. Blomberg eventually turned part of it into a car museum, and later, his daughter Marilyn, who had married into one of Asheville's oldest families, the Pattons, and her sister Barbra opened the highly successful Grovewood Gallery on the site. Harry Blomberg remained an active businessman, civic leader, and leader in the Jewish community until his death in 1991. (Courtesy of Grovewood Galleries and Ramsey Library Special Collections.)

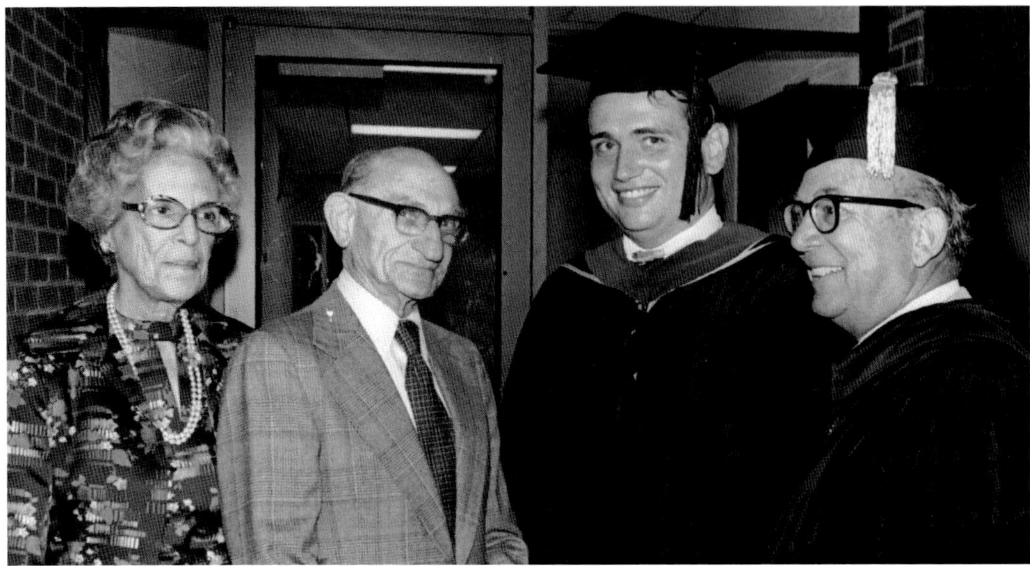

Coleman Zageir
Coleman Zageir (second from left) opened The Man Store in 1922. A men's haberdashery, the store served the Asheville community for more than 40 years. Zageir was known for treating every customer as his best, which built a fierce loyalty to the store by men throughout Asheville, many of whom bought their first suit at The Man Store. Zageir's graciousness was also seen in the numerous scholarships he gave to needy college-bound graduates from Asheville High School. (Photograph by Robbi Snyder, courtesy of Ramsey Library Special Collections.)

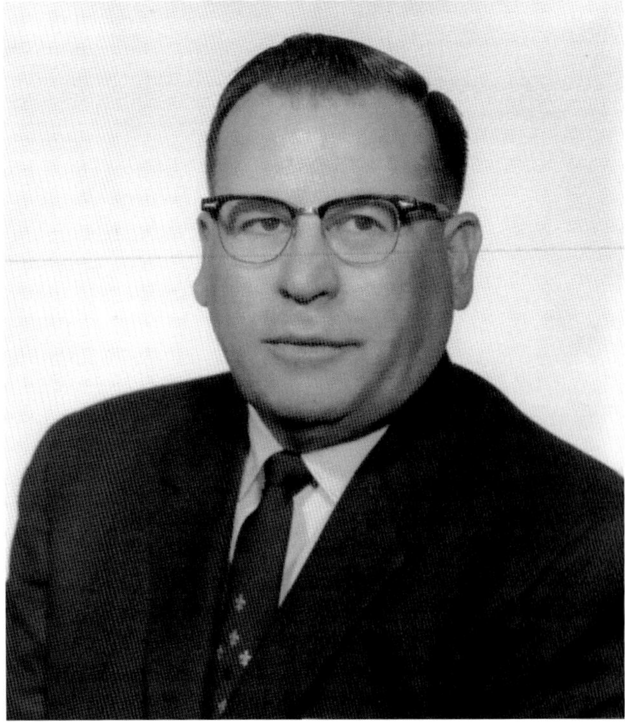

Hyman Dave
Prior to World War II, Hyman Dave moved to Asheville to help his brother run Dave Steel. The company played an important role fabricating military structures during the war. When his brother moved to Cincinnati in 1950 to open a new plant, Hyman became president of Dave Steel in Asheville. Upon his retirement, Dave, who had always been interested in food, took up the management of the Asheville Downtown City Club and the Asheville Country Club. When Dave passed in 2011, he was over 100 years old. (Courtesy of Ramsey Library Special Collections.)

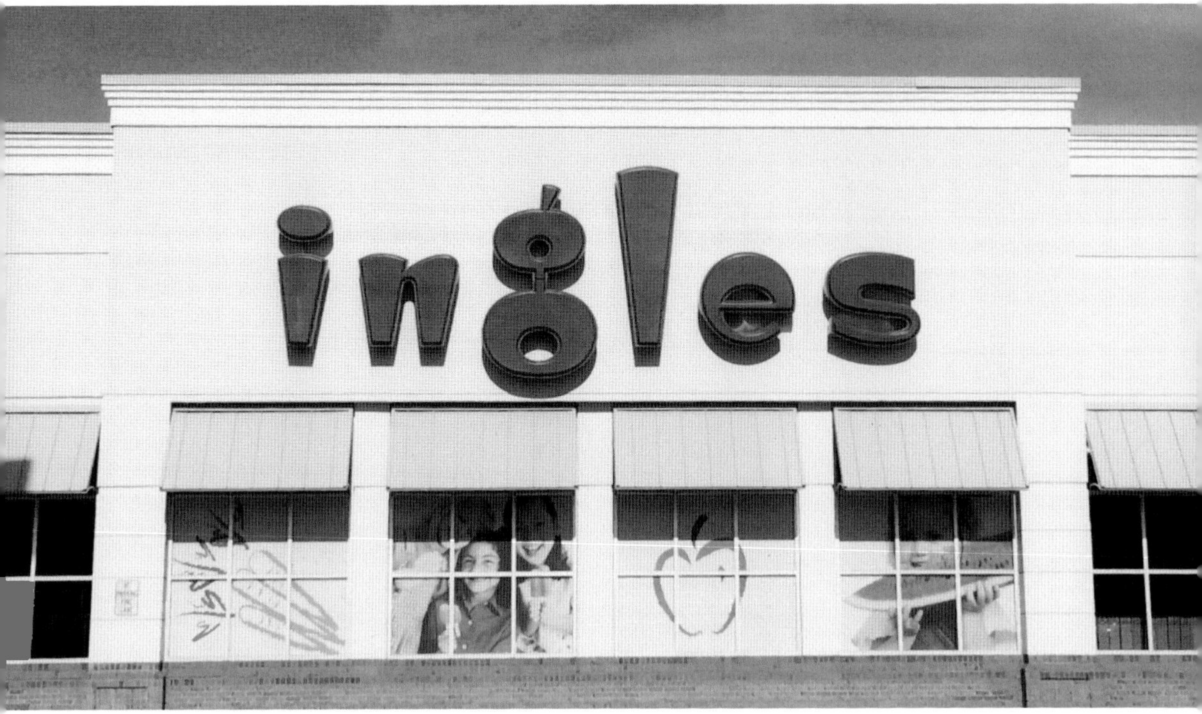

Robert P. Ingle

Bob Ingle, a third-generation grocer, was born in Asheville in 1933. In 1963, after attending the University of Miami, Ingle returned home and opened the first Ingles Supermarket. The competition was fierce, but Ingle implemented a strategy of opening stores in smaller communities typically underserved by major supermarkets. The strategy paid off, and by the time of his passing in 2011, Ingles was not only a fixture in Asheville but had grown to over 200 stores with more than $4 billion in annual sales. (Photograph by the author.)

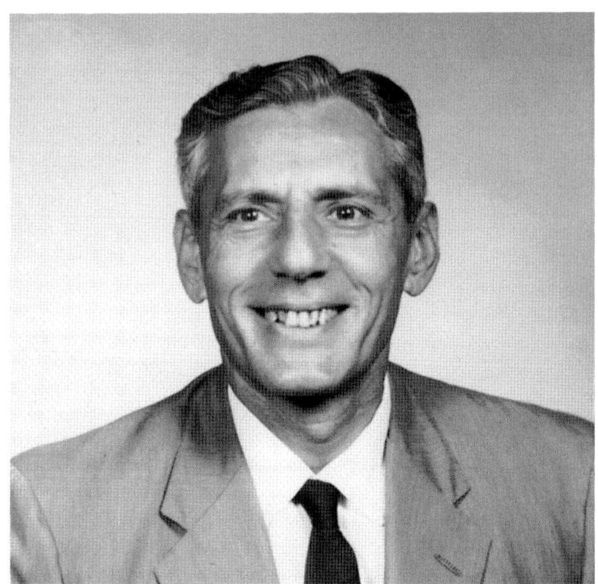

Ernest A. Mills

Ernie Mills brought Mills Manufacturing, a parachute maker, to Asheville from New York in 1952. Mills brought the plant to North Carolina because of its booming textiles industry and to Asheville because of its climate. Mills Manufacturing soon became, and remains today, one of the county's most significant employers. Mills himself became an active leader in the community, serving on numerous boards and giving generously, and often anonymously, of his resources. He passed away in 1989. (Courtesy of Ramsey Library Special Collections.)

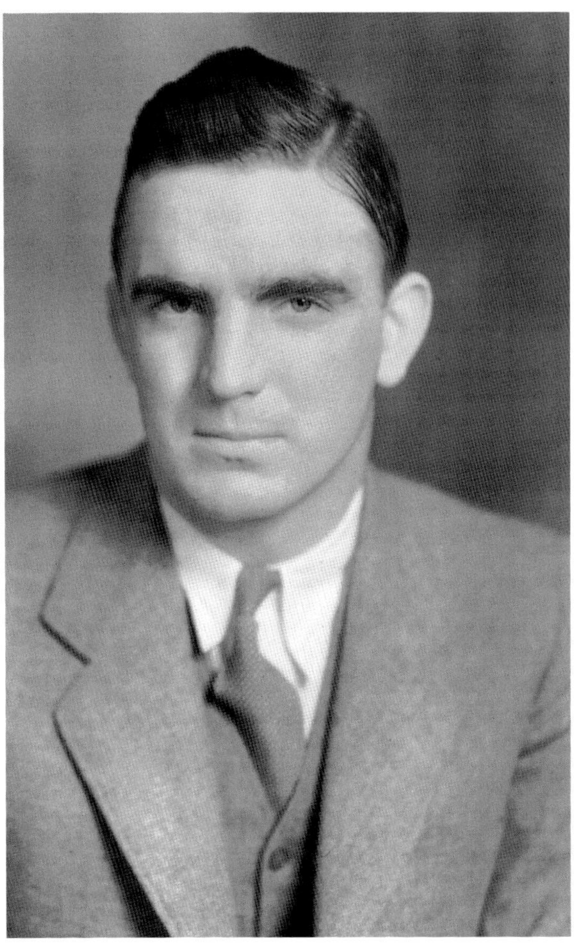

Weldon Weir
From 1950 to 1968, Weldon Weir served as Asheville's city manager, and arguably one of its most powerful leaders. Weir was known as a problem solver. If one needed something done, a pothole fixed or an oil tank filled, they asked Weir, and he would make it happen. If someone had a request, they joined him on Saturday for a hot dog in the basement of Lance's Produce. That is also where folks went to ask for a city job, or even to run for political office. In addition to being city manager, Weir also ran the Democratic political machine, which had controlled Asheville politics for decades. It was only after he retired that the machine finally collapsed, though Weir remained a powerful figure until his death in 1987. (Courtesy of Ramsey Library Special Collections.)

Roy A. Taylor
Roy Taylor graduated in 1929 as the valedictorian of the first graduating class of Buncombe County Junior College, predecessor of the University of North Carolina at Asheville. Taylor went on to serve in the Navy during World War II, and upon his return served two terms in the North Carolina General Assembly, where he played a key role in laying the foundations for what would become the state's community college system. He was later elected to Congress, where he served from 1960 to 1977. After his retirement from Congress, a 40,000-acre parcel within the Nantahala National Forest was named in his honor. In 1986, he was the first person to be granted an honorary doctorate from UNC Asheville, his alma mater. He also won its first Distinguished Alumnus Award, in 1995, the same year as his passing. (Courtesy of Ramsey Library Special Collections.)

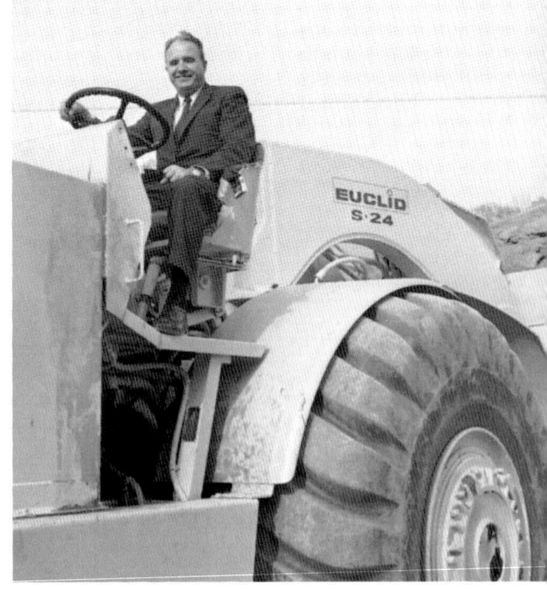

CHAPTER FOUR

Educators and Humanitarians

Since its founding, Asheville has been a city of neighbors helping neighbors, a necessity for surviving on the Appalachian frontier, but Asheville's neighborliness has always gone beyond survival to living a good life. There were those who made sure that all people in Asheville had access to books, even in the days of segregation. There was a convent of nuns who started a hospital to ensure access to health care, and there have been many philanthropists who have given generously in support of their community.

Asheville has always had a strong commitment to education, from elementary school to high school to college. In the 20th century, the city was fortunate to see the emergence of a nationally ranked community college, Asheville-Biltmore Technical Community College, and a nationally ranked public liberal arts university, the University of North Carolina at Asheville. Both, through their students, staff, faculty, and leadership, have contributed much to the community. Asheville also saw, in neighboring Black Mountain, an experimental college that, though short-lived, transformed the American arts.

It was in Asheville's schools that the earliest battles against segregation were fought, led by brave women and men who knew that a desegregated Asheville would be a better Asheville for all of its residents. So many of those who fought for civil rights in their youth stayed in Asheville and continue to lead the community in making better lives for all people.

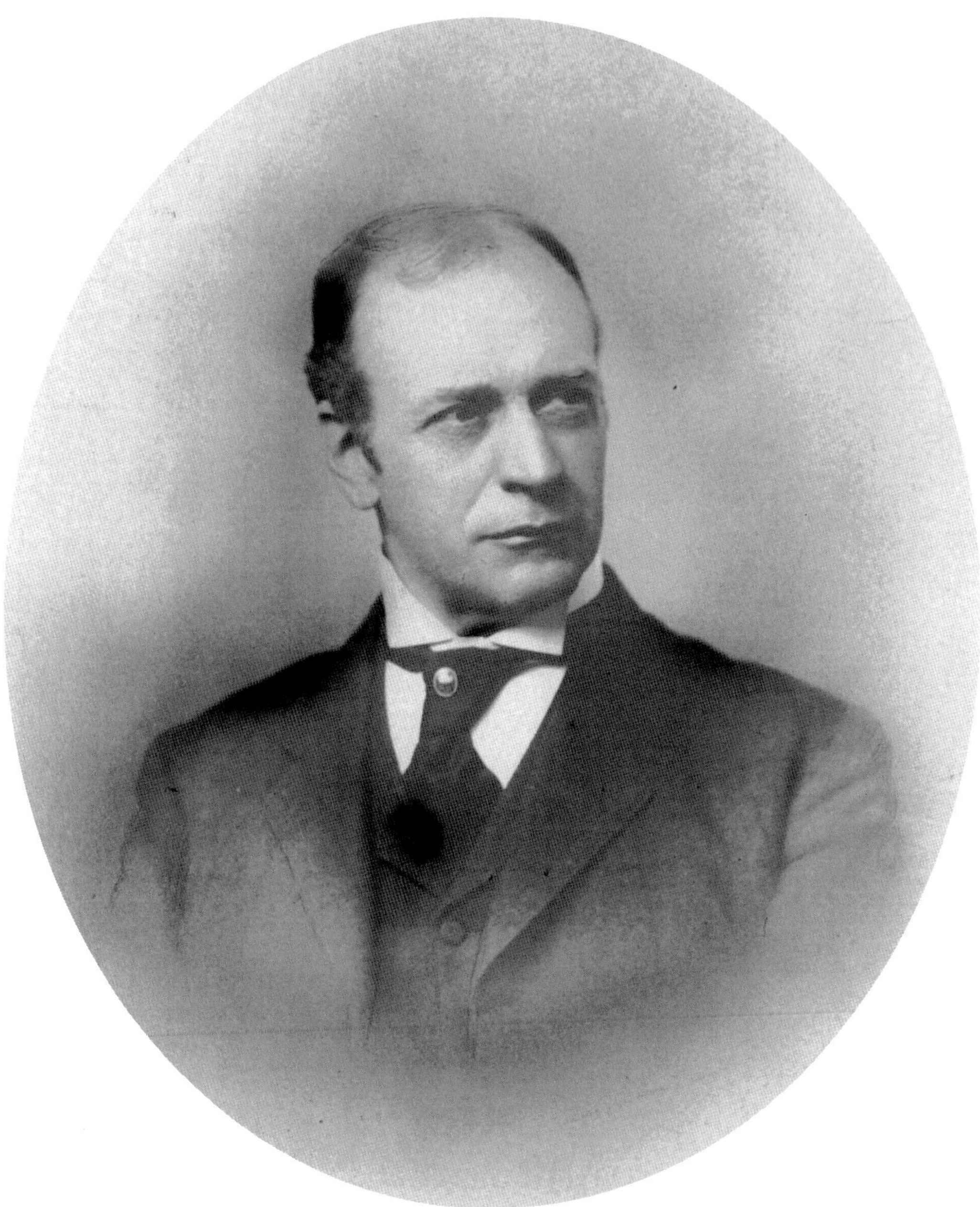

Foster A. Sondley

Foster Sondley began his law practice in Asheville in 1879. His deep knowledge of North Carolina law and history earned him a reputation as one of the state's top litigators. An avid collector of everything from firearms to gems, Sondley amassed an extraordinary collection of some 30,000 rare books and documents pertaining to North Carolina history. A gifted writer, he published works in the 1920s and 1930s on the history of Asheville and Buncombe County that are still considered seminal. Upon his passing in 1931, he left his book collection to the City of Asheville, and it formed the core of the Sondley Reference Collection at Pack Memorial Library. (Courtesy of the North Carolina Collection, Pack Library.)

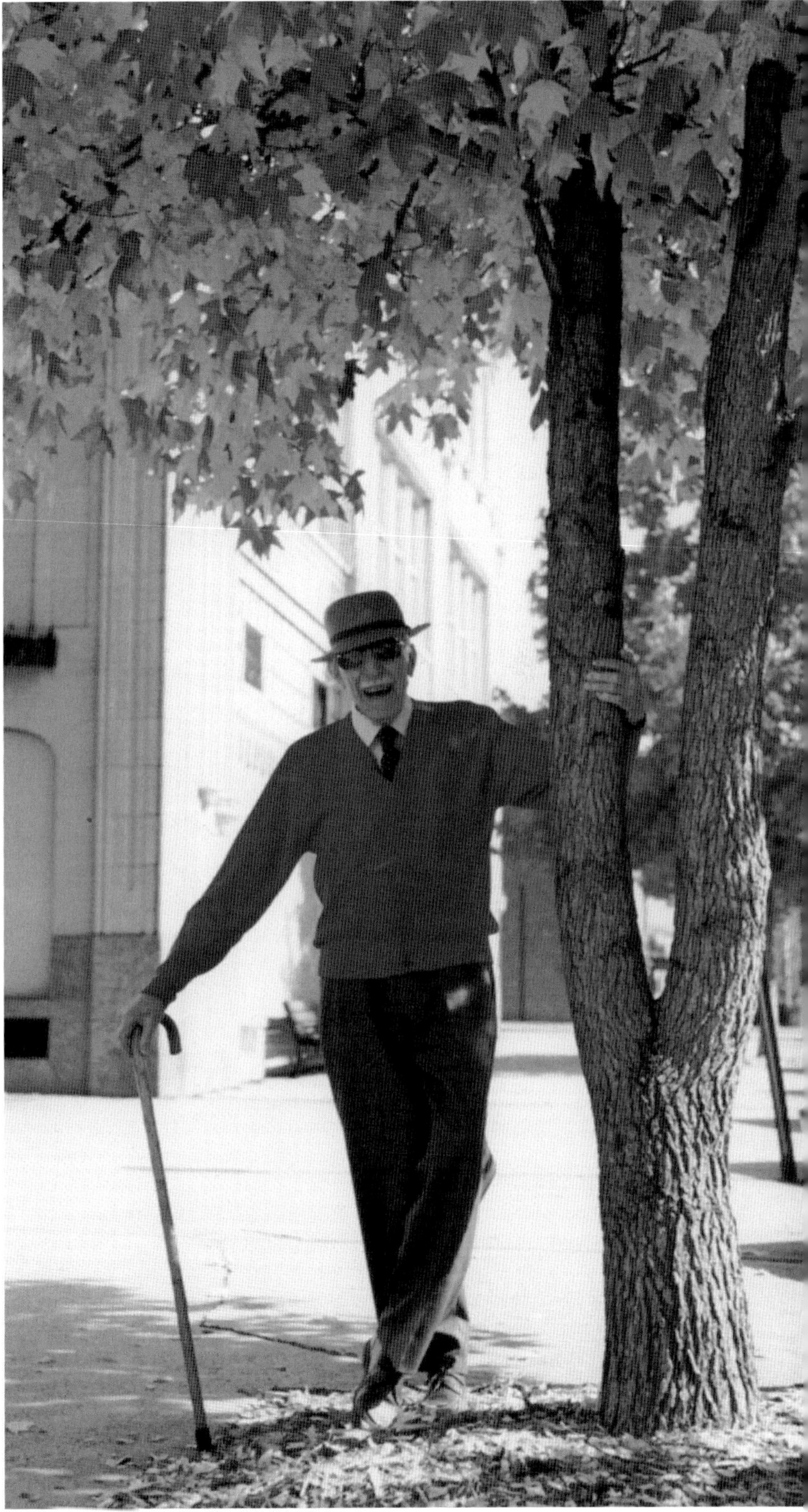

Anthony Lord
After earning his degrees, Anthony "Tony" Lord returned to Asheville in 1928 to join his father in the architectural firm Lord & Lord. The Great Depression suspended Lord's career, and he turned to blacksmithing, earning a significant reputation as an artisan blacksmith, with commissions for the Washington National Cathedral and Yale University, his alma mater. By the late 1930s, he resumed his practice and designed a notable new building in the International style for the *Asheville Citizen-Times*, the first of his numerous major commercial and civic projects throughout the region. During World War II, he was one of the founding partners of the Six Associates firm, which gained a significant reputation throughout the Southeast. Lord was also known for his decades of volunteer leadership in service to the Asheville-Buncombe Library System, of which he served as chair for some 20 years, including in 1961 when the library was desegregated. Lord died in 1993. (Courtesy of the North Carolina Collection, Pack Library.)

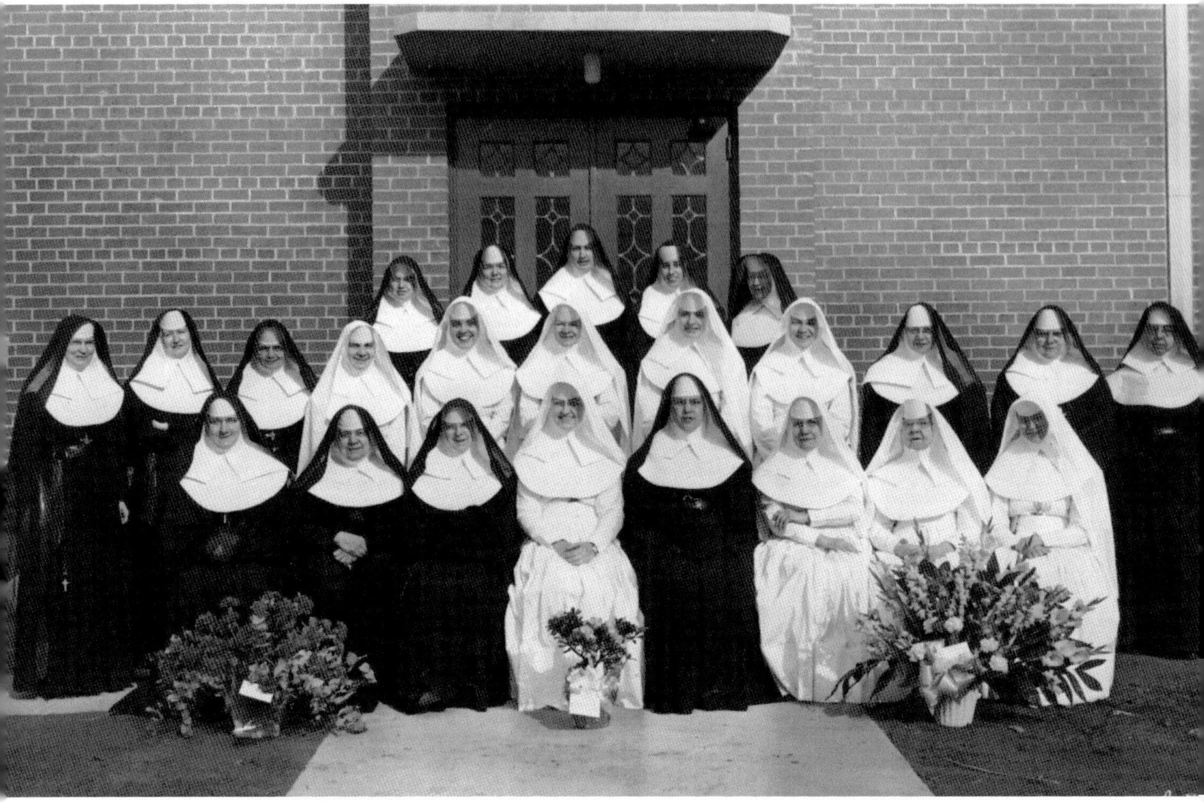

Sisters of Mercy

Founded by Catherine McAuley in Dublin, Ireland, in 1831, the Sisters of Mercy came to the United States in 1843. They expanded their ministry to Asheville in 1895 with the opening of a tuberculosis sanitarium, which eventually expanded to the 338-bed St. Joseph's Hospital. They ran it for nearly 100 years until selling it to Mission Health Care in 1998. In 1985, the Sisters expanded their operations to include an urgent care network in Asheville, which they still operate today. (Courtesy of the North Carolina Collection, Pack Library.)

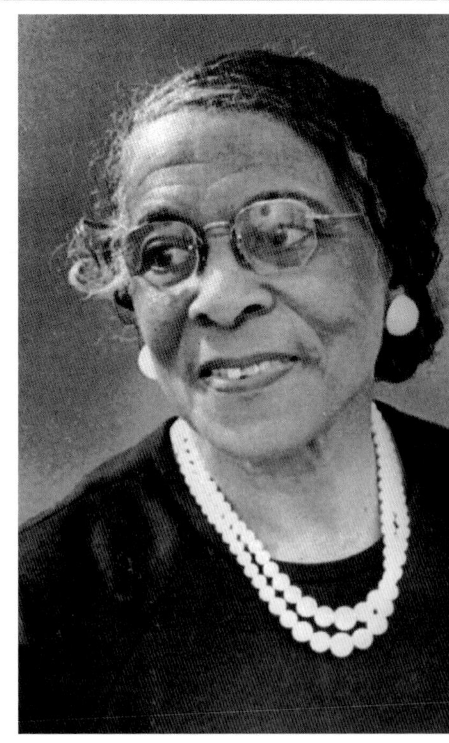

Irene O. Hendrick

In 1926, finally heeding calls to create a public library for African Americans, the City of Asheville hired Irene Hendrick to organize the city's first black library, and she became its first librarian the following year. The library was located at the Young Men's Institute, an institution built by and for the African American community in the late 1800s. The Market Street Branch Library, or the "Colored Library," as it was known at the time, remained in operation until 1961, when the Asheville Student Committee on Racial Equality desegregated the main public library. (Courtesy of the North Carolina Collection, Pack Library.)

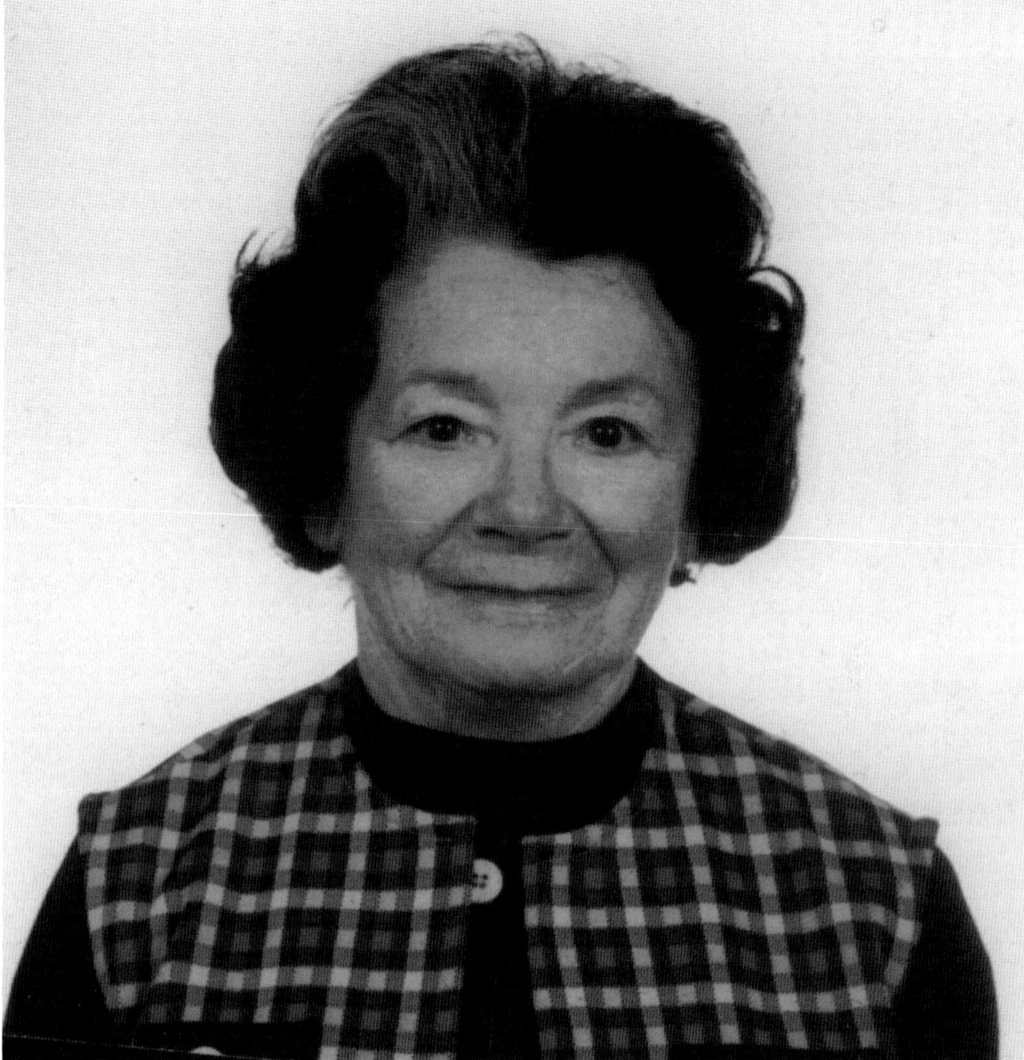

Sprinza Weizenblatt

One of Asheville's most beloved physicians, Sprinza Weizenblatt trained in Vienna as an ophthalmologist and was convinced to move to Asheville in 1928 by a local ophthalmologist, Harry Briggs, whom she met at a conference. Weizenblatt quickly developed a reputation as one of the city's most outstanding physicians, noted not only for her skill but also for her generosity. No matter the color of their skin or the size of their wallets, all were welcome at Weizenblatt's practice. She kept a significant bank of cash at the front desk and instructed her staff to dip into the cashbox if a patient could not pay and tell them an anonymous benefactor had paid for the doctor's services. In her later years, Weizenblatt's generosity, often anonymous, supported several of the area's colleges. An avid traveler and patron of the fine arts, Weizenblatt journeyed often to New York and Europe for the symphony, theater, and opera. An equally strong outdoor enthusiast, she took up surfing in her 70s and went backpacking across the Alaskan wilderness in her 80s. She remained active until her passing in 1987. (Courtesy of Ramsey Library Special Collections.)

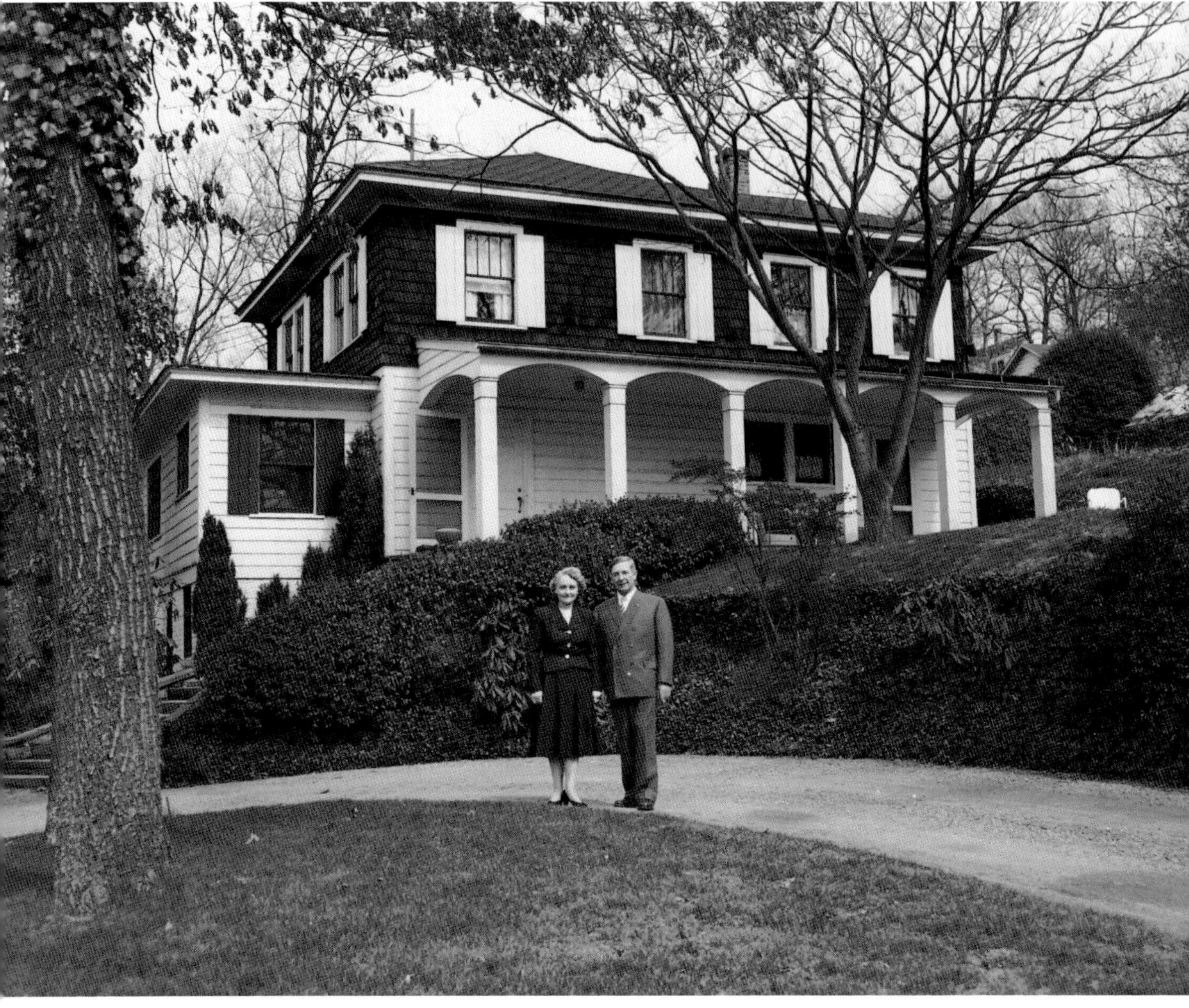

Charles G. "Buzz" Tennent

Born in 1894, Buzz Tennent studied at the University of North Carolina at Chapel Hill. As editor of *The Tarheel*, the student newspaper, he convinced young Thomas Wolfe to join the staff. A landscape architect by profession, Tennent is noted for his work in developing the original landscape of the University of North Carolina at Asheville's current campus in north Asheville. During his lifetime, Tennent was also highly involved with Rotary International and served as the international head of the organization in the 1950s. Tennent remained active in civic affairs until his death in 1979. (Courtesy of Ramsey Library Special Collections.)

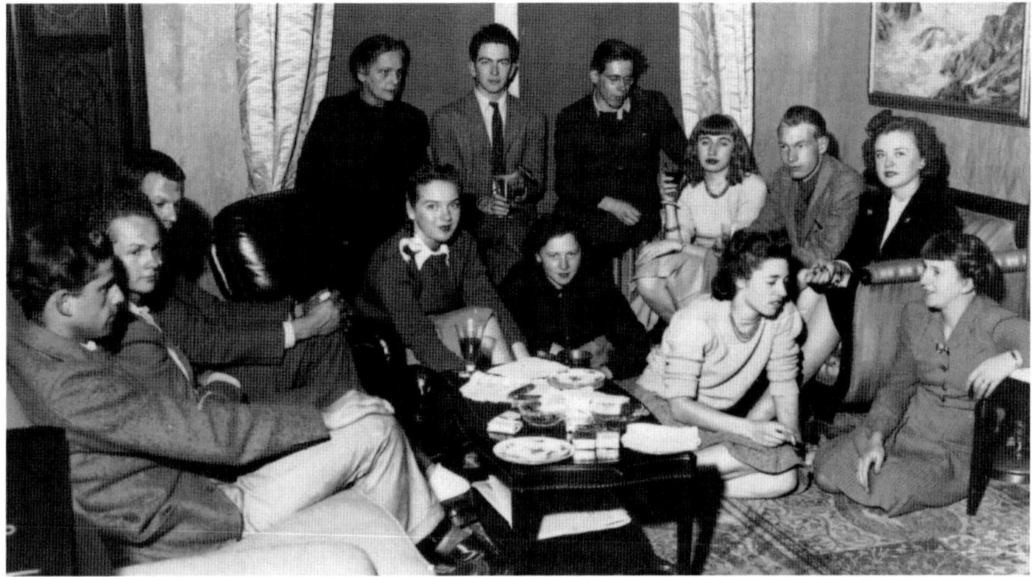

Black Mountain College Faculty

In 1933, in the midst of the Great Depression, John A. Rice, a controversial scholar from Rollins College, established the experimental Black Mountain College based on John Dewey's principle of progressive education. Owned by the faculty and supported by physical labor from students, faculty, and staff alike, the college attracted an extraordinary group of faculty and students, several of whom had fled Nazi Germany and many of whom went on to become very famous and highly influential 20th-century artists and thinkers, including Buckminster Fuller, Willem and Elaine de Kooning, Robert Rauschenberg, Josef and Anni Albers, Jacob Lawrence, Merce Cunningham, John Cage, Cy Twombly, Kenneth Noland, Ben Shahn, Franz Kline, Arthur Penn, M.C. Richards, Francine du Plessix Gray, Charles Olson, Robert Creeley, and Dorothea Rockburne. The impact of Black Mountain College on American arts is significant and reverberates to this day. (Both, courtesy of Black Mountain College Museum and Ramsey Library Special Collections.)

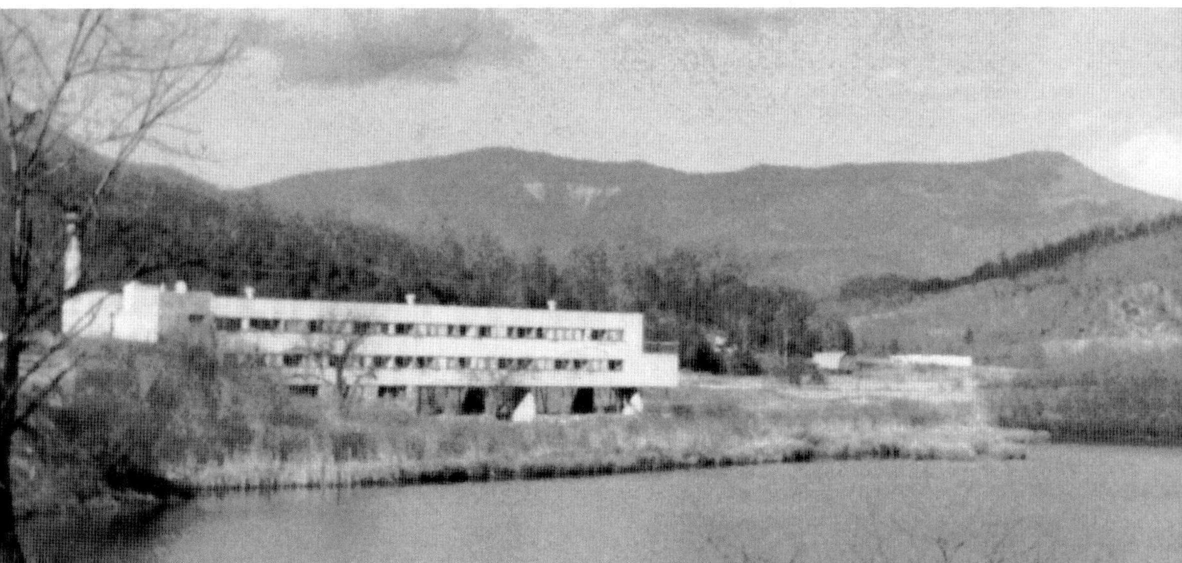

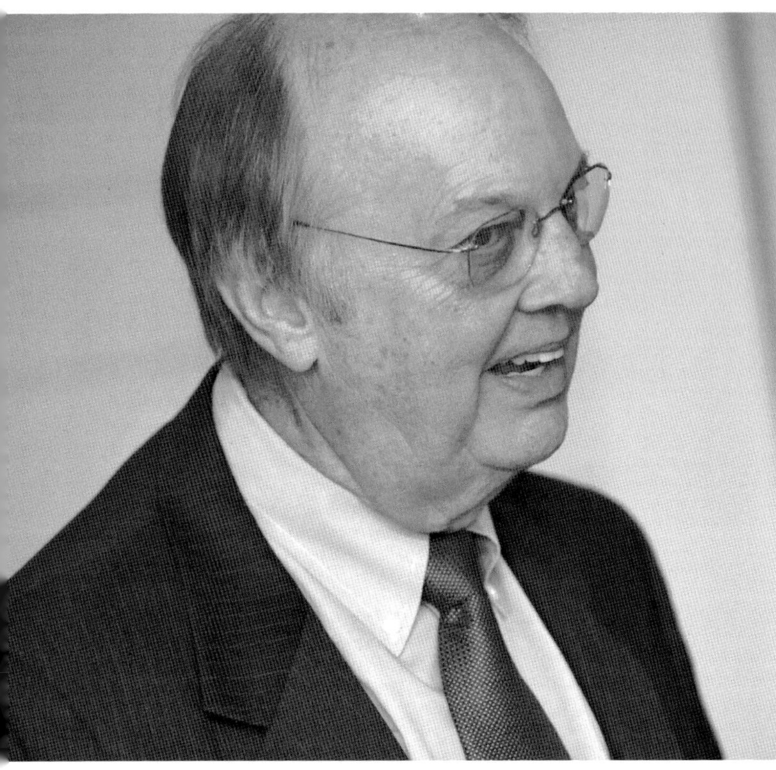

K. Ray Bailey

K. Ray Bailey served as the president of Asheville Buncombe Technical Community College for 17 of his more than 40 years at the college. During that time, the institution grew to include over 25,000 students on three campuses. The ENKA Campus was a gift of the BASF Corporation and is the largest gift ever given to a community college in the United States. After his retirement in 2007, Bailey went on to serve on the Buncombe County Commission until 2012, and has since remained active in area economic development. (Left, photograph by Perry Hebbard, courtesy of UNC Asheville Communication and Marketing; below, photograph by Aaron Dahlstrom.)

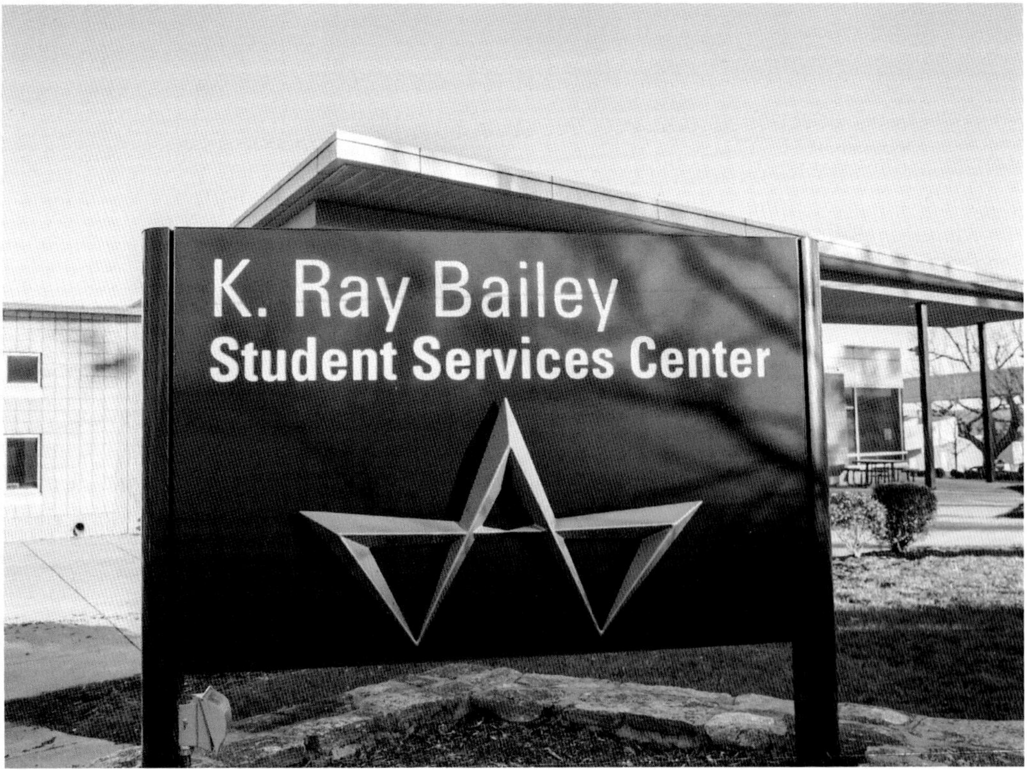

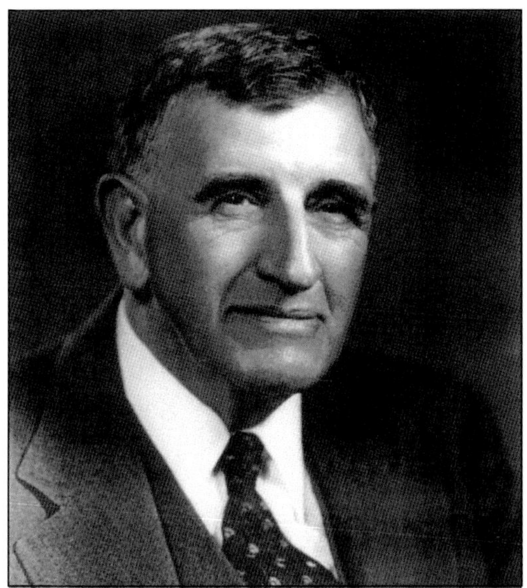

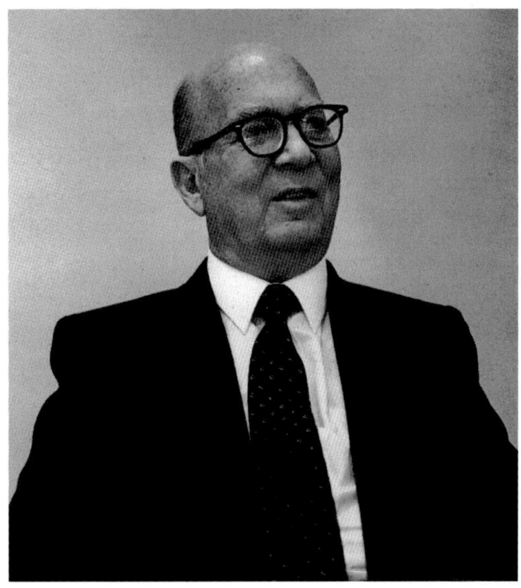

UNC Asheville Chancellors

Founded in 1927 as Buncombe County Junior College, the University of North Carolina at Asheville has played a significant role in shaping the Asheville community. Established by A.C. Reynolds (above, left), superintendent of Buncombe County Schools, as a free junior college, the college has gone through several name changes, including Biltmore College and Asheville-Biltmore College, and has been located at six different campuses. Since joining the University of North Carolina system in 1969, UNC Asheville has evolved into one of the nation's leading liberal arts universities. Much of this came at the hands of a group of extraordinary leaders who shaped not only the college but the community as well. William E. Highsmith (above, right) was the first to serve as chancellor, from 1962 to 1984, followed by (below, from left to right) David G. Brown (1984–1990), Samuel Schuman (1991–1993), Patsy. B. Reed (1994–1999), James H. Mullen Jr. (1999-2005), and Anne Ponder (2005–2014). (Above, both courtesy of Ramsey Library Special Collections; below, courtesy of UNC Asheville Communication and Marketing.)

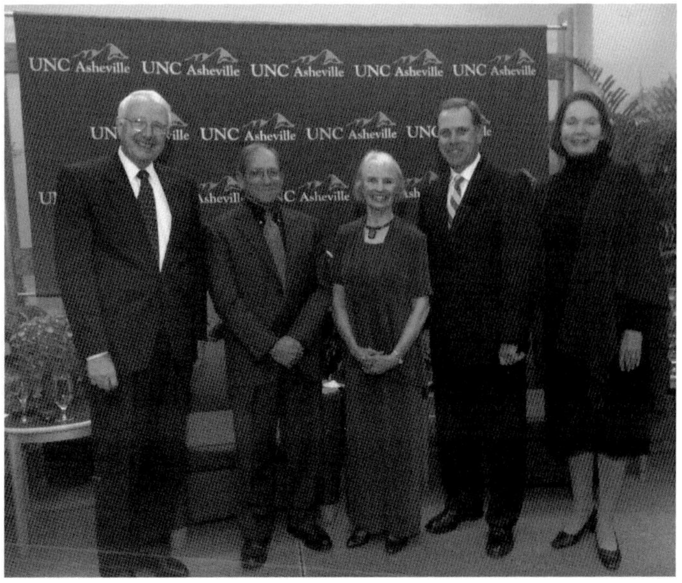

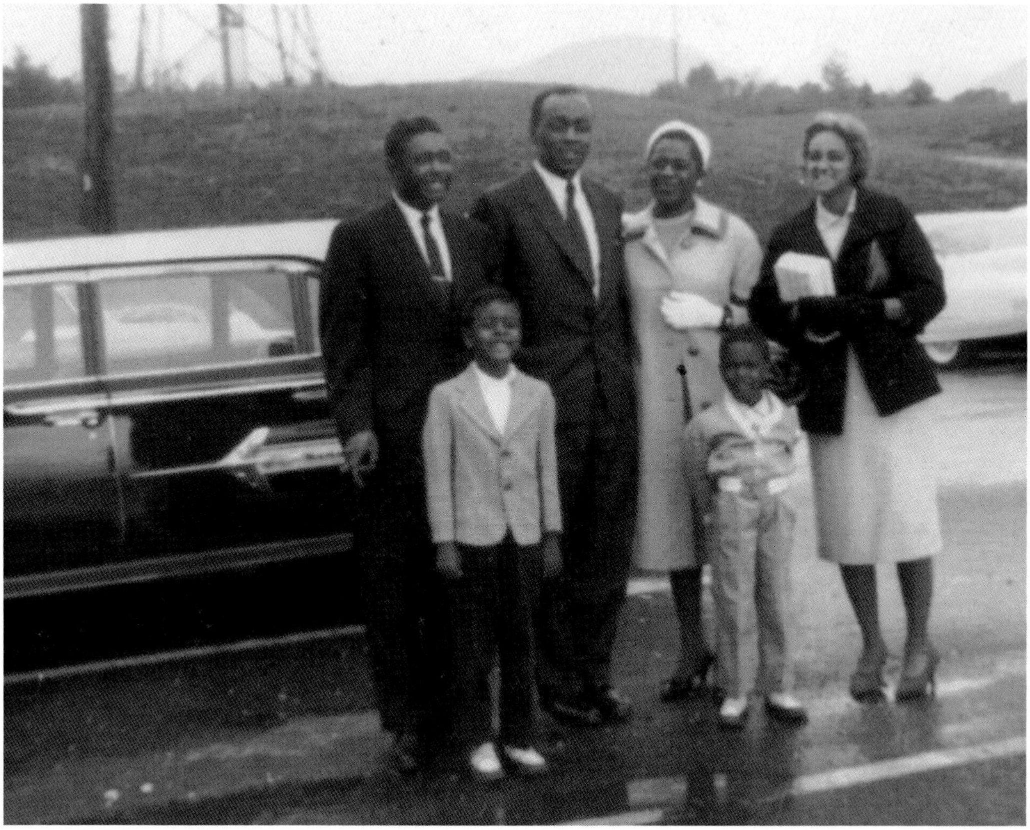

Julia and Jesse Ray Sr.

Julia and Jesse Ray met in Asheville after Jesse's mother had encouraged him to correspond with a beautiful girl whose picture he had seen in a Pittsburgh newspaper. They married in 1935, and a few years later opened their first funeral services business, providing funeral services for generations of African American families. During World War II, Jesse served as a civilian embalmer and played an important role in the removal and reinterment of soldiers' remains from temporary to permanent graves. After the war, both of the Rays were very active in civic affairs in Asheville, including desegregation and economic development. They served on numerous boards and have been extremely well-respected members of the community. Jesse died in 1994, but the family continues in the funeral services business under the name Ray and Allen Funeral Services. (Above, courtesy of Ramsey Library Special Collections; right, courtesy of Ray and Allen Funeral Services.)

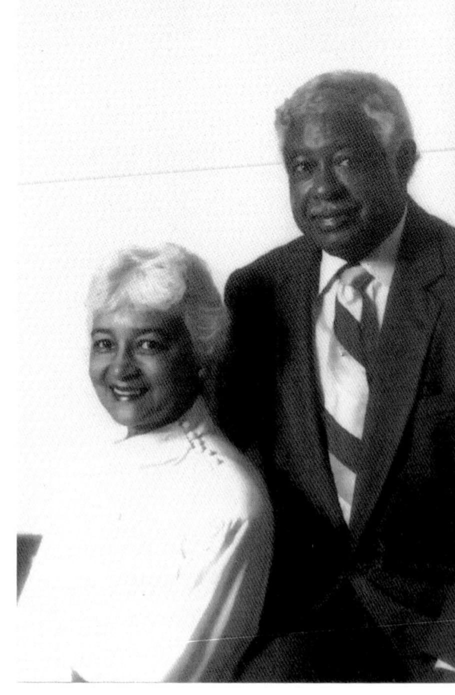

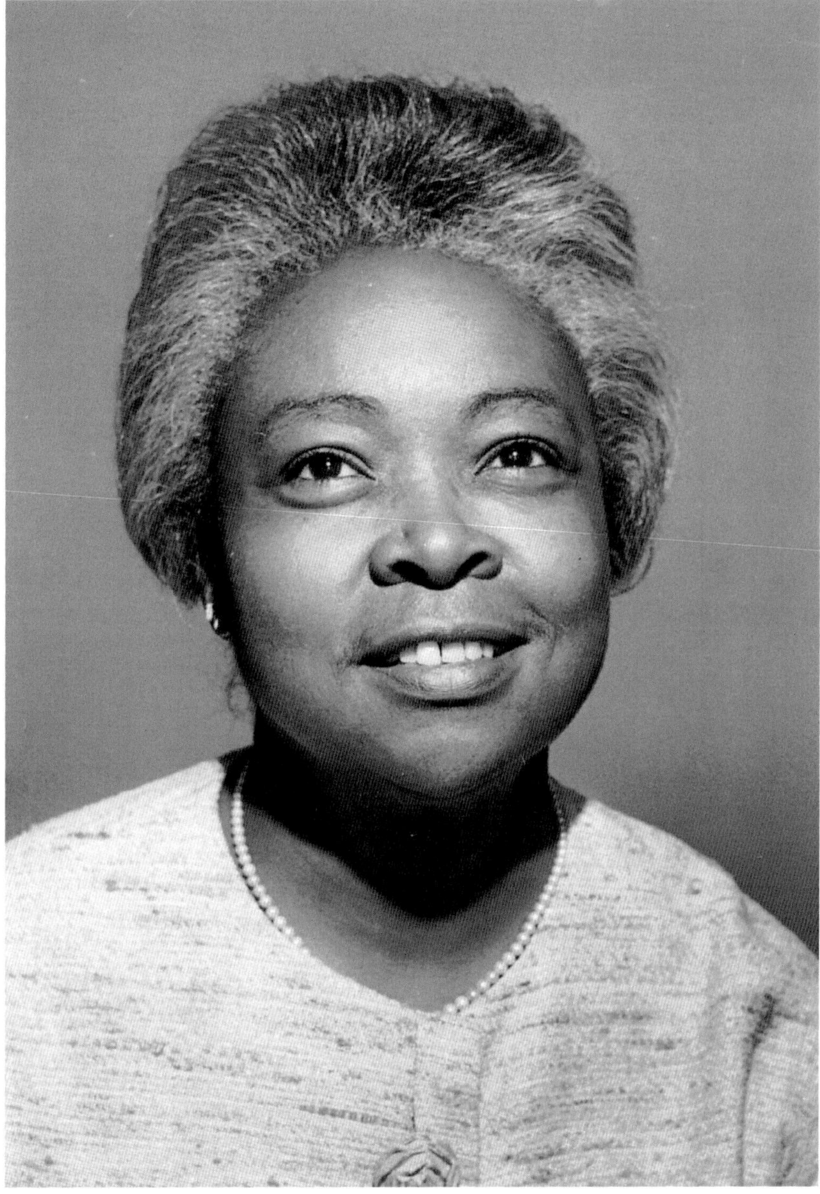

Thelma Caldwell

Thelma Caldwell arrived in Asheville in 1960 to become director of the Phyllis Wheatley Branch of the Asheville YWCA, the segregated branch for African Americans. Caldwell quickly and thoughtfully began her work to create a racially blended YWCA, carefully pulling in supporters from both facilities to begin a series of Black-White Dialogues to uphold the YWCA's new national mission, which included "the elimination of racism wherever it exists, and by whatever means necessary." The effort was controversial and had supporters and detractors on both sides. It took seven years, but Caldwell was victorious, and in the late 1960s became the executive director of the newly merged YWCA. Caldwell was the first African American director of a YWCA in the South and only the second in the nation. Her success in Asheville led her to advise YWCAs all over the world. (Courtesy of Ramsey Library Special Collections.)

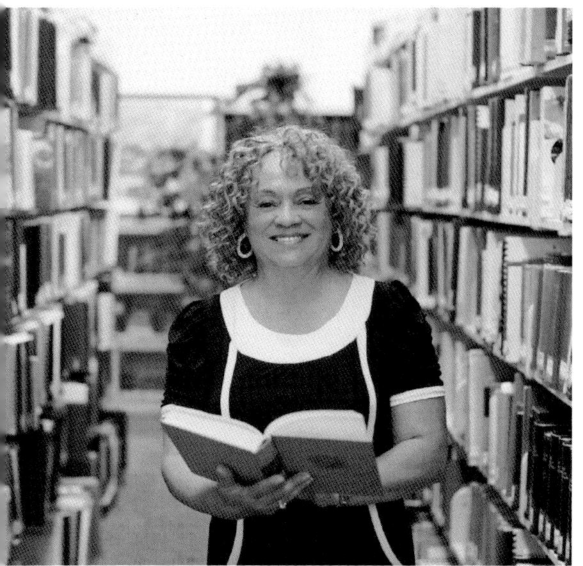

Oralene Simmons

Oralene Simmons grew up in neighboring Madison County, and in 1961 became the first African American student to be admitted to and graduate from Mars Hill College. Her family's history with the college went back to its founding, when her great-great-grandfather, Joe Anderson, a slave, was held as collateral for the loan that originally built the college. Simmons went on to build a long career at the Asheville Parks and Recreation Department, where, in 1982, she led the founding of the annual Dr. Martin Luther King Jr. Prayer Breakfast, now an Asheville institution. For her leadership honoring Dr. King, Simmons has received the North Carolina Order of the Long Leaf Pine and the King Holiday Award from Coretta Scott King. (Photograph by Tim Robison, courtesy of Tim Robinson Creative.)

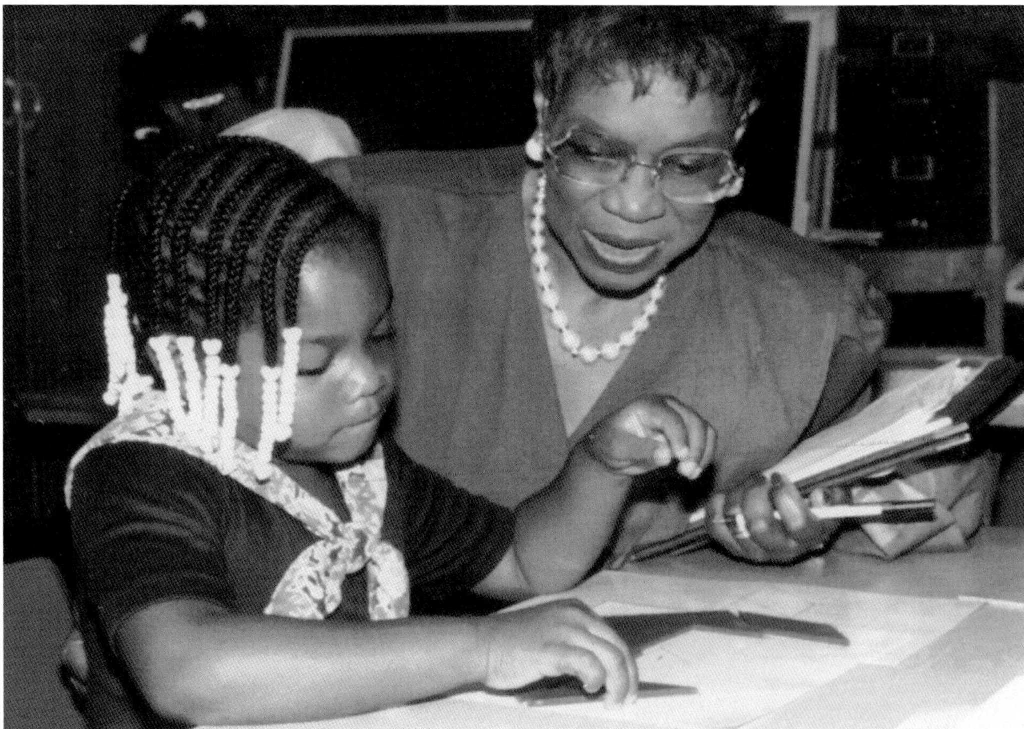

Beatrice Francine Mitchell Delany

Francine Delany was the first African American to graduate from Asheville-Biltmore College, predecessor of the University of North Carolina at Asheville, and was a member of the college's first baccalaureate class in 1966. Delany went on to become a teacher, and, eventually, principal of Isaac Dickson School, one of North Carolina's first "alternative" elementary schools. She was also instrumental in helping community members form the city's first charter school, the Francine Delany New School for Children, named in her honor after her passing. (Courtesy of Ramsey Library Special Collections.)

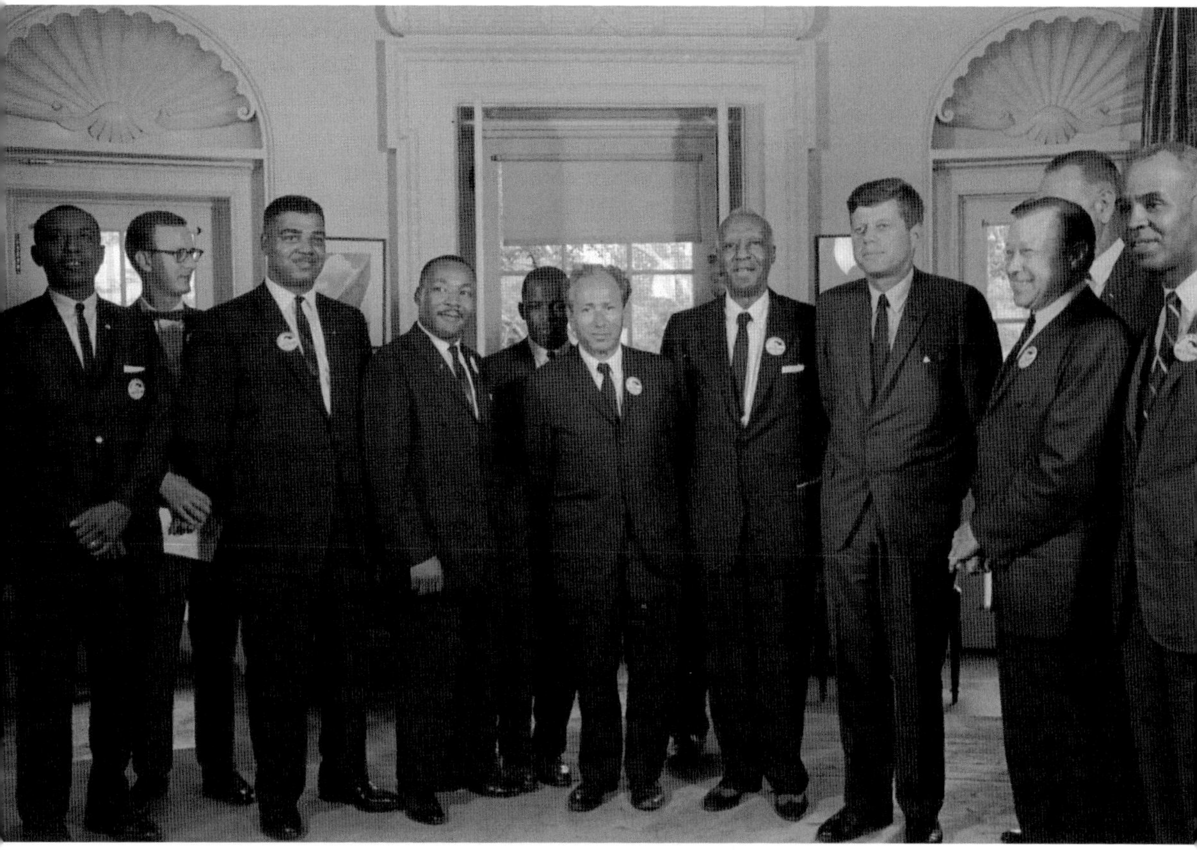

Floyd B. McKissick

Floyd McKissick (far left, facing forward), head of the Congress of Racial Equality (CORE) in the mid-1960s, was born in Asheville in 1922. As a young man, McKissick was active with the NAACP and participated in his first protest in Asheville. After returning from Army service in World War II, McKissick became a lawyer and was active in a number of civil rights cases. In 1963, he became the national chairman of CORE, and in 1966, he replaced James Farmer as the head of CORE until 1968. After CORE, McKissick tried to build a planned community, Soul City, in Warren, North Carolina, which was designed to advance minorities and the poor. Though the project received funding, it ran into difficulties and never developed as planned. McKissick later became a judge in North Carolina. (Courtesy of the Library of Congress.)

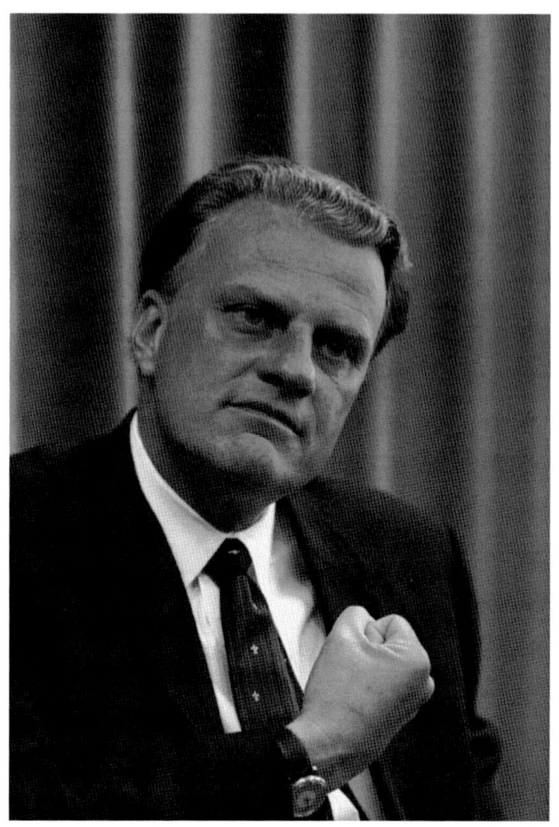

Billy Graham

Often called "America's Pastor," Billy Graham began his career as a Christian evangelist in the 1940s with his first radio program, "Songs in the Night." Graham went on to have a storied career, building close ties with US presidents and other global leaders, as well as leading more than 400 crusades in 185 countries. In the 1970s, Graham purchased acreage outside of Asheville, which in the 1980s became the Billy Graham Training Center at The Cove. Graham eventually moved to the area, where he retired with his wife, Ruth. (Right, courtesy of the Library of Congress; below, courtesy of the North Carolina Collection, Pack Library.)

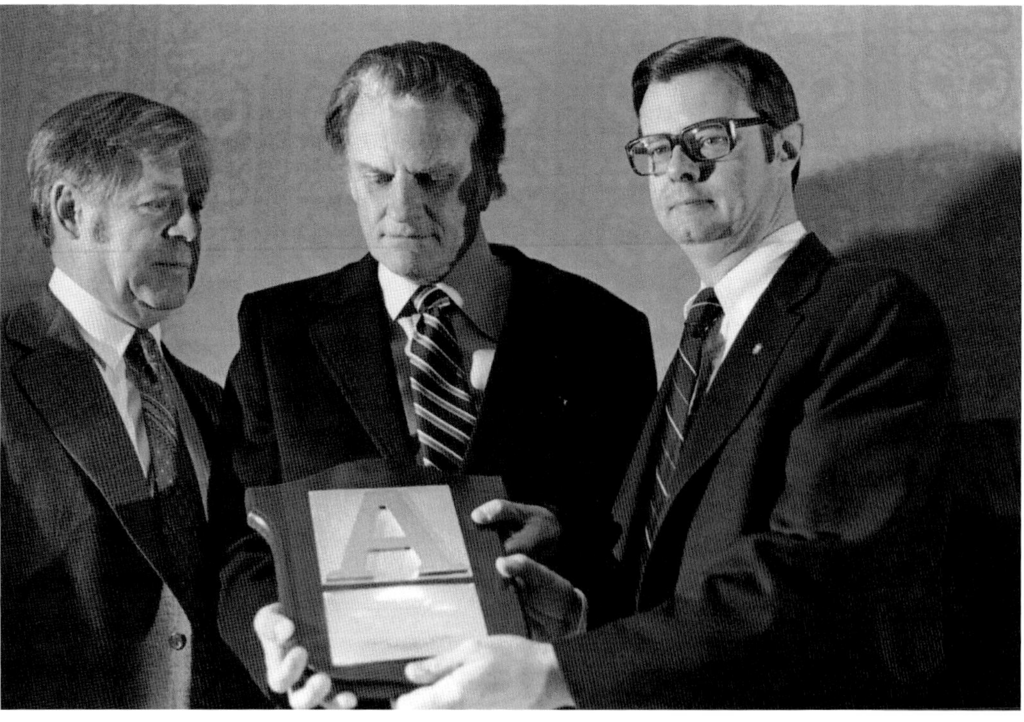

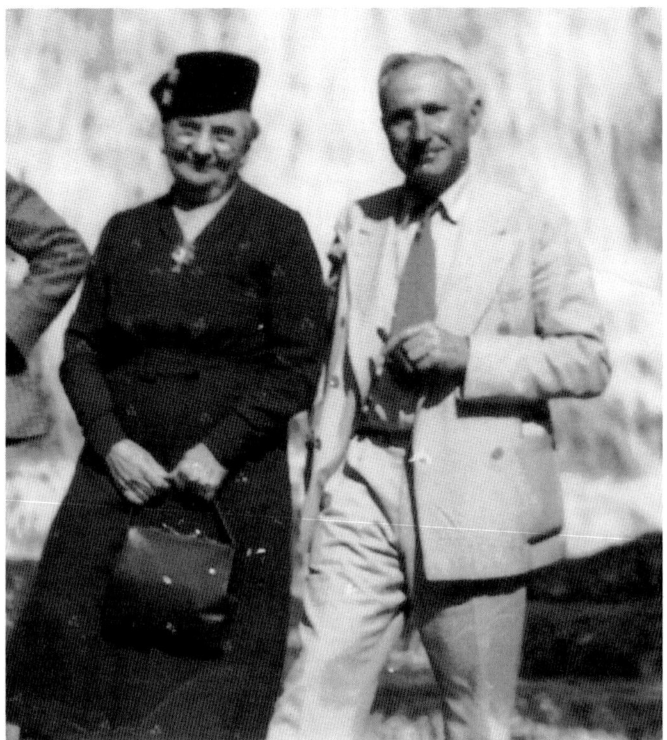

Janet and Irving Reuter
Janet and Irving Reuter moved to Asheville in 1937 after Irving's retirement from his post as the longtime head of Oldsmobile. In 1954, the Reuters established the Janirv Foundation (derived from their first names), funded by their significant wealth. Over the next 60-some years, until it closed in 2012, the foundation gave tens of millions of dollars to hundreds of projects in Asheville. The legacy of their generosity in Asheville is significant. (Courtesy of Ramsey Library Special Collections.)

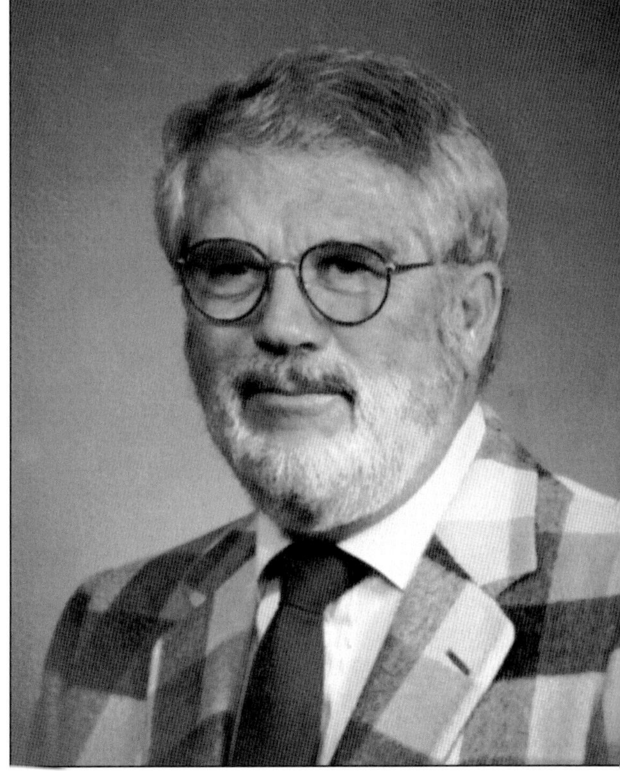

Joe P. Eblen
Born in 1925 in Tennessee, Eblen moved to Asheville after serving in the Navy in World War II and receiving degrees from the University of Tennessee and Vanderbilt to teach and coach sports. Eblen loved sports and worked as an official for some 70 years. In the 1950s, he left teaching to join his father-in-law in running Biltmore Oil, which he eventually expanded to include a chain of convenience stores, Eblen Short Stop Stores. In 1991, Eblen grew concerned that there was no local organization to directly assist individuals and families with illness or disability regardless of income. In 1991, a yard sale raised $400, and Eblen Charities was born. It assisted 300 families in its first year. Eblen turned to William Murdoch to lead the organization, and, by the time of Eblen's death in 2013, Eblen Charities had grown into a multimillion-dollar philanthropic organization with 70 programs helping tens of thousands of people each year. (Courtesy of Rock Eblen.)

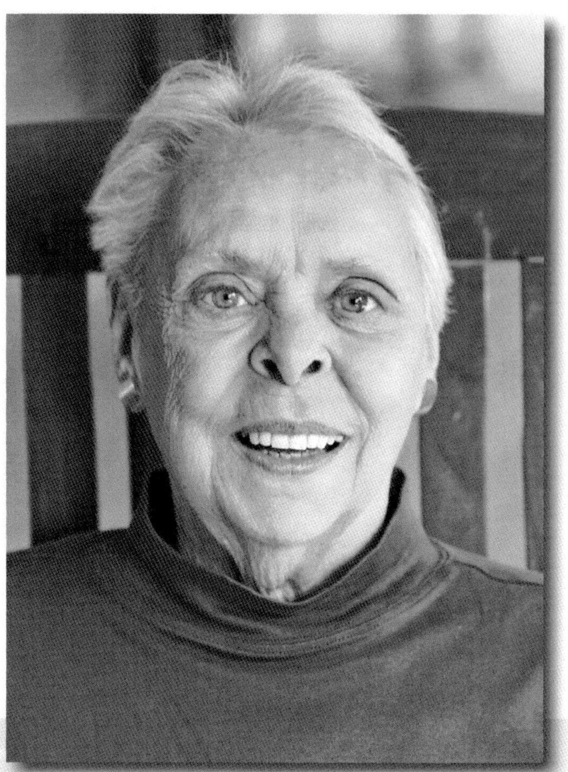

Adelaide Daniels Key

Born in 1935 into the prominent Daniels family, publishers of the *Raleigh News & Observer*, Adelaide Key sold her shares in the family business in 1990, shortly after she moved to Asheville. While a successful business owner in both Franklin, North Carolina, and Asheville, she is best known for her seemingly tireless philanthropic work. Through her foundation, Key established a service learning center at UNC Asheville and a special school for children with dyslexia housed at Carolina Day School. She also founded the Lewis Rathbun Center, which provides free lodging and support services to patients and their families traveling to Asheville for medical treatment. The recipient of two honorary doctorates, Key served on the boards of numerous colleges, foundations, and nonprofit organizations. Key died in 2014. (Left, photograph by Roger Bargainnier, courtesy of Roger Bargainnier and Asheville Living Treasures; below, photograph by Aaron Dahlstrom.)

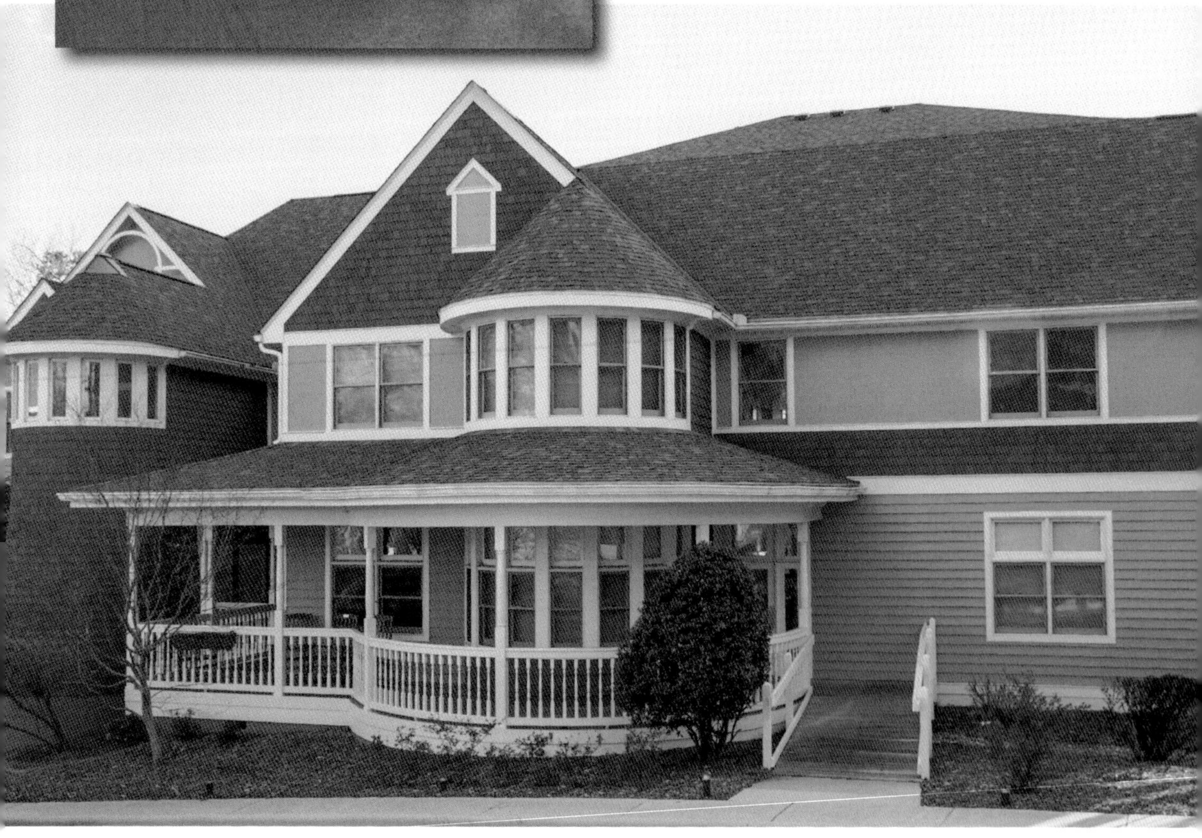

CHAPTER FIVE

Authors, Artists, and Musicians

The arts are strong in Appalachia. From music, crafts, ceramics, and painting, to the written and spoken word, the arts have always been an essential part of Asheville's culture. In music, Ashevillians have kept the old traditions alive while also introducing the world to new forms of music. Many great musicians were born here, but as many have been drawn to the musical energy of Asheville to call it their home later in life. Some unexpected actors, too, have gotten their starts in theater in Asheville.

From the first Cherokee stories told around a fire to the many nationally celebrated writers who call Asheville home, this is a community of words. There were the Jazz Age writers who defined the Roaring Twenties, and the Southern writers who used Asheville itself as their backdrop. While many have seen their works made into film, the best stories in Asheville are still often told in a small group gathered on the front porch.

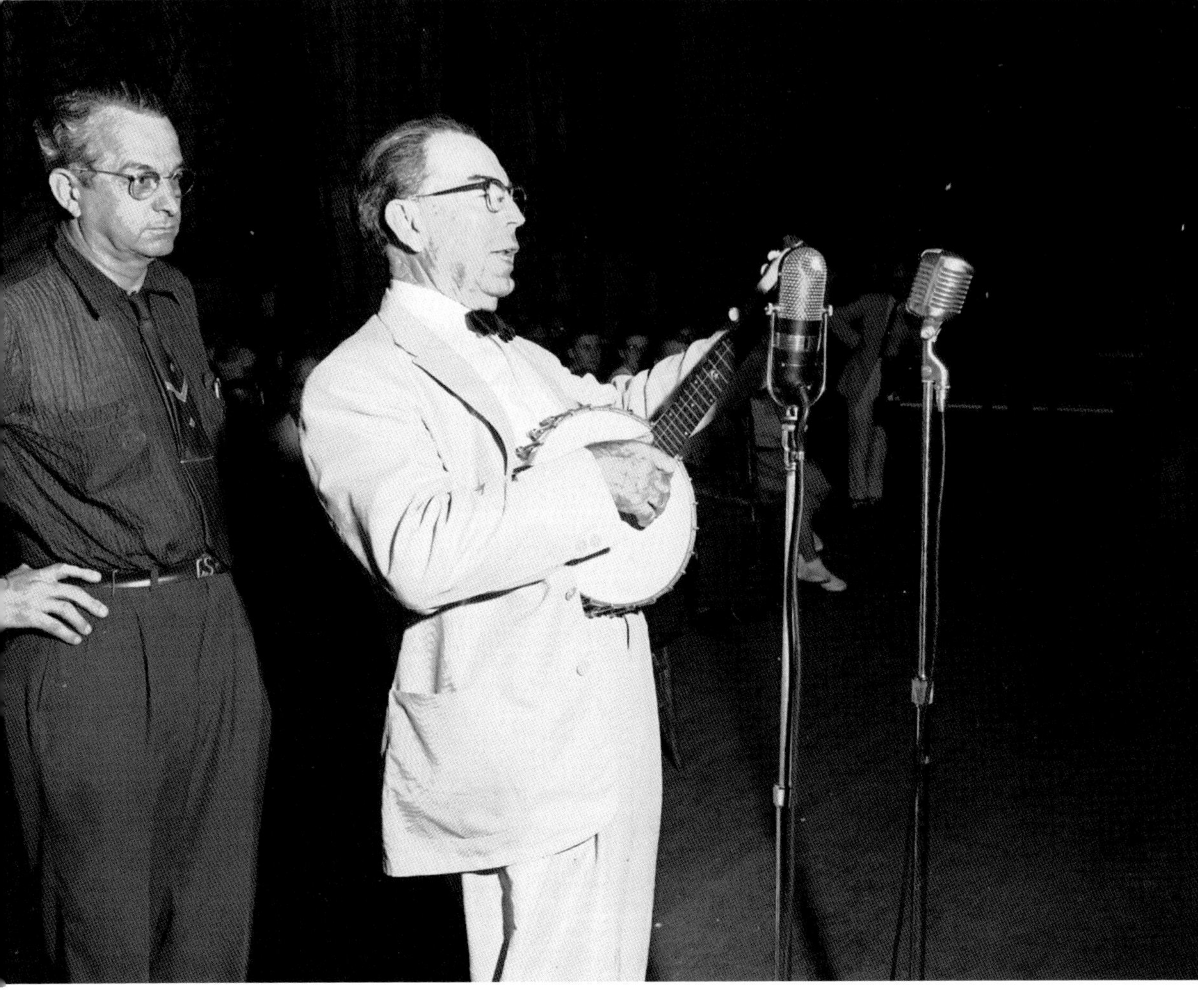

Bascom Lamar Lunsford
Often called the "Minstrel of the Appalachians," banjo player Bascom Lamar Lunsford spent most of the 20th century preserving and advancing traditional mountain music. Lunsford was a man of many talents and worked as a lawyer, teacher, publisher, legislative reading clerk, and even a fruit tree and honey salesman. His travels as a salesman gave him the opportunity to learn music from families across the mountains. In 1928, Lunsford founded Asheville's Mountain Dance and Folk Festival, which continues to this day. Lunsford performed often, usually in a white shirt and black bow tie, as a way to battle hillbilly stereotypes. During his lifetime, he was invited to perform before presidents and royalty and worked closely with the Library of Congress and the Smithsonian to preserve folk traditions. He died in 1973. (Courtesy of Ramsey Library Special Collections.)

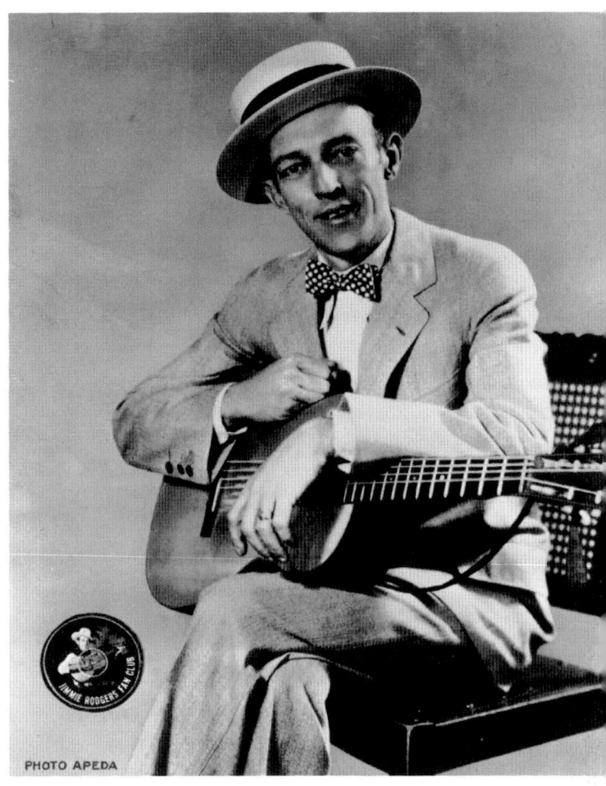

Jimmie Rodgers

Widely acknowledged as the "Father of Country Music," Jimmie Rodgers began his commercial music career in Asheville in 1927. Rodgers had moved to the city that year, possibly due to his tuberculosis. On April 18, he performed for the first time on the radio on WWNC, Asheville's first radio station, founded earlier that same year. Rodgers recruited the Tenneva Ramblers from Bristol, Tennessee, to be his band, and the Jimmie Rodgers Entertainers secured a weekly slot on the station. Unfortunately, the show was short-lived, but while in Asheville, Rodgers had connected with Ralph Peer, a representative of the Victor Talking Machine Company, to make a recording. The national success of Rodgers's first recordings, often marked by his unique yodeling, led him to become a very popular early recording artist. Days after recording a studio album in 1933, Rodgers collapsed from a pulmonary hemorrhage, a complication from his years of fighting tuberculosis. (Courtesy of the Southern Folklore Collection, The Wilson Library, UNC Chapel Hill.)

Bill Monroe

Bill Monroe, the award-winning mandolin player and "Father of Bluegrass Music," first performed on the radio with the Blue Grass Boys on February 2, 1939, at 1:30 p.m. on WWNC's "Mountain Music Time" radio show, atop Asheville's triangular-shaped Flat Iron Building. Monroe and his band stayed in residence in Asheville only three months, but, during that time, they began to craft the sound that would come to be known as bluegrass music, so named after Monroe's band. From these humble beginnings evolved a uniquely American music genre. (Courtesy of the Southern Folklore Collection, The Wilson Library, UNC Chapel Hill.)

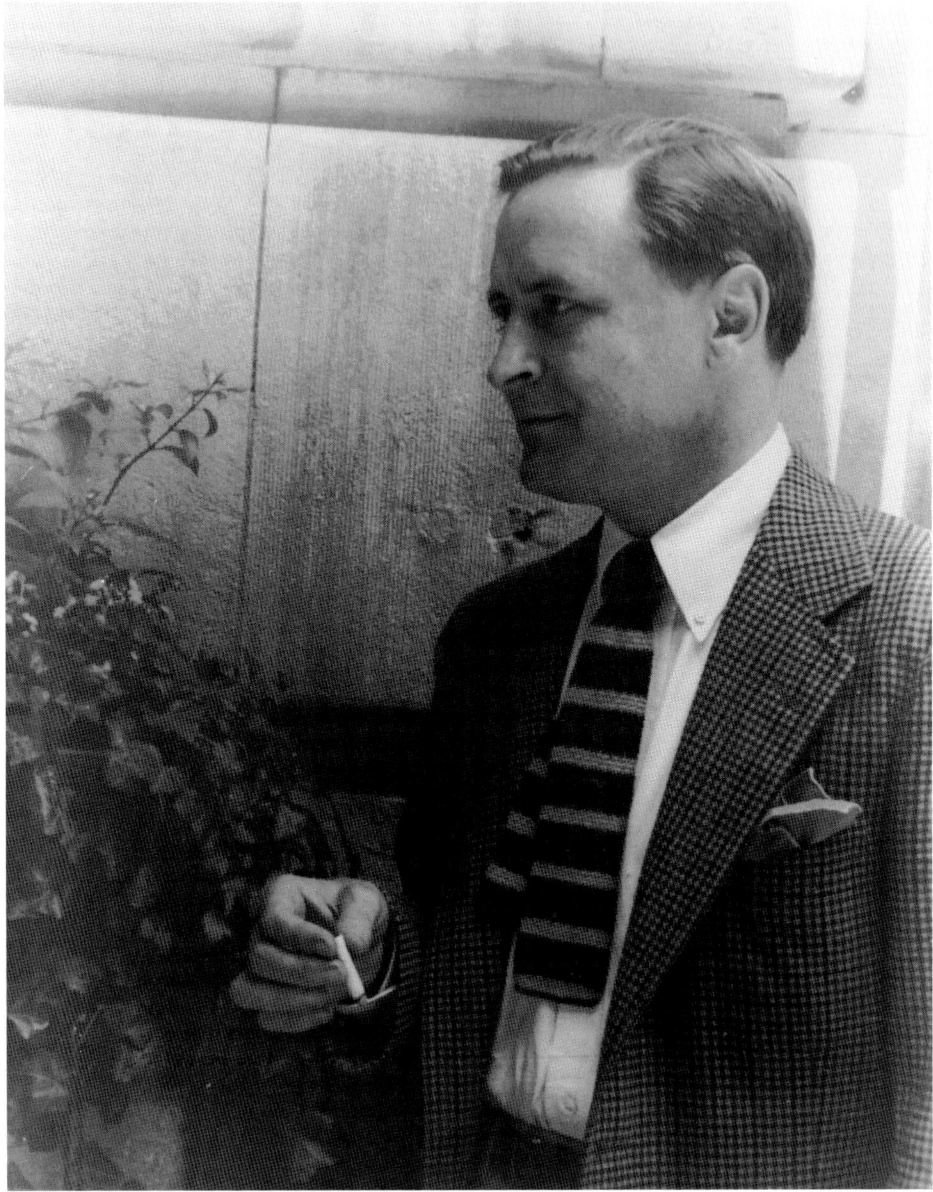

F. Scott Fitzgerald

F. Scott Fitzgerald, the noted Jazz Age author, moved to Asheville in the summer of 1935 to live at the Grove Park Inn. He had come to Asheville both for inspiration and for a lung ailment, likely tuberculosis. He had hoped Asheville would give him the rest and inspiration he needed to write his fourth novel, a follow-up to *The Great Gatsby*. The following year, Fitzgerald returned to Asheville and the Grove Park, both for his writing and to be near his wife, Zelda, whom he had checked into Asheville's Highland Hospital for her mental health. Nonetheless, Fitzgerald made sure his room overlooked the entrance to the inn, so he could see the arrival of wealthy socialites, several of whom were his known lovers. The author would return one last time in 1937 before moving to Hollywood to write for film. In poor health much of his life as a result of his alcoholism, Fitzgerald died of a heart attack in California in 1940. (Photograph by Carl Van Vechten; courtesy of the Library of Congress.)

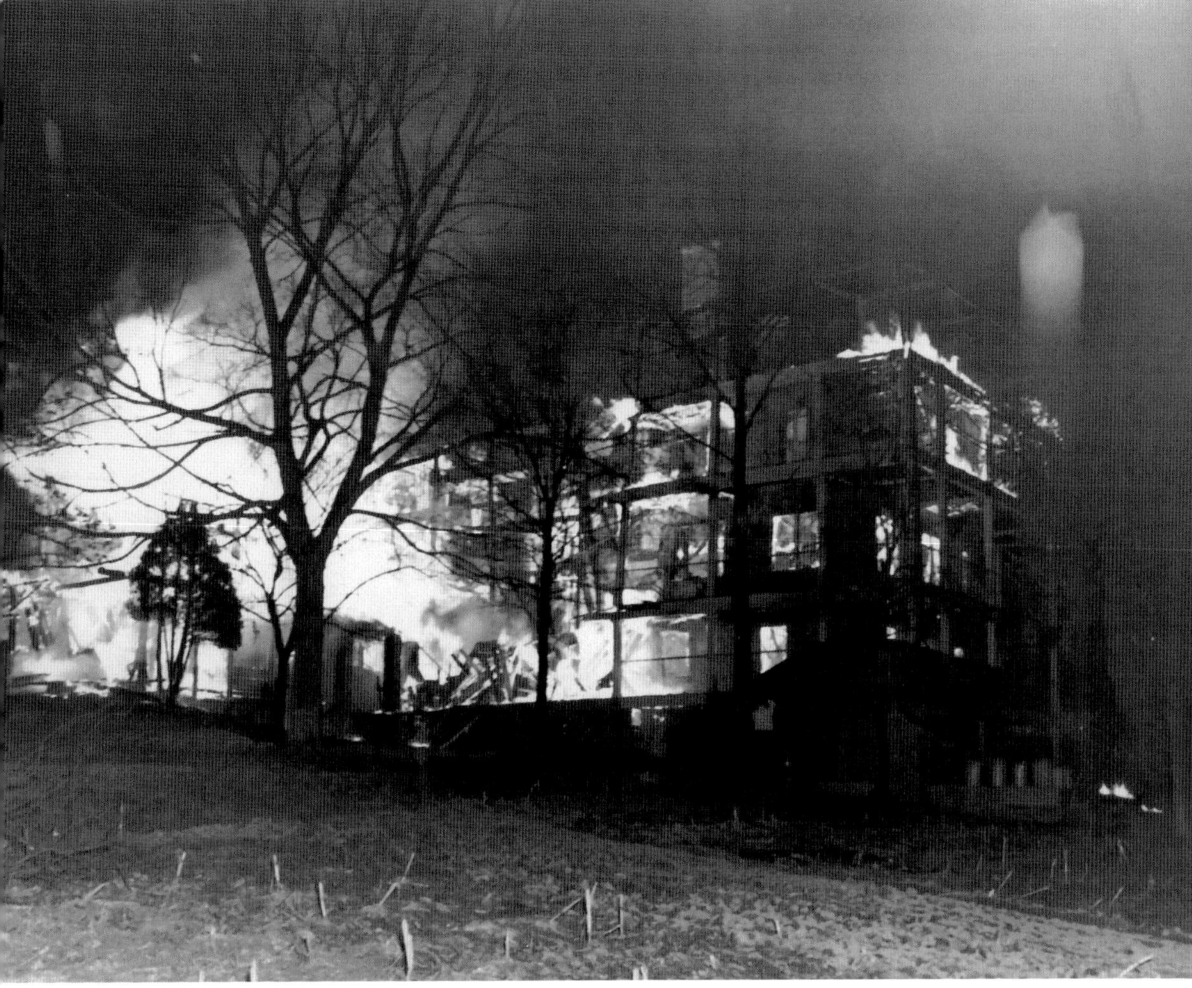

Zelda Fitzgerald

Zelda Fitzgerald, wife of noted author F. Scott Fitzgerald, first came to Asheville in 1936 when Scott had her admitted to Dr. Robert S. Carroll's Highland Hospital. Zelda had been diagnosed with schizophrenia, though today it is believed that she had bipolar disorder. Zelda's mental health had been in decline since 1930, with much of it believed to have been related to her and Scott's tumultuous relationship, her isolation when he was writing, and his lack of support and even anger toward her own career goals, including ballet and writing, especially her semiautobiographical novel, *Save Me the Waltz*. Zelda and Scott last saw each other in Asheville in 1938. She was released from Highlands in 1940 but returned by 1943. She, along with eight other patients, died at the hospital in 1948 as a result of a fire set by a former patient who had come to work for Highlands. Her death was barely noticed at the time, and it was not until 1950 that public interest in her and Scott resurged. (Courtesy of the North Carolina Collection, Pack Memorial Library.)

William Sydney Porter (O. Henry)

Born in Greensboro, North Carolina, in 1862, noted short story writer William Sydney Porter began his literary career in the late 1890s while incarcerated for embezzlement, a charge he denied until his dying day. While in prison, he wrote short stories under the pseudonym O. Henry to disguise his imprisonment from publishers. A prolific writer, his stories were noted for their warm characters and ironic endings. O. Henry was released on good behavior after only three years and moved to New York to write full time. While on a trip back home to North Carolina, he chanced to meet his childhood sweetheart, Sarah "Sallie" Lindsey Coleman. They married in 1907, and three years later moved to Sallie's hometown, Asheville, for Porter's failing health. He did not find Asheville conducive to his writing and returned to New York, only to die soon thereafter in 1910. Sallie had his body taken to Asheville, where he was buried in Riverside Cemetery. (Courtesy of the North Carolina Collection, Pack Library.)

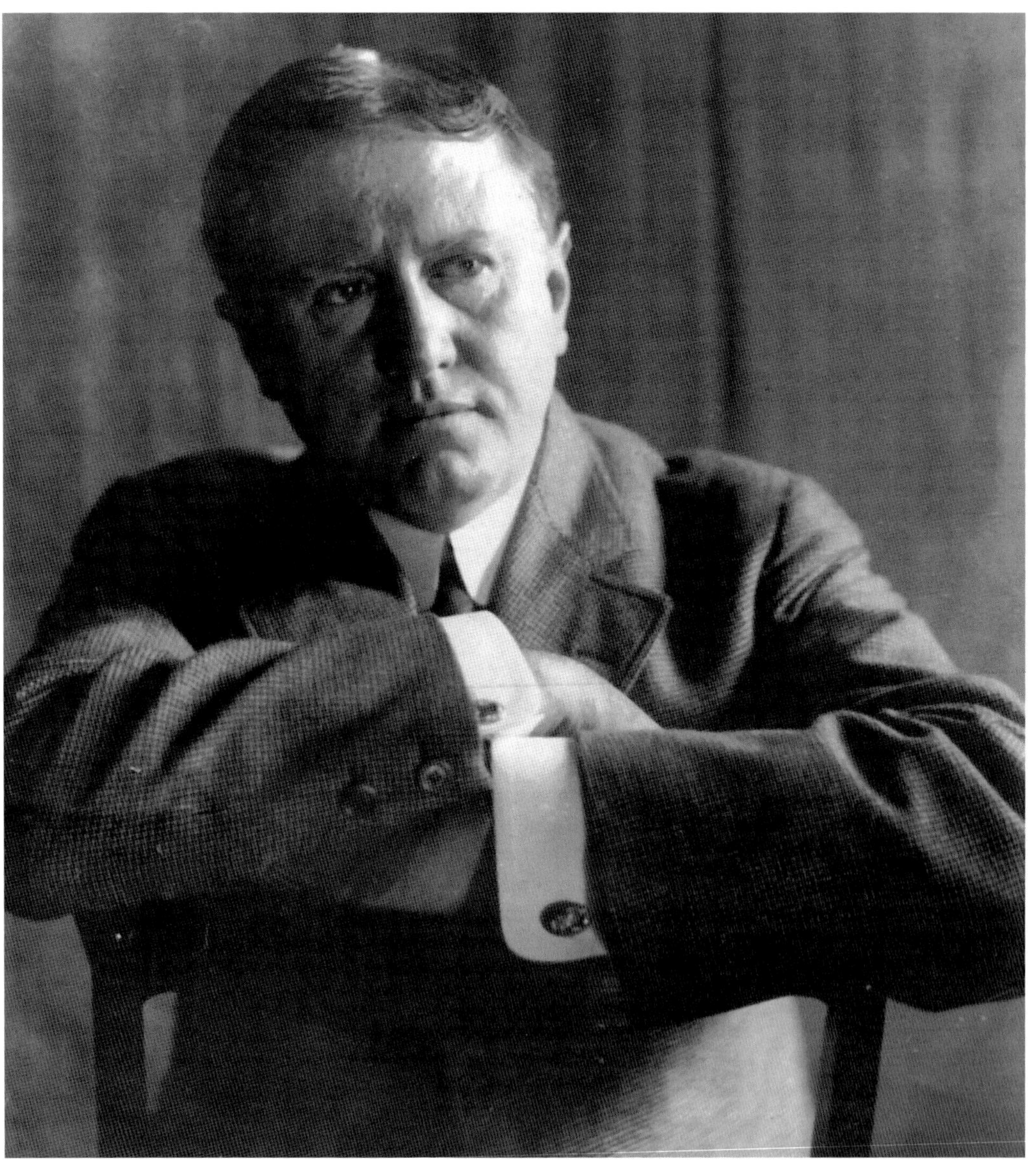

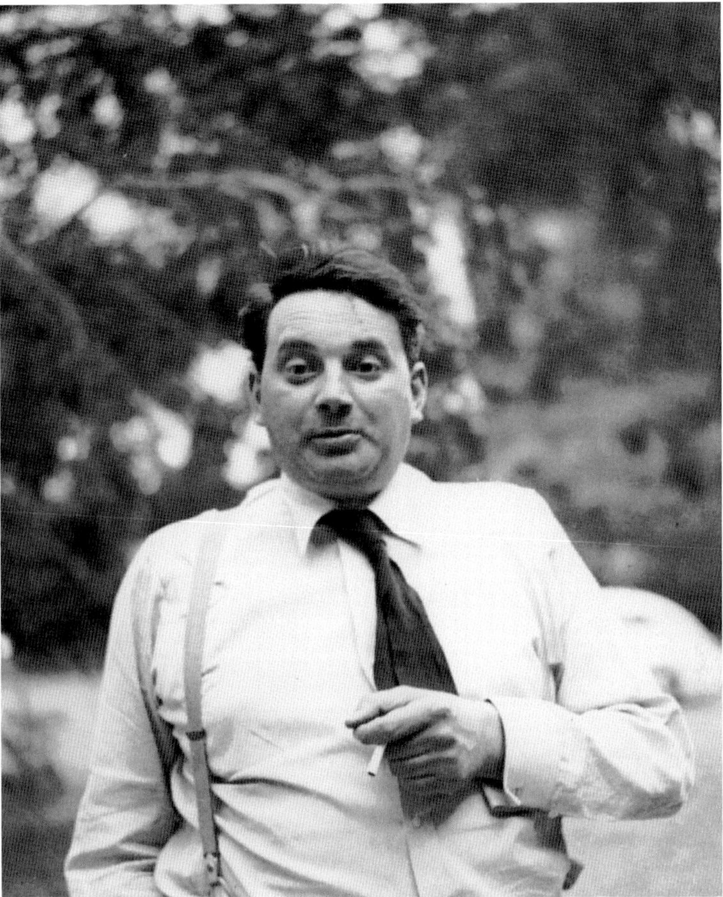

Thomas Wolfe

The great American novelist Thomas Wolfe was born in Asheville in 1900, his father a stonecutter and his mother a boardinghouse operator. The youngest of seven children, Wolfe grew up away from most of the family and lived with his mother in her boardinghouse, a few blocks from the family home, where his father lived. It was his father who stirred Wolfe's interest in the classics, like Shakespeare, which inspired him to take up writing. Quiet but bright, Wolfe enrolled at the University of North Carolina at Chapel Hill at the age of 15, and by 20 was in graduate school at Harvard University. After Harvard, he took a teaching position at New York University, which gave him a chance to travel. On one of several voyages to Europe he met the love of his life, Aline Bernstein, a married woman 19 years his senior. Though their relationship was at times turbulent, Bernstein became one of Wolfe's strongest supporters, and in 1928 helped him find a publisher for his first novel, *O Lost*. After several rejections, the manuscript was picked up by Charles Scribner's Sons publishers, where Maxwell Perkins, who had discovered the likes of Ernest Hemingway and F. Scott Fitzgerald, became Wolfe's editor. *O Lost* was published in 1929 as *Look Homeward, Angel*, a thinly veiled autobiography that caused quite a stir in Asheville. Wolfe quickly became a literary sensation, and set out to work on his second title. *Of Time and the River* was published in 1935, and, though it was very well received, Wolfe was stung by the words of a number of literary critics. He recovered and traveled west in 1938 for inspiration for his third novel. Unfortunately, a bout of pneumonia aggravated an old medical condition, and Wolfe was dead only a few days before his 38th birthday. He was buried in Asheville. Due to the amount of material he left at his death, several more novels were published posthumously, cementing his position as a great American author. (Courtesy of the North Carolina Collection, Pack Library.)

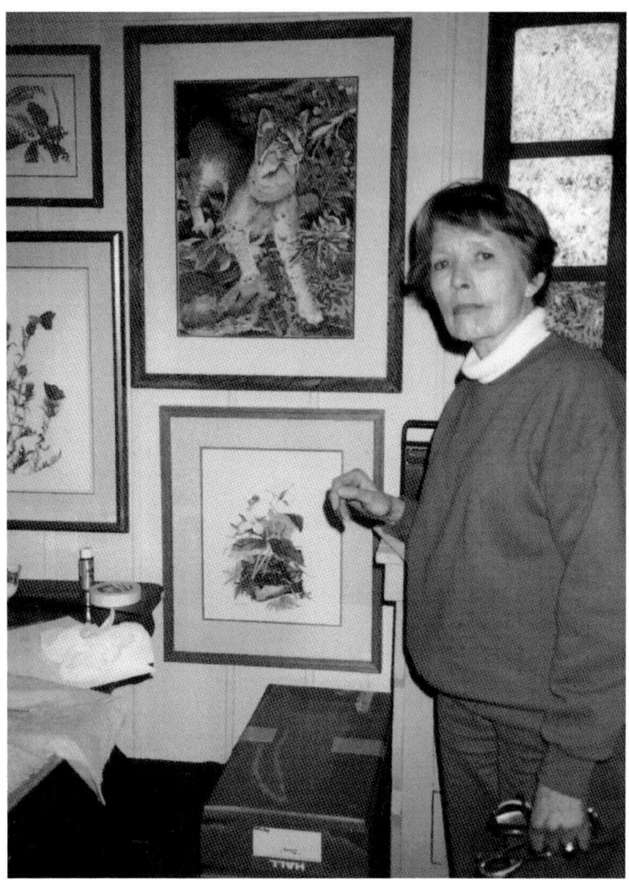

Sallie Ellington Middleton
Renowned wildlife watercolor artist Sallie Middleton moved to Asheville in the 1920s as a young girl with her parents, Margaret and Kenneth Ellington. Kenneth, an architect, was in practice with his brother, famed architect Douglas Ellington. Kenneth encouraged his daughter's curiosity and passion for nature. Their nature walks in Chunn's Cove when she was a girl inspired and informed her work later in life. Middleton was a prolific painter, producing hundreds of works before her death in 2009. (Courtesy of Ramsey Library Special Collections.)

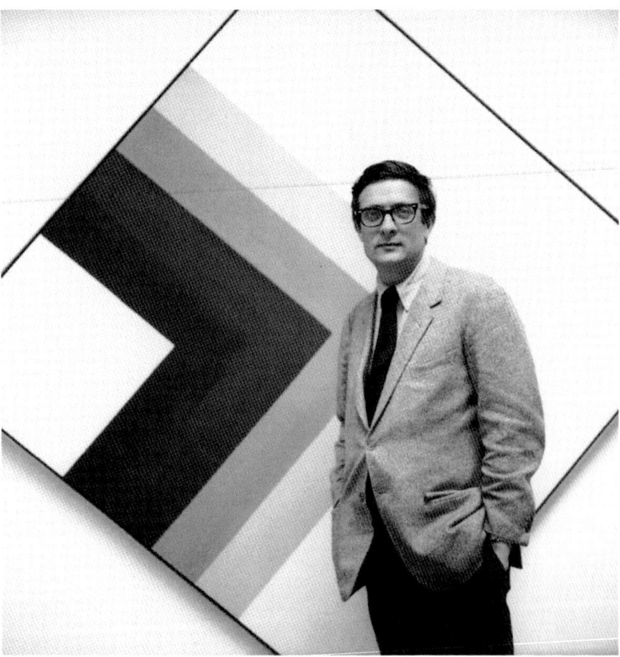

Kenneth Noland
Born in Asheville in 1924, Kenneth Noland studied at Black Mountain College after his return from World War II. Studying under Ilya Bolotowsky, who introduced him to neoplasticism, and Josef Albers, who introduced him to Bauhaus theory and color theory, Noland became one of the key figures in the color field painting movement, a style closely related to abstract expressionism. Often centering his works around targets, chevrons, and stripes, Noland experimented often with color and pioneered the use of shaped canvases. He died in 2010, leaving behind an extraordinary body of work. (Courtesy of the estate of Kenneth Noland.)

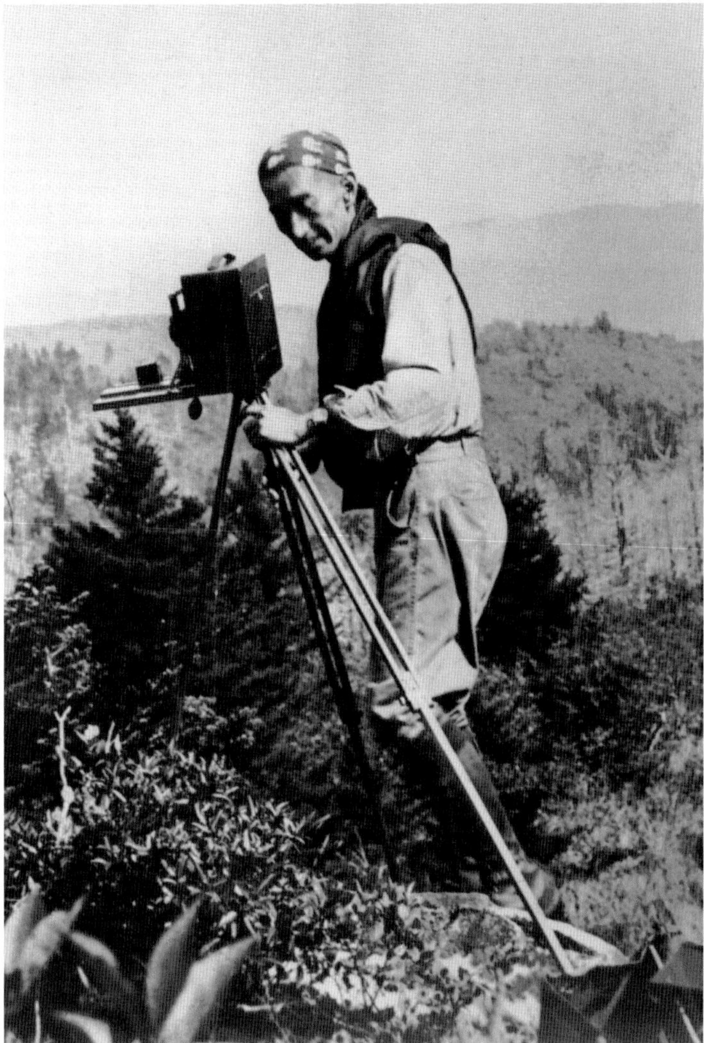

George Masa

Noted photographer George Masa, born Masahara Izuka, immigrated to the United States from Japan around 1901, possibly to study mining. He would eventually make his way to Asheville in 1915, where he changed his name and began working as a laundryman, then a bellhop, and finally a valet at the Grove Park Inn. While at Grove Park, Masa began taking photographs of guests, which he sold to earn extra money. He eventually went out on his own and started Plateau Studios. Masa became the photographer of all of Asheville's most prominent families, but also became noted for his extraordinary mountain landscape photographs. His love for the mountains eventually led to a partnership between Masa and the author Horace Kephart. The two became the leading voices in convincing the federal government to stop unmanaged logging and create the Great Smoky Mountains National Park. Masa's photographs were important in influencing key governmental leaders, as well as John D. Rockefeller, who helped fund the park. Masa also played a key role in the development of the Appalachian Trail. With camera and journal in hand, he scouted, laid out, and marked the entire North Carolina portion of the trail. Masa died of the flu in 1933, a year before the Great Smoky Mountains National Park was opened. In 1961, Masa Knob, a peak of 5,680 feet, was named in his honor. (Courtesy of the North Carolina Collection, Pack Library.)

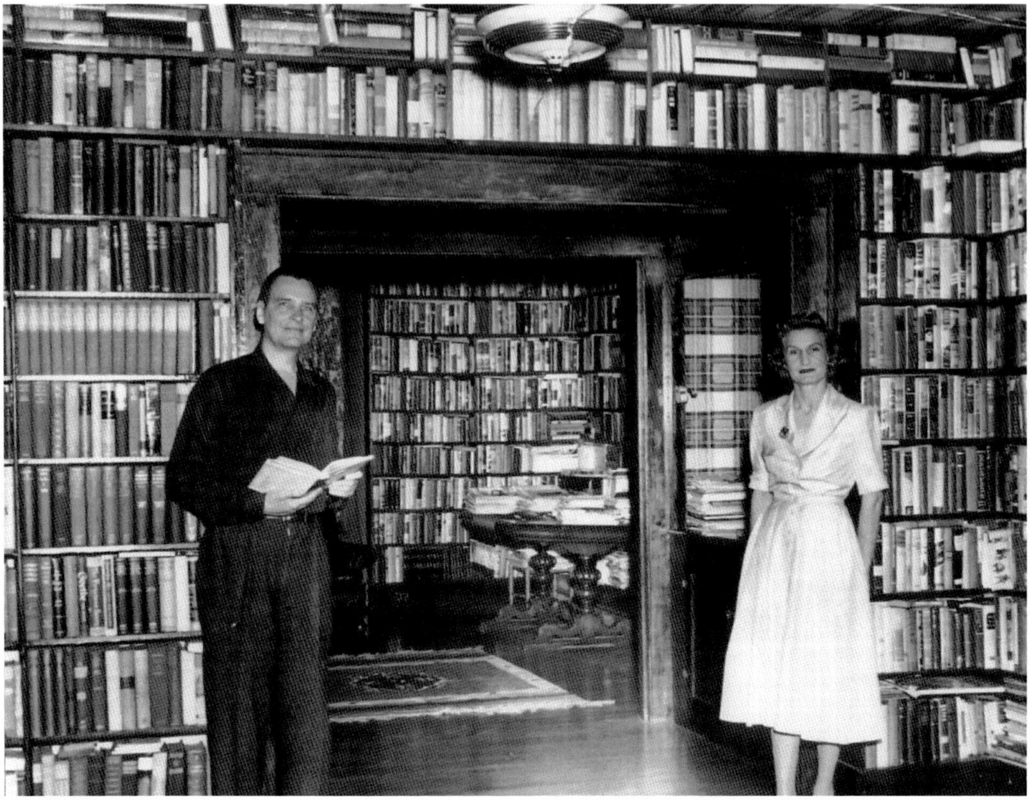

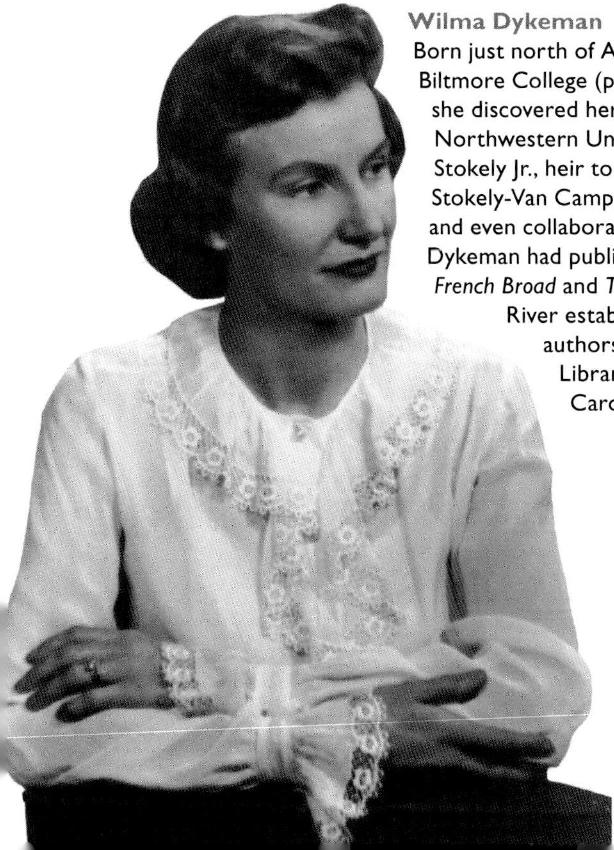

Wilma Dykeman

Born just north of Asheville in 1920, Wilma Dykeman graduated from Biltmore College (predecessor of UNC Asheville) in 1938, where she discovered her talents as a writer. Soon after graduating from Northwestern University in 1940, she met her husband, James R. Stokely Jr., heir to the Stokely Brothers Canning Company (later Stokely-Van Camp). Stokely encouraged Wilma's work as a writer and even collaborated on several books. Before her passing in 2006, Dykeman had published 18 books, including her highly acclaimed *The French Broad* and *The Tall Woman*. Her work on the French Broad River established her as one of the earliest environmental authors. (Above, courtesy of Jim Stokely and Ramsey Library Special Collections; left, courtesy of the North Carolina Collection, Pack Library,)

John Ehle

Best known for his fiction set in the Appalachian South, John Ehle was born in Asheville in 1925. He served in the Army during World War II and went on to receive two degrees from the University of North Carolina at Chapel Hill, where he later served on the faculty. A highly awarded writer, Ehle has written 17 books, 11 fiction and 6 nonfiction. *The Winter People* and *The Journey of August King* have both been adapted into films. Ehle is married to the award-winning actress Rosemary Harris and is the father of award-winning actress Jennifer Ehle. (Courtesy of the North Carolina Collection, Pack Library.)

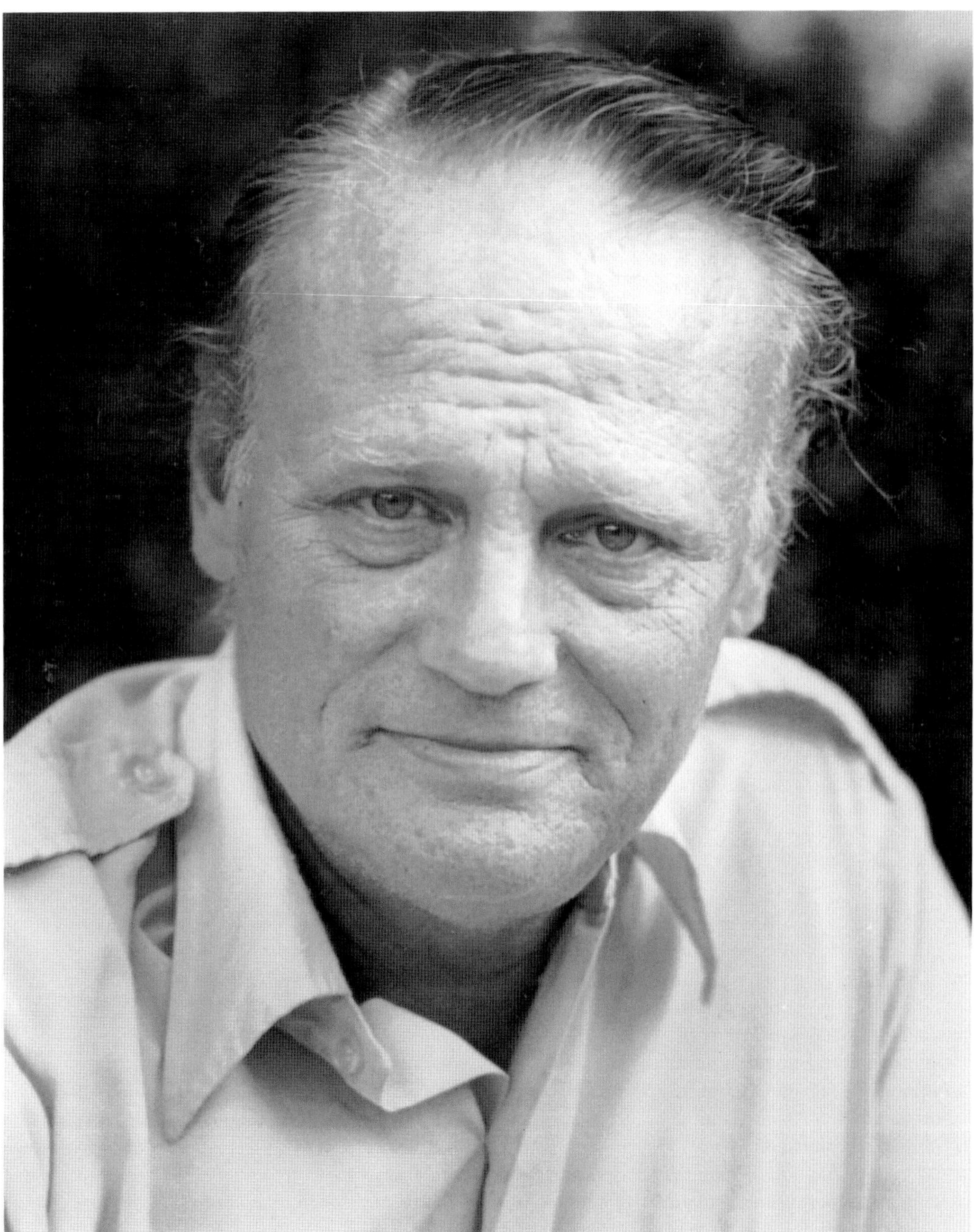

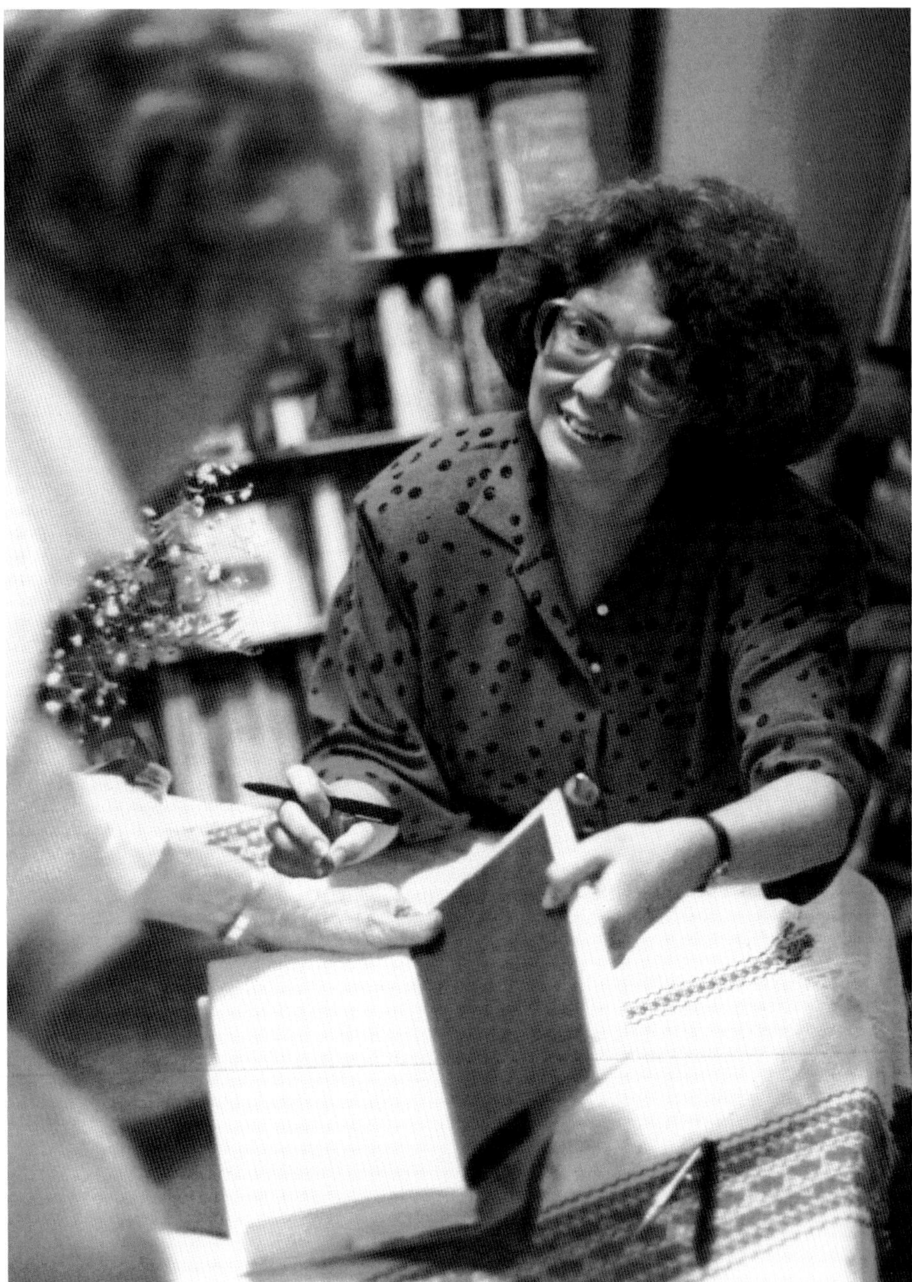

Gail Godwin

Nationally noted novelist Gail Godwin moved to Asheville as a young girl with her mother around 1940 after her parents' divorce. Reared by her mother and grandmother, Godwin's works are often noted for their strong female protagonists. Though she left Asheville in her high school years after her mother remarried, Godwin eventually began writing about Asheville, though she had avoided it for many years because of Thomas Wolfe's close association with the city. Godwin has published some 20 books and received numerous nominations, awards, recognitions, and fellowships over her 40-year career. (Courtesy of the North Carolina Collection, Pack Library.)

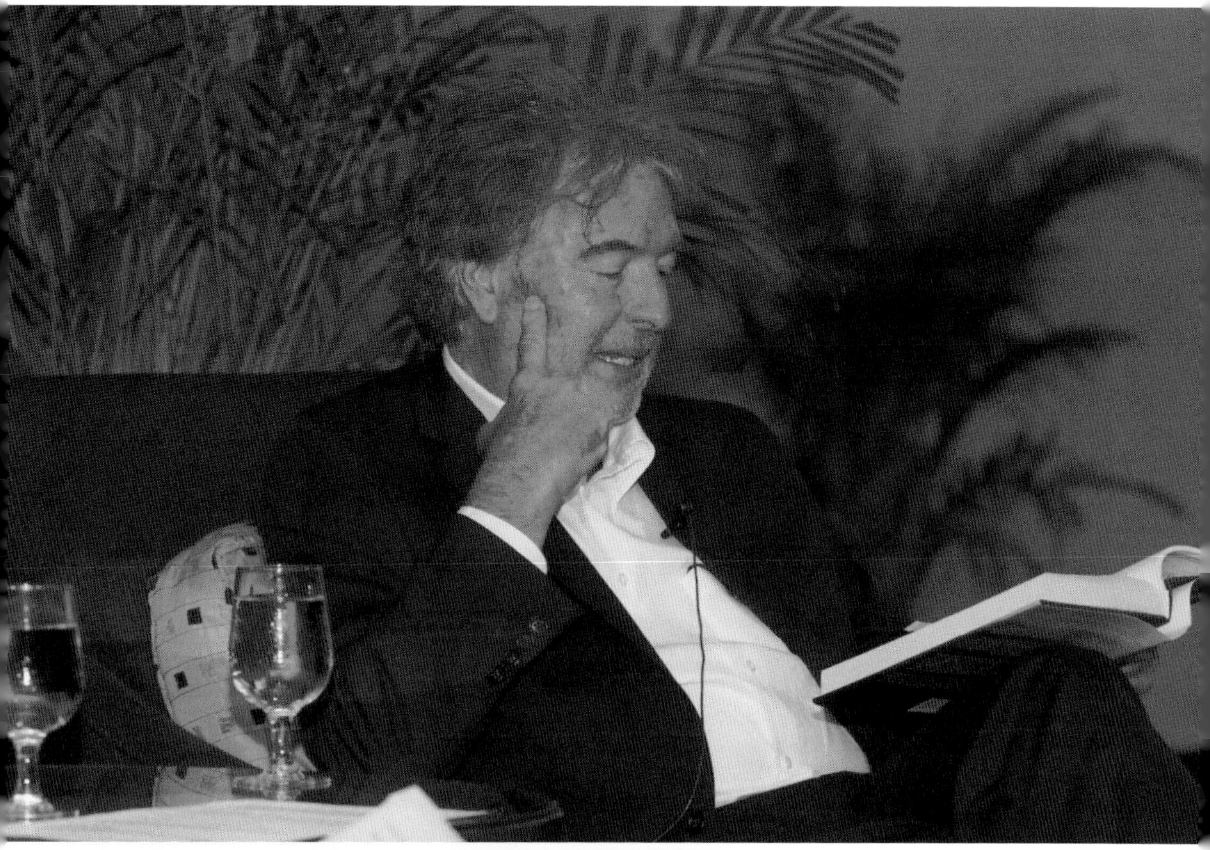

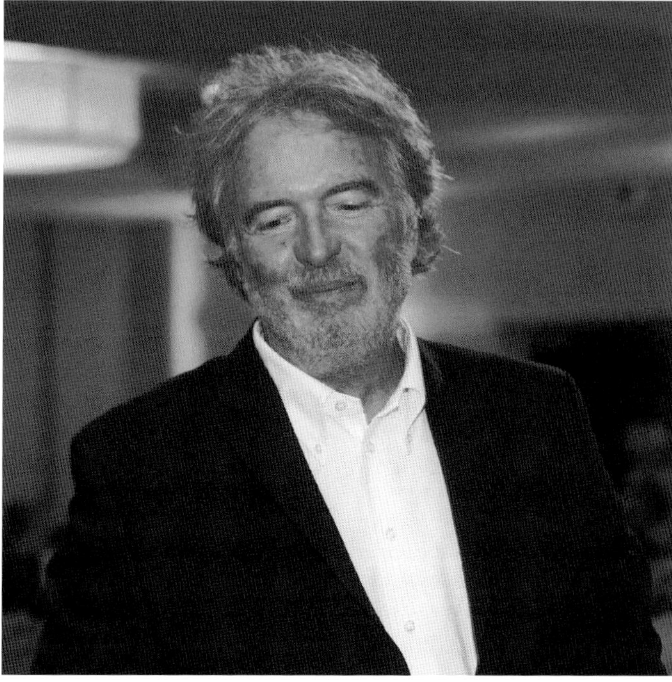

Charles Frazier
Born in Asheville in 1950, award-winning novelist Charles Frazier published his first novel, *Cold Mountain*, in 1997. The book, which sold more than three million copies, earned the National Book Award, sat atop the New York Times Best Seller List for more than a year, was adapted to film, and was released as a movie under the same title in 2003. Frazier published his second novel, *Thirteen Moons*, in 2006, and his third, *Nightwoods*, five years later. (Both, courtesy of the Literacy Council of Buncombe County.)

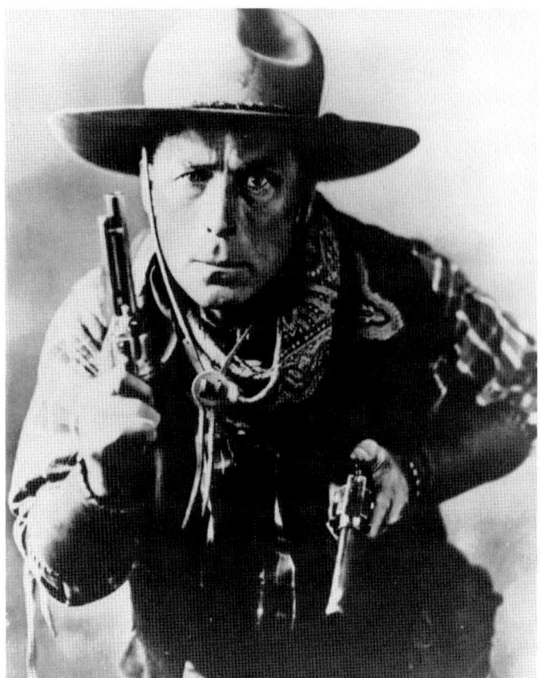

William S. Hart
William S. Hart, the original movie cowboy, directed shows at the Asheville Opera House at the beginning of the 20th century while developing his career as a stage actor. Hart would enter film in 1914 and lead the creation of the original Western genre. After starring in the lead of the movie *The Bargain*, Hart became one of the most famous actors of the silent movie era. His last film was the self-produced *Tumbleweeds*, in 1925. (Courtesy of the North Carolina Collection, Pack Library.)

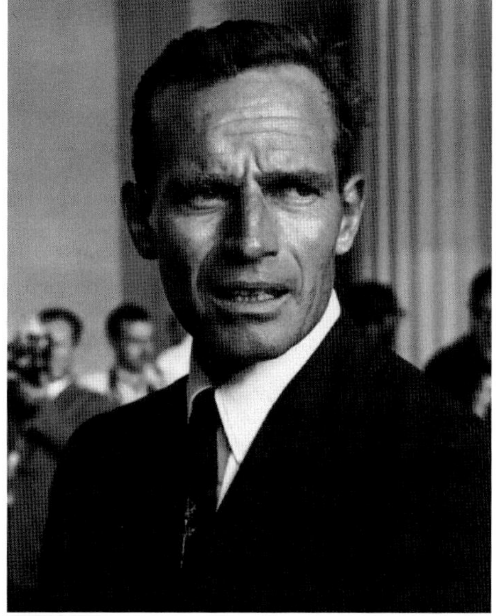

Charlton Heston
Known for his roles in *The Ten Commandments* and *Ben-Hur*, Academy Award–winning actor Charlton Heston began his stage career in 1947 in Asheville. Heston and his wife, Lydia Clark, served as artistic codirectors for the Asheville Community Theatre (ACT) the year before Heston got his first Broadway stage role as a supporting actor in a revival of Shakespeare's *Antony and Cleopatra*. The couple earned $100 per week for their work and lived in what is now the Beaufort House Inn. ACT's main auditorium is named in honor of the Hestons. (Courtesy of the National Archives.)

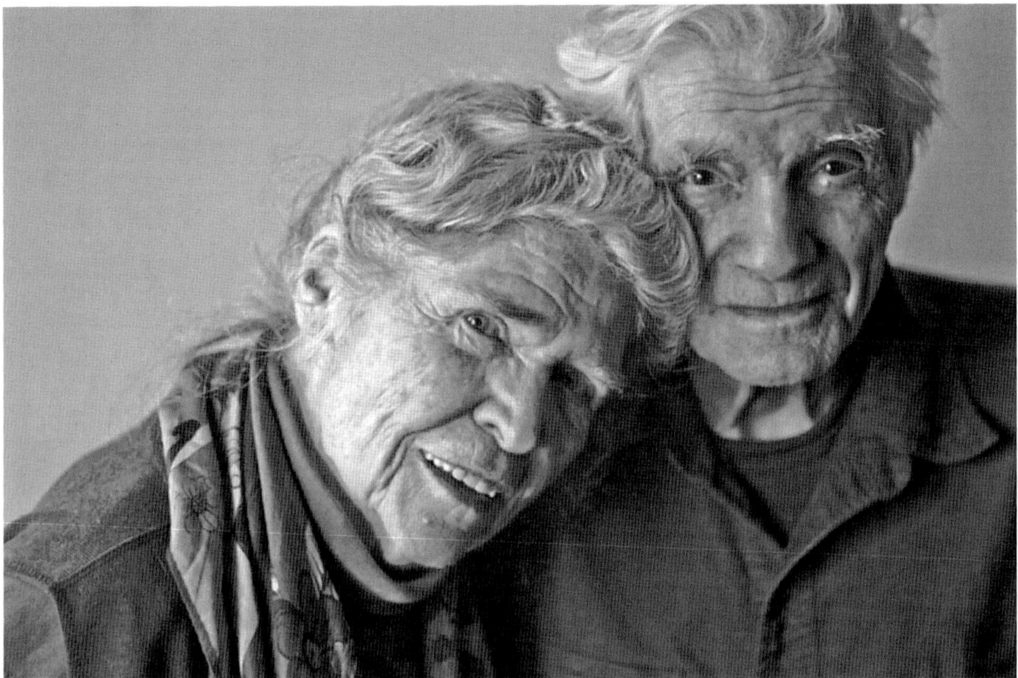

Hazel and John Robinson

Hazel and John Robinson moved to Asheville in 1971 because Hazel had grown up in the area as a child. John worked at Beacon Manufacturing, and Hazel reengaged her lifelong interest in theater at the Asheville Community Theatre. After attending an outdoor theater production while visiting her mother-in-law, Hazel became convinced that Asheville needed an outdoor Shakespeare company, and in 1973, the Montford Park Players was born. Since staging its first production, *As You Like It*, the Montford Park Players has grown into a year-round company, with its summer home at the Hazel Robinson Amphitheater in the Montford neighborhood and its winter home at the Asheville Masonic Temple. (Photograph by Roger Bargainnier; courtesy of Roger Bargainnier and Asheville Living Treasures.)

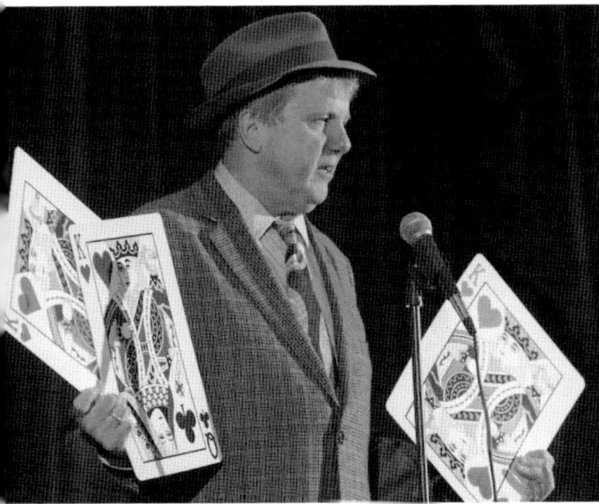

Harry L. Anderson

Best known for his roles as Judge Harry Stone in the television series *Night Court* (1984–1992) and Dave Barry in the series *Dave's World* (1993–1997), actor, writer, director, and magician Harry Anderson and his wife, Elizabeth, moved to Asheville in 2006 following Hurricane Katrina. The Andersons had moved to New Orleans in 2002 and opened Sideshow, a magic and curiosities shop in the French Quarter, and Oswald's Speakeasy, a nightclub. Declining tourism and concerns over the reelection of Ray Nagin as mayor led them to sell their businesses and move to Asheville. (Photograph by Steven Masker, courtesy of Steven Masker Photography.)

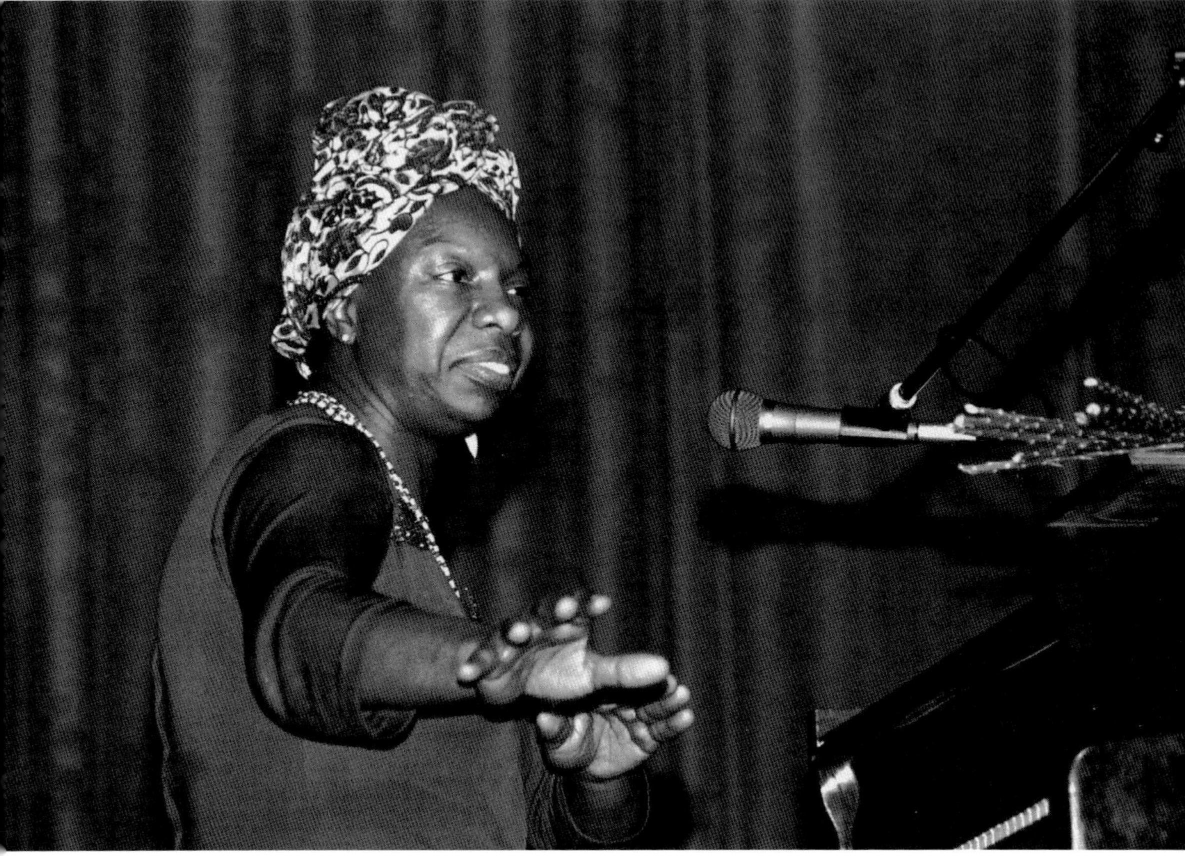

Nina Simone

Born Eunice Kathleen Waymon in nearby Tryon, the internationally renowned pianist, songwriter, jazz singer, and civil rights activist Nina Simone studied at Asheville's Allen High School, a boarding school for African American girls, in the 1940s. Upon graduation, Simone was rejected for admission at the prestigious Curtis Institute of Music in Philadelphia (she believed strongly it was because of her race), but eventually studied at Julliard in New York. Later, to fund private lessons, she began singing at Midtown Bar & Grill in Atlantic City. There, she took on the name Nina Simone so her mother, a Methodist minister, would not know she was singing at a bar. By the late 1950s, Simone had acquired commercial success, and gained notoriety in the 1960s for her signature style, which in many ways became a soundtrack for the civil rights movement. Simone left the United States in the early 1970s in protest of the country's involvement in Vietnam and lived the last 30 years of her life abroad. Her influence on music is immeasurable. Nominated for 15 Grammys, she received the Hall of Fame Award in 2000 for her earlier recording of "I Loves You Porgy," from the musical *Porgy and Bess*. Simone died in France in 2003. (Photograph by Roland Godefroy.)

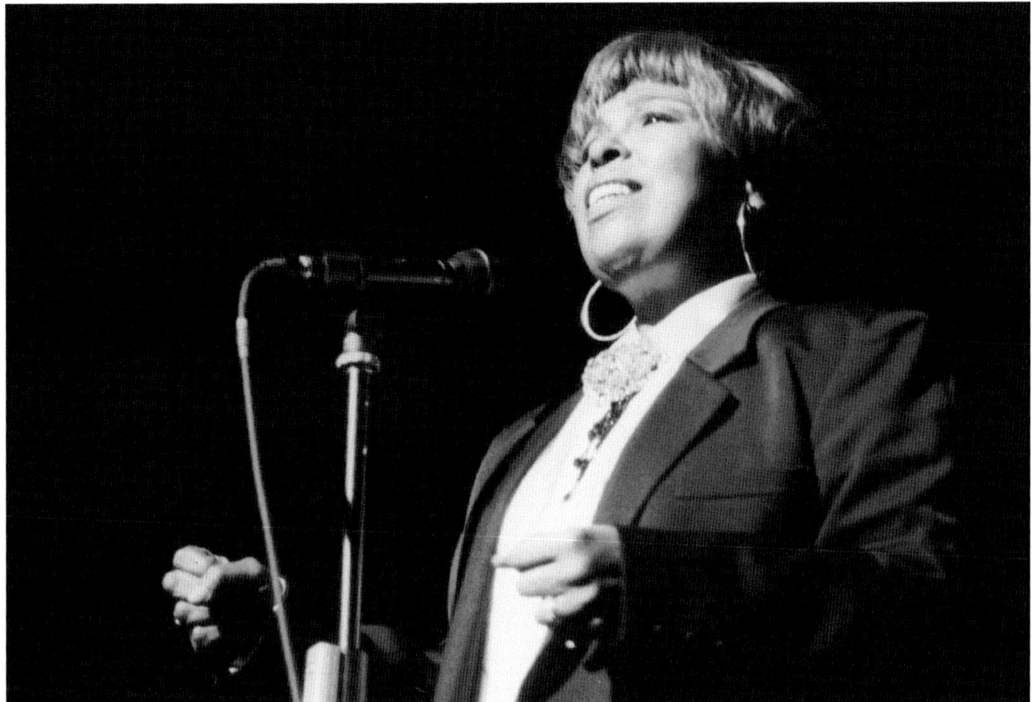

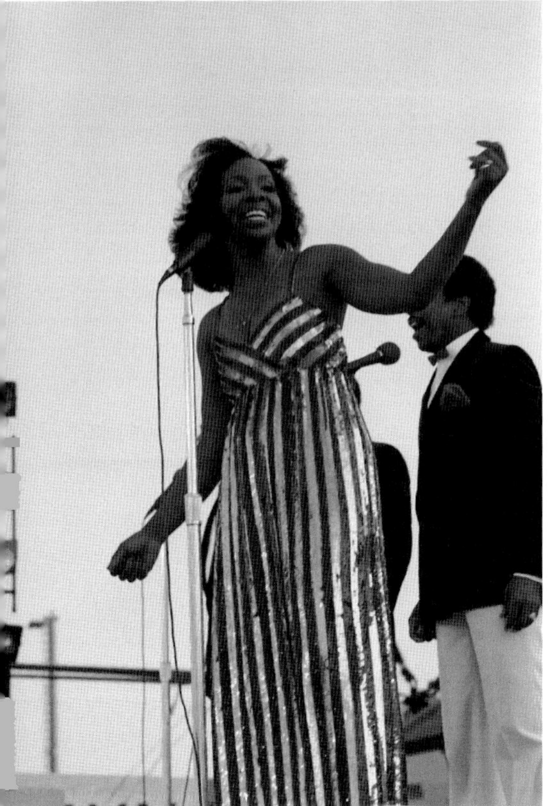

Roberta Flack

Multiple Grammy Award–wining singer-songwriter Robert Flack was born just outside of Asheville in the community of Black Mountain in the late 1930s. At age four her family moved to Arlington, Virginia, where she was first exposed to the likes of great singers such as Mahalia Jackson and Sam Cooke. At 15, she earned a piano scholarship to Howard University. She was later discovered by Les McCann in a Washington, DC, nightclub and released her first album shortly thereafter with Atlantic Records, in 1969. Over her career, Flack has released more than two dozen albums and nearly four dozen singles. (Photograph by Roland Godefroy.)

Gladys Knight

The "Empress of Soul," Gladys Knight moved to the Asheville area in 2007 and lives in the nearby community of Fairview. Knight is best known for her R&B recordings in the 1960s and 1970s with her group Gladys Knight & the Pips. Knight, who maintains a regular tour schedule as well as an active television career, has won seven Grammy awards and numerous other accolades. (Courtesy of the National Archives.)

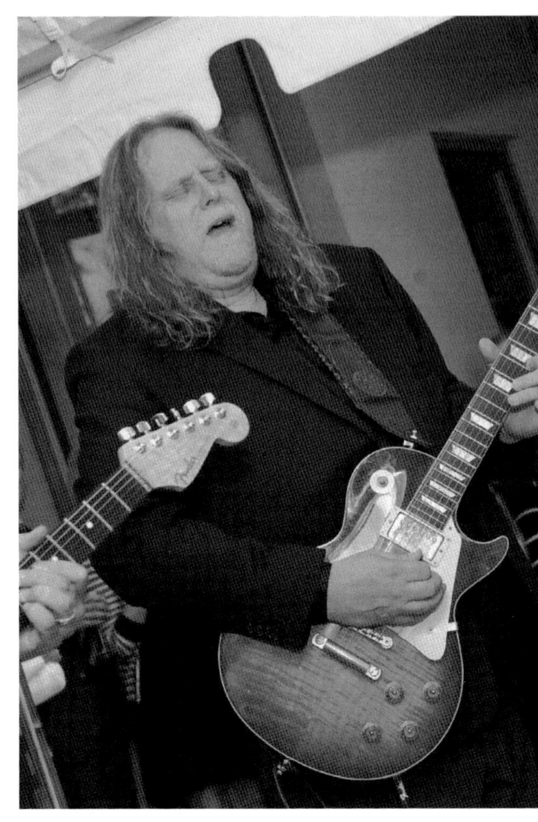

Warren Haynes
Named one of the top 25 guitar players of all time by *Rolling Stone*, Haynes grew up in Asheville in the 1960s and 1970s, where he began to play the guitar at age 12. Since first beginning his professional career with David Allan Coe, Haynes has been a member of the Allman Brothers Band, Phil Lesh and Friends, and The Dead, and is a founding member of Gov't Mule. Each year, Haynes returns to Asheville to host the always-sold-out Warren Haynes Christmas Jam, which brings together top talent in the rock community to raise money for Habitat for Humanity. In 2013, Haynes received an honorary doctorate from UNC Asheville for his professional and philanthropic contributions. (Photograph by Perry Hebbard; courtesy of UNC Asheville Communication & Marketing.)

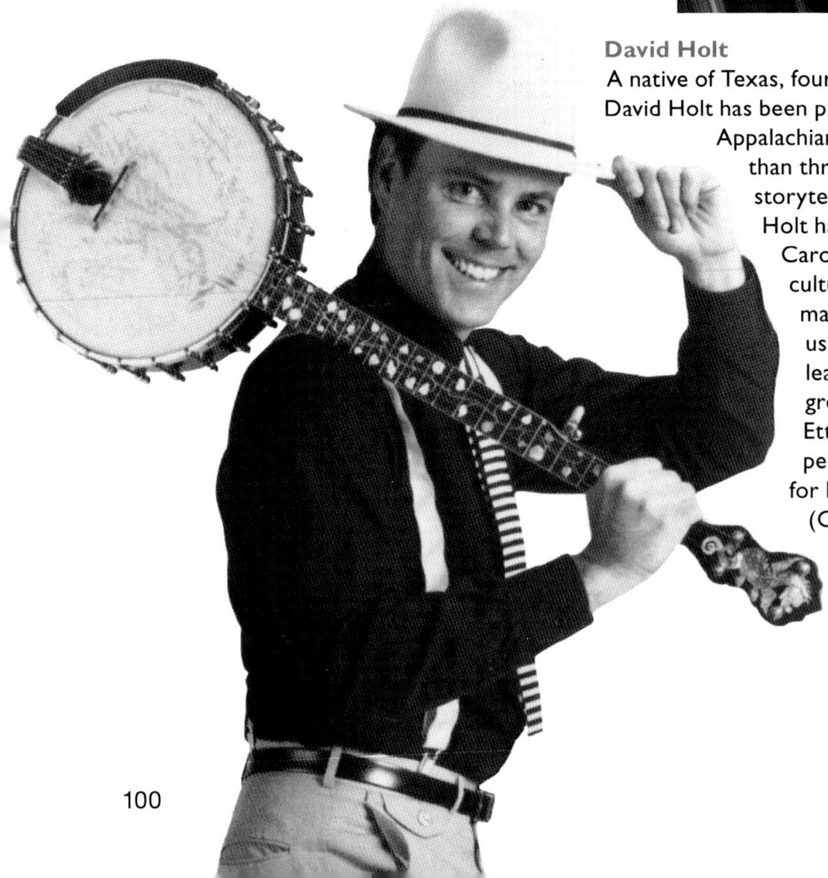

David Holt
A native of Texas, four-time Grammy award winner David Holt has been preserving and advancing Appalachian mountain music for more than three decades. Known for his storytelling as much as his music, Holt has shared Western North Carolina's traditional mountain culture throughout the world. A master of a range of instruments, usual and unique, Holt has learned from numerous musical greats such as Doc Watson and Etta Baker. In addition to his performances, Holt hosts shows for PBS and National Public Radio. (Courtesy of the North Carolina Collection, Pack Library.)

CHAPTER SIX

The Famous, Both Near and Far

Even in the early days of Asheville, folks like Daniel Boone, Davy Crocket, and Francis Asbury passed through. After the city earned its reputation as a health resort and tourist destination, many of the famous or would-be-famous came to make Asheville their home, either for a few weeks or for the rest of their lives.

Biltmore, with its more than 30 guest rooms, brought a regular parade of the wealthy and famous, including such luminaries as Edith Wharton and Henry James. Likewise, the numerous resort hotels saw folks like Henry Ford, Harvey Firestone, and Thomas Edison. Asheville's reputation was strong, and people wanted to rub shoulders with the social elite.

Then there are those who came from Asheville and found fame as performers and professional athletes. The Asheville Tourists minor league baseball team alone has sent over 500 players to the major leagues. There are also the war heroes whose service to the country was recognized nationwide.

Asheville's own local celebrities are often like family members. There is the television anchor who has been behind the news desk for more than 30 years, and the radio personality with whom locals drank their coffee every morning for more than 40 years while he read their favorite columnists, who had been writing in the newspaper for as long.

Celebrity sightings are commonplace in Asheville, where an old Appalachian attitude of "live and let live" prevails and few are interrupted by autograph seekers. It is not even uncommon to hear a story of somebody in line at a barbeque joint who, after recognizing the voice of the person in line behind them, turned around to say, "Oh, good afternoon, Mr. President."

Davy Crockett

Davy Crockett met Elizabeth Patton in 1814 when he brought her deceased husband's belongings to her, the wish of Crocket's best friend, James, who had died in the Battle of Horseshoe Bend. Soon thereafter, Crockett's wife died and he began to court Elizabeth. Though she was reluctant to marry him, the two were wed in 1815. Her concerns proved well-founded, however, as Crockett was an absentee husband and father most of the time, as a hunter, guide, and member of Congress. Crockett eventually moved to Texas without his family and died in the Battle of the Alamo. Elizabeth followed to claim land granted to her for her husband's service. (Courtesy of the North Carolina Collection, Pack Library.)

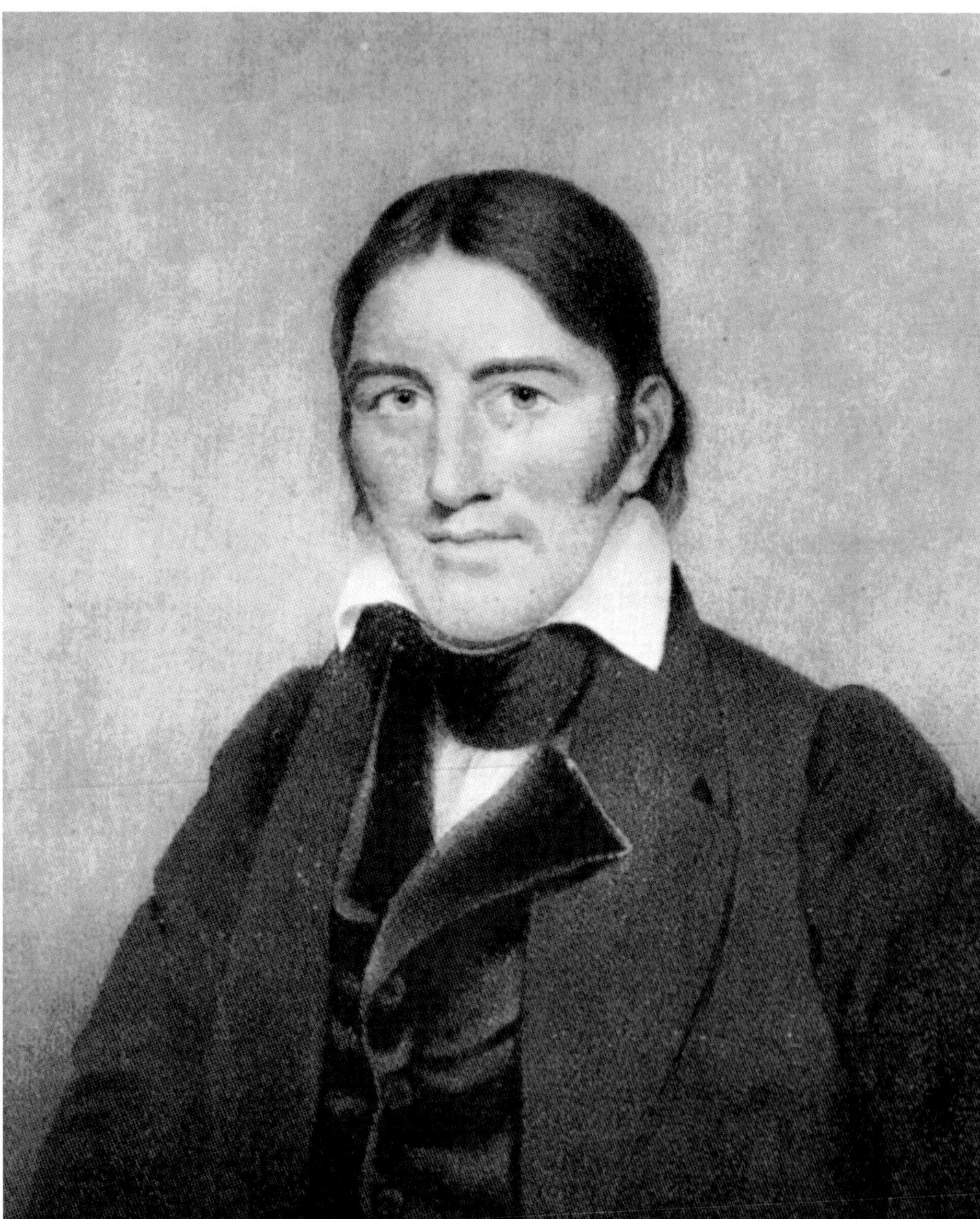

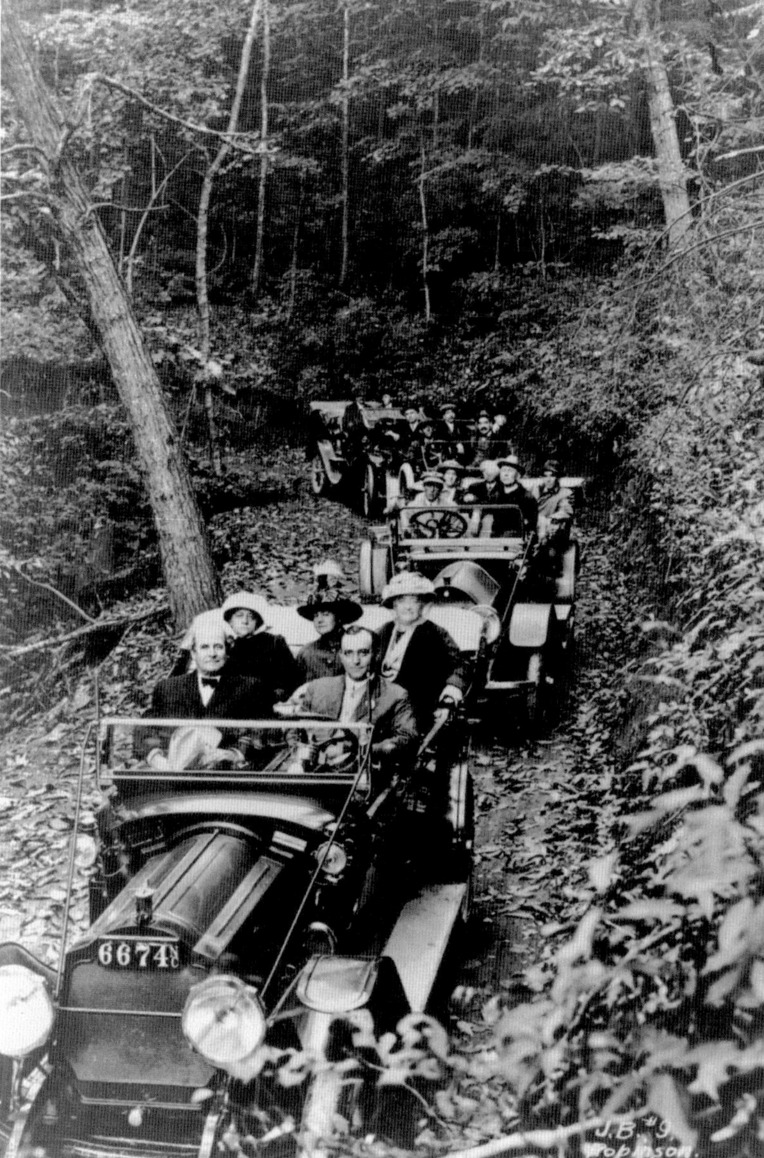

William Jennings Bryan

William Jennings Bryan (front left) was one of the nation's leading Democratic politicians for more than 30 years at the turn of the 20th century. Bryan unsuccessfully ran for president three times. It was during his first bid, in 1896, at the young age of 36, that Bryan first came to Asheville. Bryan's "stump speech" whistle-stop train tour of the United States was the first of its kind by a presidential candidate. Prior to Bryan, presidential candidates did not tour, but instead sent agents out on their behalf. Despite his losses, Bryan remained a powerful force in the Democratic Party and was eventually appointed secretary of state by Woodrow Wilson, a post he would resign in 1915 because of differences between the pacifist Bryan and President Wilson as the United States considered its role in World War I. Immediately before his appointment and during his service as secretary, Bryan, widely hailed as one of the country's great orators, visited Asheville several times to speak, including at the opening of the Grove Park Inn in July 1913. Much taken by Asheville, Bryan and his wife soon bought a tract of land from E.W. Grove in his Grove Park neighborhood that surrounded the inn. Bryan bought the land both for real estate speculation and to build his retirement home. The house, designed by noted local architect Richard Sharp Smith, was completed in 1917, but unfortunately, the need to move to Florida for Bryan's wife's health led them to sell and leave Asheville after only three years. A few years later, Bryan, a lawyer by training, would fight against Darwinism and evolution as the prosecuting attorney in the famous 1925 Scopes Trial in Tennessee. Five days after the end of the trial, Jennings died in his sleep from a heart attack. (Courtesy of the North Carolina Collection, Pack Library.)

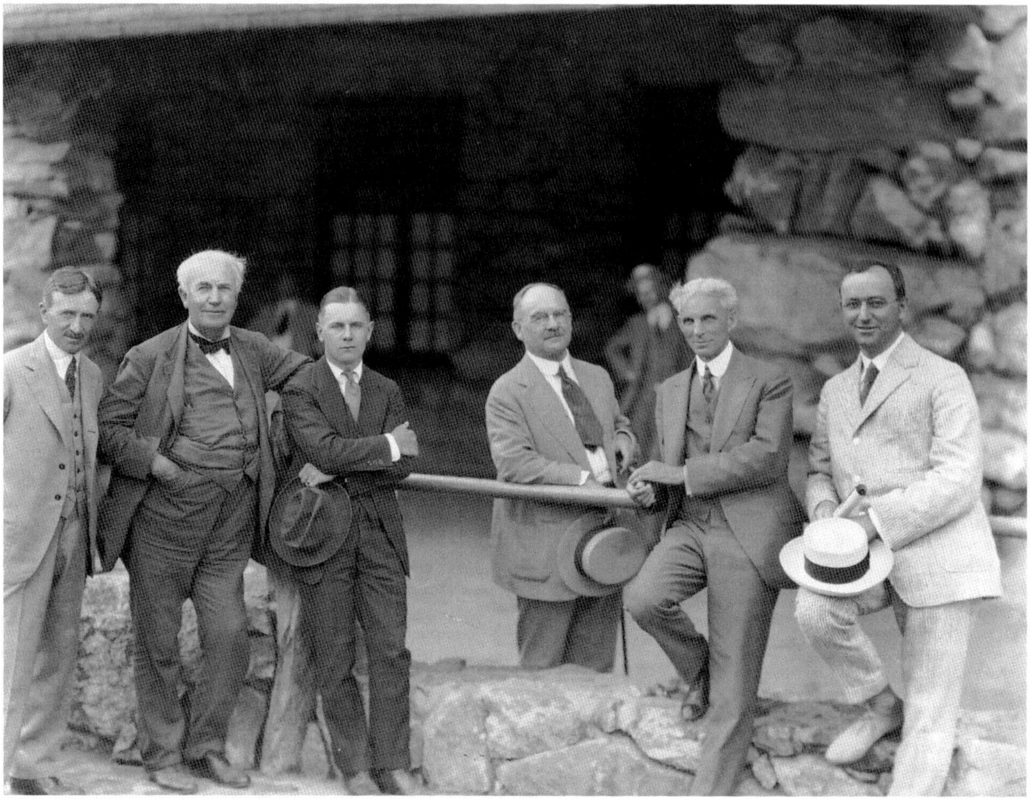

Famous Visitors

As Asheville's reputation as a resort destination grew in the late 1800s and early 1900s, the wealthy and famous often frequented Asheville. With more than 30 guest rooms at Biltmore, Edith and George Vanderbilt hosted hundreds from the who's who of American society, including overnight guests such as authors Edith Wharton and Henry James, as well as those who just passed through, such as Pres. Theodore Roosevelt (right). Likewise, the Grove Park Inn proudly displays hundreds of photographs of all of the presidents, movie stars, and business leaders who have stayed at the inn over the past 100 years. Asheville itself remains a destination for the famous, with celebrity sightings a regular occurrence year-round. The 1918 photograph above is representative of Asheville's many famous visitors. It shows, from left to right, rubber magnate Harvey Firestone Sr., inventor Thomas Edison, Firestone's son Harvey Jr., medicine manufacturer and owner of the Grove Park Inn E.W. Grove, automaker Henry Ford, and Grove Park Inn operator Fred Seely. (Above, courtesy of the Omni Grove Park Inn and Ramsey Library Special Collections; right, courtesy of the Library of Congress.)

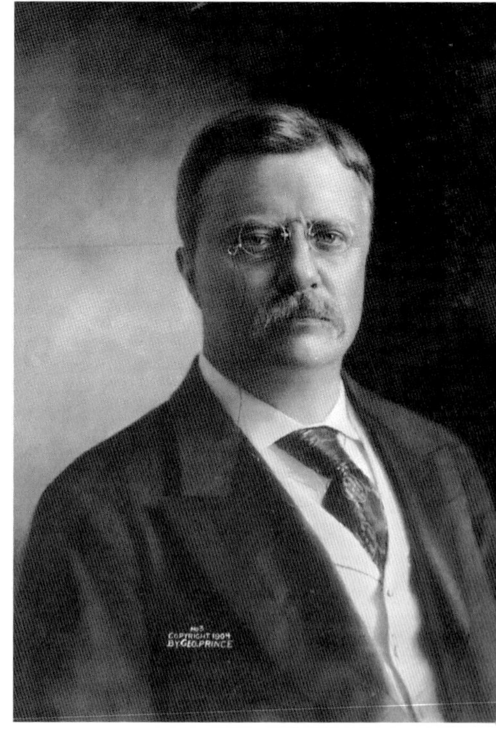

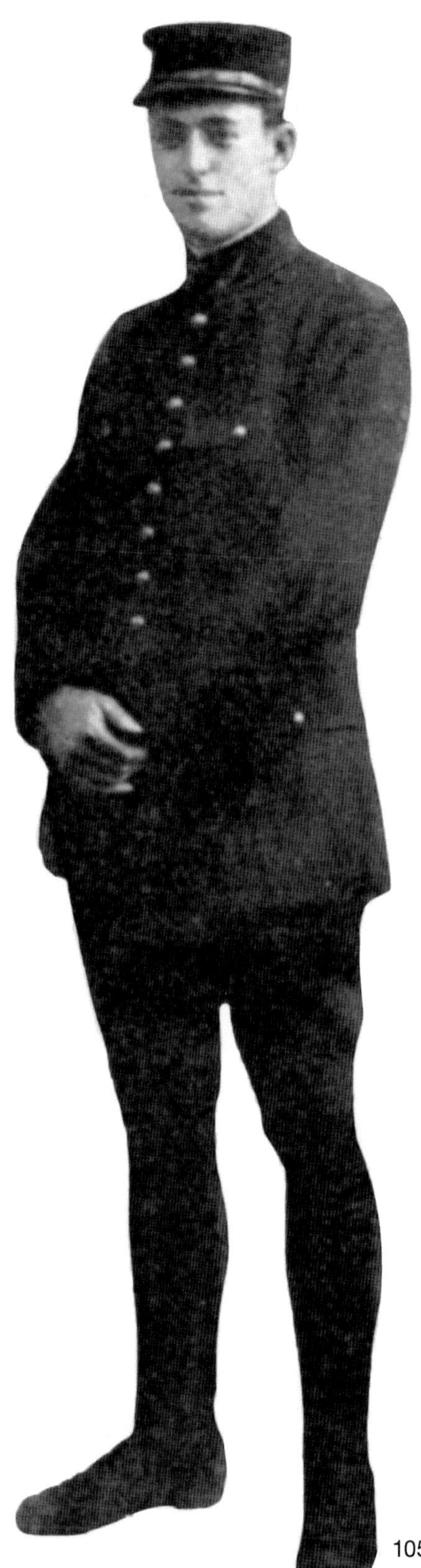

Kiffin Y. Rockwell
Kiffin Rockwell moved with his family to Asheville during his high school years in the early 1900s. After graduating, Rockwell attended Virginia Military Institute and Washington & Lee University and later began a career in advertising. When World War I broke out in Europe, Rockwell and his brother Paul traveled to France and joined the French Foreign Legion. In 1915, Paul was badly injured and left the French military to become a war correspondent. Kiffin asked to join the Service Aeronautique and became one of the first Americans to join the Escadrille Americaine (later called the Lafayette Escadrille). In May 1916, he became the first American to shoot down an enemy plane during the war. A courageous pilot, he was killed in combat a few months later and buried with military honors. (Courtesy of the North Carolina Collection, Pack Library.)

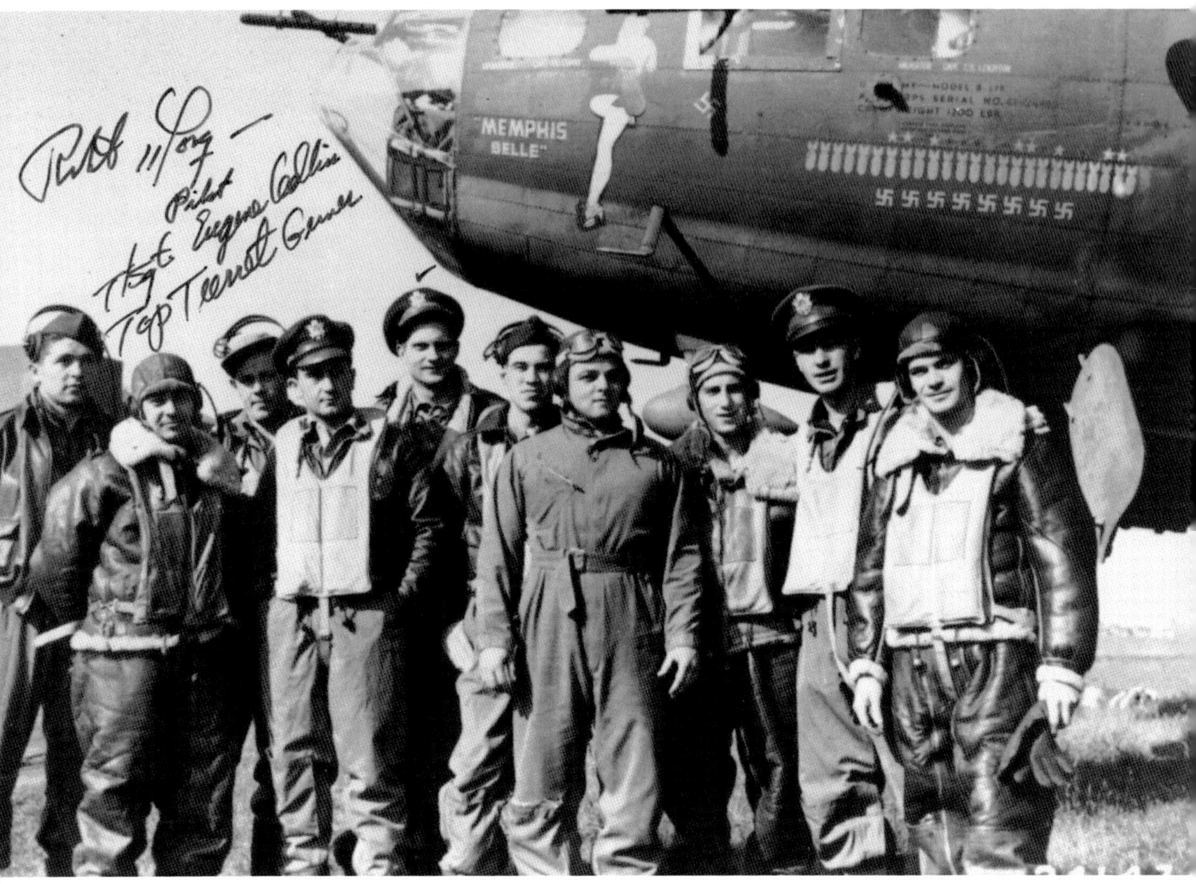

Robert K. Morgan

Born in Asheville in 1918, Robert Morgan entered the Army Air Corps in 1940 and earned his pilot's wings the next year. Between 1942 and 1943, Morgan and the crew of the *Memphis Belle* (so named after a Tennessee girlfriend of Morgan's) were celebrated as the first to successfully complete 25 heavy combat missions in the European Theater during World War II. Morgan, his crewmates, and the plane became legends and were brought back to the United States to rally support for the war. During a stop in Asheville in 1943 as part of the war bonds tour, Morgan orchestrated an amazing stunt, flying the *Memphis Belle* down Patton Avenue and across Pack Square, banking the wings 60 degrees to pass between city hall and the county courthouse. Later, Morgan would also fly 26 successful missions in the Pacific Theater piloting a new B-29 Superfortress, but he is best remembered for piloting the *Memphis Belle*. Morgan lived the rest of his life in Asheville, passing in 2004. (Courtesy of the North Carolina Collection, Pack Library.)

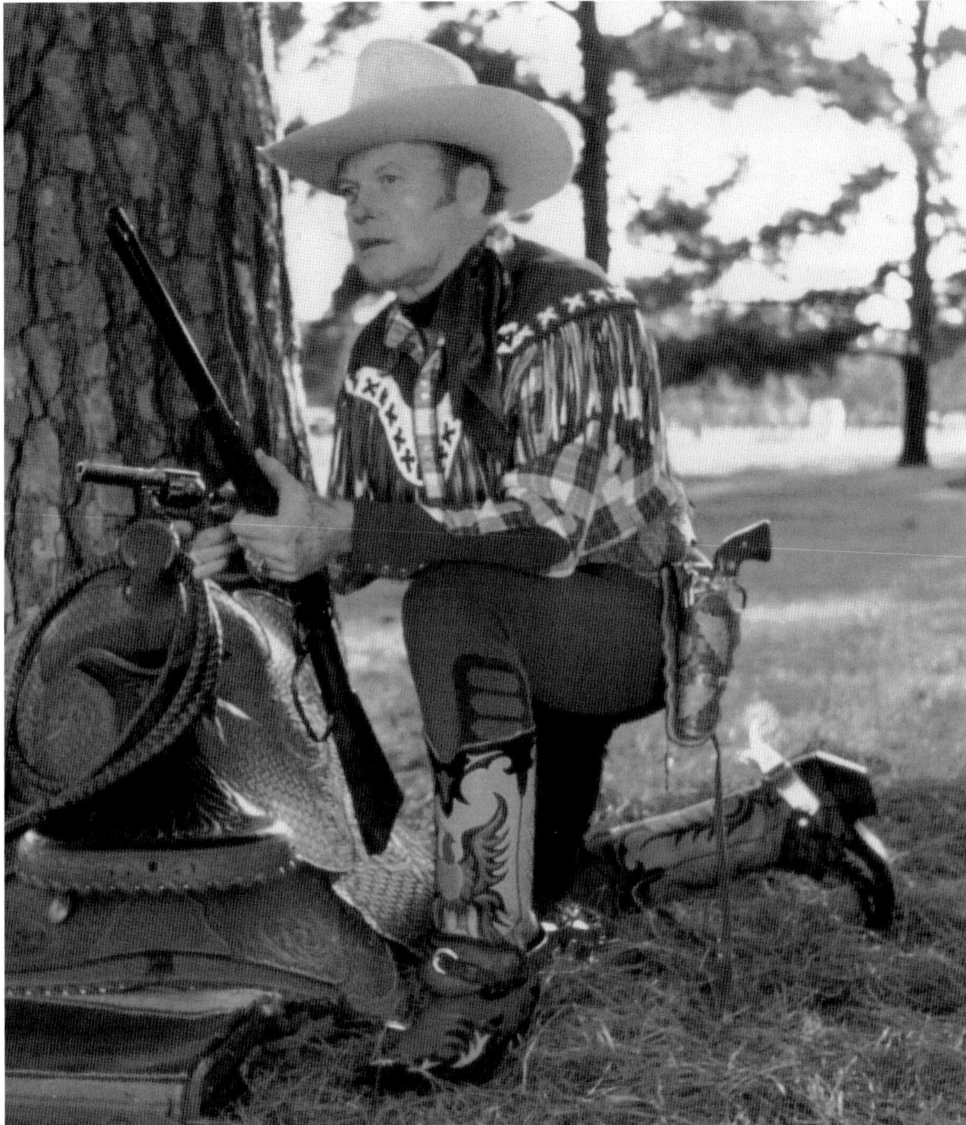

Joe Bowman

Known internationally as the "Straight Shooter" and the "Master of Triggernometry," Joe Bowman was one of the world's leading sharpshooters. Born in 1925, Bowman grew up in Asheville, where he and his brother Mark watched Tom Mix and Gene Autry Westerns, which fueled his interest in marksmanship. His family eventually moved to Texas, where he learned to be a boot maker as well as a marksman. After serving in World War II, Bowman became internationally famous for his incredibly fast gun slinging. He eventually trained not only actors in Western films but also FBI agents and SWAT teams. Bowman gave thousands of sharpshooting demonstrations in front of rodeo crowds, heads of state, and royalty. Besides his amazing speed, he was known for his precision, ably demonstrated by his ability to hit tiny saccharine tablets at 30 yards, as well as his famous axe trick. Bowman would light two candles on each side of an ax blade and then fire a .22-caliber rifle at the leading edge of the blade. This would split the bullet, the two pieces of which would extinguish the candle flames. The consummate cowboy, Bowman died in 2009 as one of the embodiments of Western popular culture. (Courtesy of Mark Bowman.)

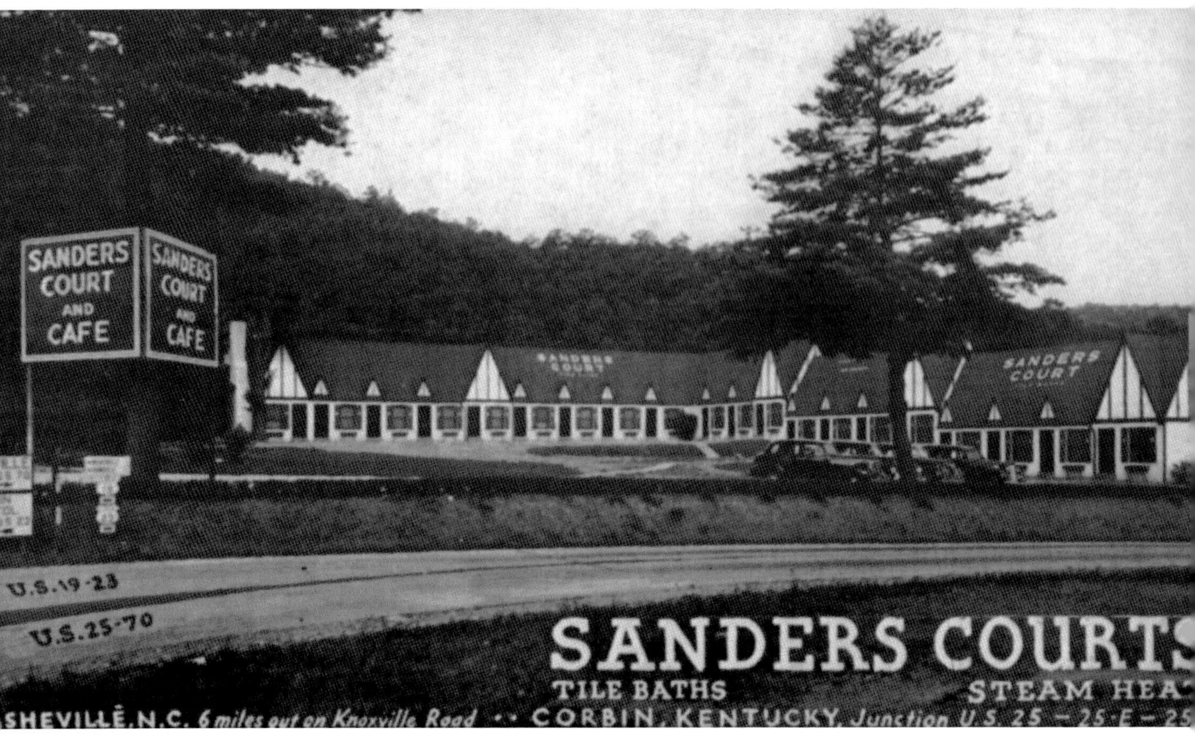

Harlan Sanders

Harlan Sanders, or Colonel Sanders, as he is more popularly known, opened his first restaurant in the early 1930s in Corbin, Kentucky. Some 40 years old, he had already been a farmhand, railroad man, insurance salesmen, steamboat ferry owner, lawyer, and even amateur obstetrician. He opened the restaurant and a motel as additions to a gas station he owned. The restaurant was highly lucrative, and Sanders tried to start a restaurant chain in 1937 but was unsuccessful. Two years later, he moved to Asheville to open another Sanders Motor Court with a motel and restaurant. The coming of World War II forced Sanders to close his Asheville business after only a few years, but it was during his time in Asheville that he developed his famous pressure-cooking method of frying chicken, which would eventually become the hallmark of his famous Kentucky Fried Chicken restaurants. (Courtesy of the North Carolina Collection, Pack Library.)

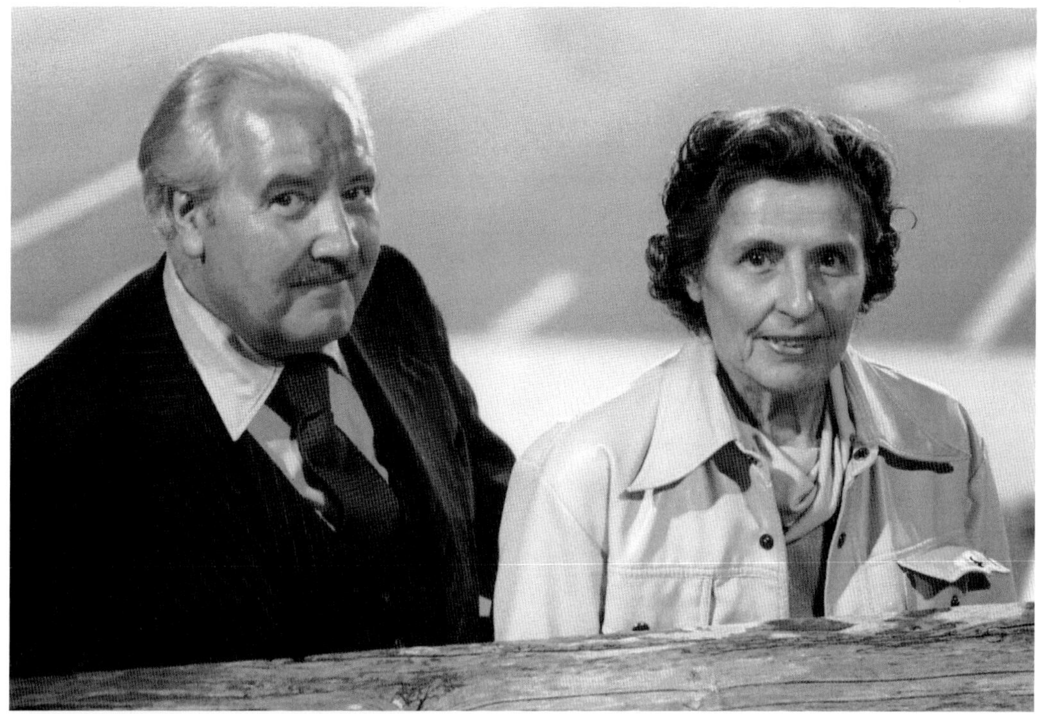

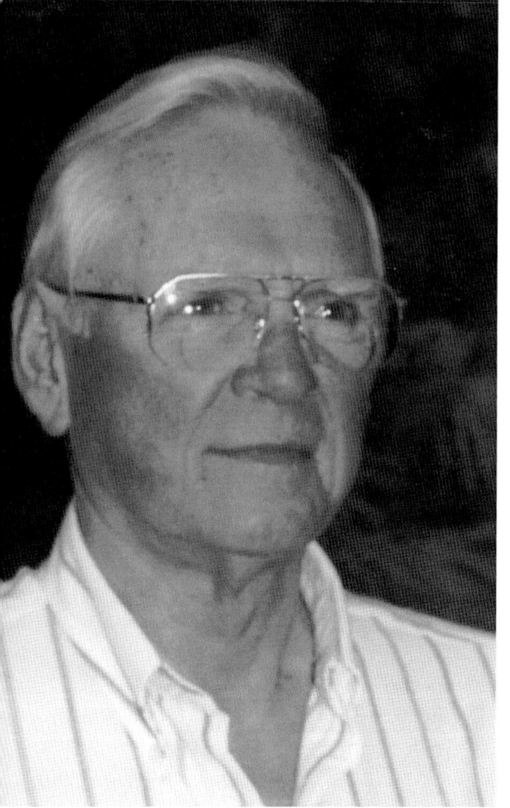

John Parris
John Parris began his career in journalism writing for the local paper in nearby Sylva. He went on to be a correspondent for several papers as well as the United Press and Associated Press wire services. In 1955, he began writing a regular column for the *Asheville Citizen-Times* called "Roaming the Mountains." The extremely popular column celebrated the history, heritage, and culture of Appalachia and led to several popular books written by Parris before his passing in 1999. (Courtesy of Western Carolina University Communications and Public Relations.)

Bob Terrell
Bob Terrell joined the staff of the *Asheville Citizen-Times* newspaper in 1949. Over the next 50 years, he would become one of the city's most read writers and columnists. A sportswriter for many years, in 1967, Terrell began the often humorous human interest column for which he was best known. Terrell retired in 1986 to write books and work with Billy Graham. He died in 2009. (Courtesy of the North Carolina Collection, Pack Library.)

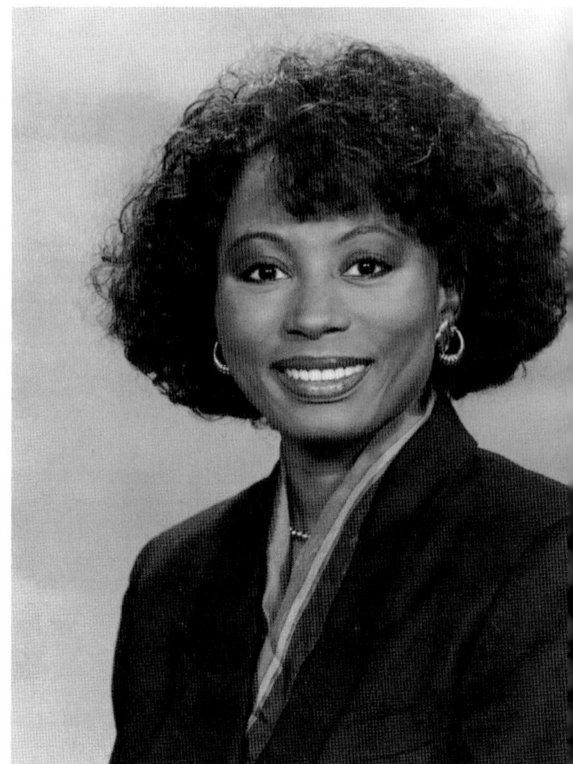

Darcel Grimes Lloyd
Originally from Washington, DC, Darcel Grimes (Lloyd) came to Asheville in 1981 from Mississippi to anchor the late evening news on WLOS-TV. More than three decades later, Grimes has become one of the longest-serving local news anchors in the nation and an icon among Ashevillians. Highly respected by colleagues and viewers alike, Grimes is well known for her mix of wit and serious journalism, as well as her leadership in the community. (Courtesy of the North Carolina Collection, Pack Library.)

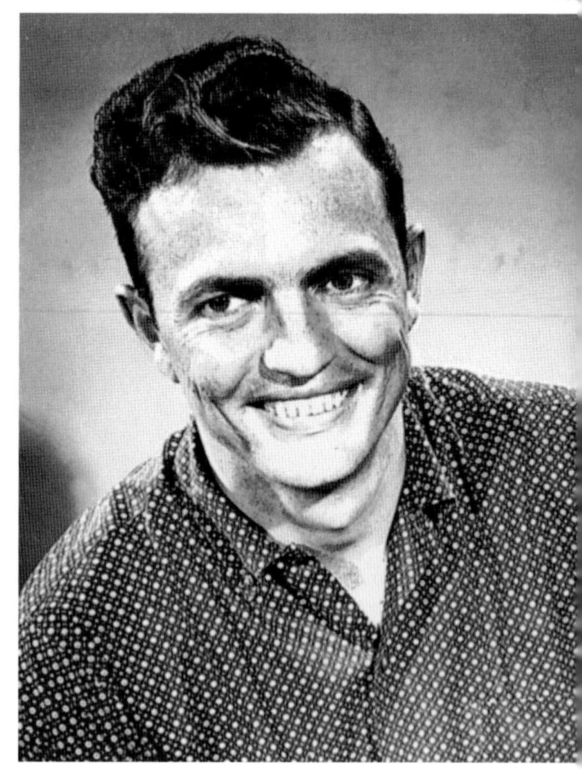

Scotty Rhodarmer
Scotty Rhodarmer joined the staff at WWNC Radio in 1954 after graduating from the University of North Carolina at Chapel Hill. Over the next 50 years, Rhodarmer became the most beloved voice on the radio in Asheville. Thousands of Ashevillians woke up to him every morning to listen to his distinctive voice as he read the newspaper and spun stories while they drank their coffee. At several times in his career, Rhodarmer achieved the largest audience share of any radio personality in America. He retired from WWNC in 2004. (Courtesy of Melanie Fox.)

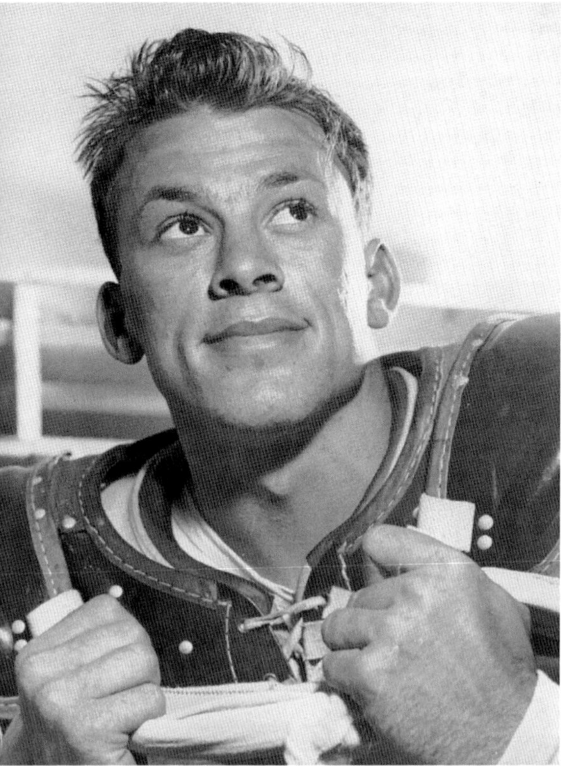

Charles "Choo Choo" Justice
Charlie "Choo Choo" Justice was one of the most celebrated players in football in the late 1940s. Justice had served in the Navy during World War II, where he earned the moniker "Choo Choo" because he looked like a runaway train dodging tackles for the Navy Training Center team. After the war, Justice had a highly celebrated career playing football for the University of North Carolina at Chapel Hill. He was the runner-up twice for the Heisman Trophy. In the 1950s, he played professional ball for a few seasons for the Washington Redskins, but worked most of his life in the oil and insurance businesses. (Courtesy of the North Carolina Collection, Pack Library.)

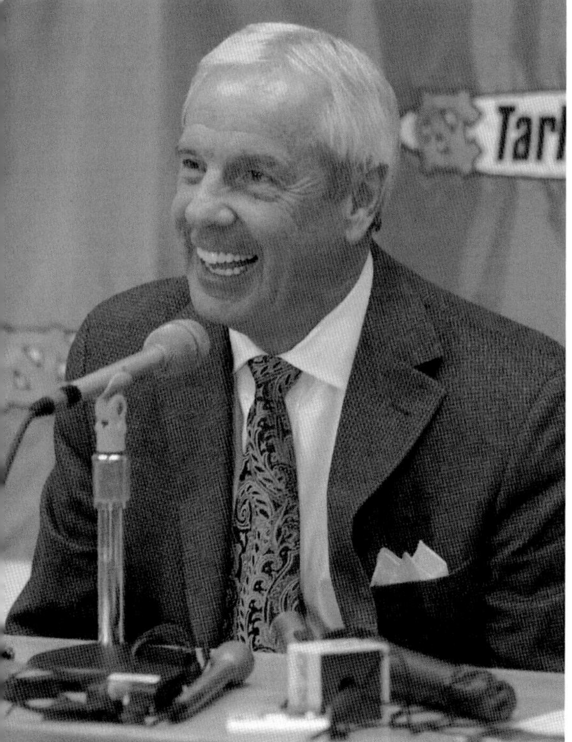

Roy Williams
Coach Roy Williams began his sports career at T.C. Roberson High School in Asheville, where he lettered in basketball and baseball. He went on to play basketball at the University of North Carolina at Chapel Hill under legendary coach Dean Smith. He later served as an assistant coach for Smith before taking over the University of Kansas program in 1988. Williams returned to UNC Chapel Hill as head coach in 2003. During his career, he has taken seven teams to the Final Four. (Photograph by Zeke Smith.)

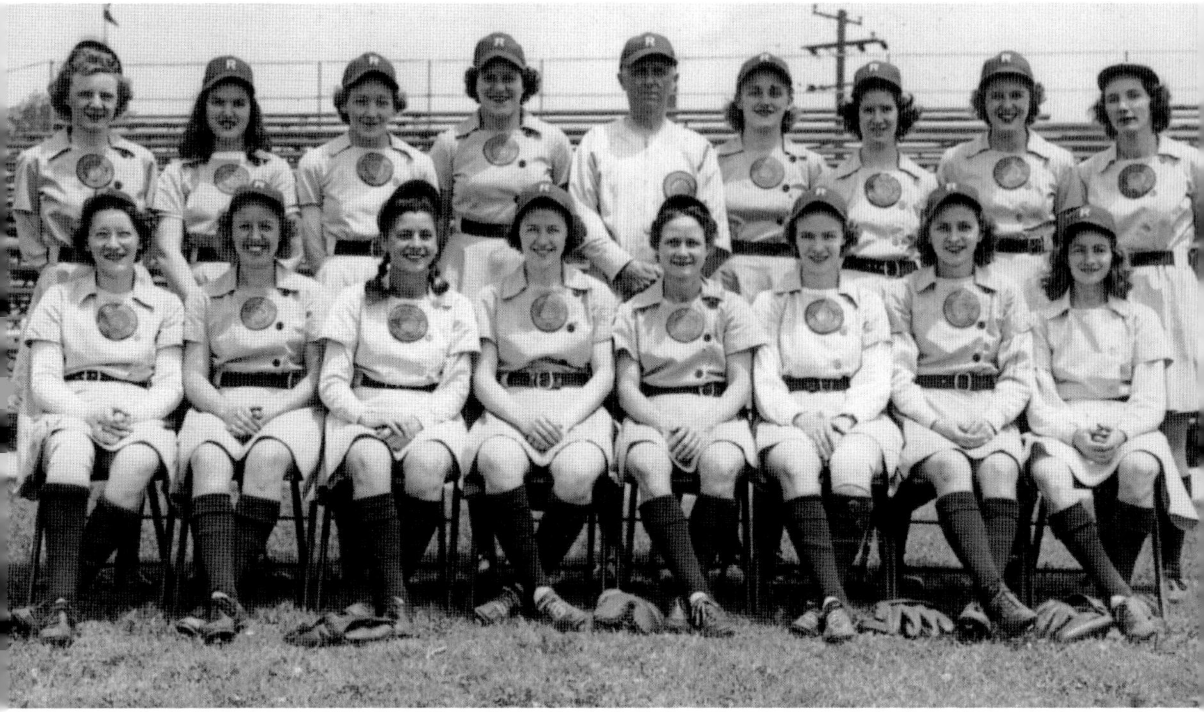

Dorothy Montgomery
Born in Asheville in 1924, Dorothy Montgomery (first row, fourth from left) was a utility infielder who played in the All-American Girls Professional Baseball League. She practiced with the Racine Belles in 1945 but was cut. She returned in 1946 and played for the Muskegon Lassies. She did not make the cut in 1947 and returned to school, going on to become a registered cytologist for 28 years. She died in 2009. (Courtesy of the Center for History.)

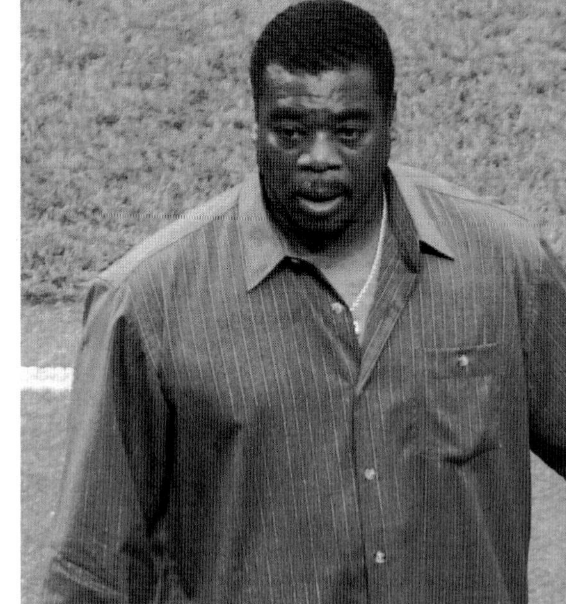

Eddie Murray
Eddie Murray played for the Asheville Orioles during the 1974 and 1975 seasons. During the 1975 season, the coach, Jimmie Shaffer, suggested that a struggling Murray try playing as a switch-hitter. The experiment worked, and Murray became one of the greatest switch-hitters of all time. He went on to spend most of his professional career with the Baltimore Orioles and was inducted into the Baseball Hall of Fame in 2003. (Photograph by Keith Allison.)

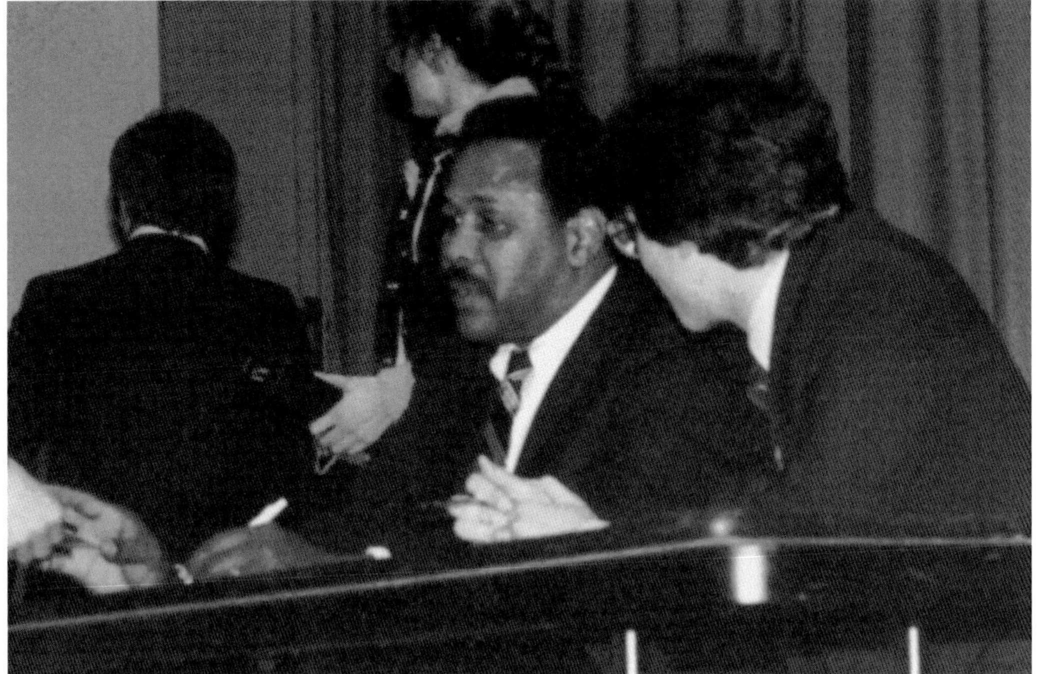

Willie Stargell
Baseball Hall of Famer Willie Stargell played for the Asheville Tourists minor league team during the 1961 season. The team was the farm club for the Pittsburgh Pirates at the time. While playing for the Tourists, Stargell was nicknamed "On the Hill Will" for the long home runs he hit into the hillside far beyond the right-field fence. Stargell made his major league debut the next season for the Pirates and was with the team for 21 years. (Photograph by Ed McDonald.)

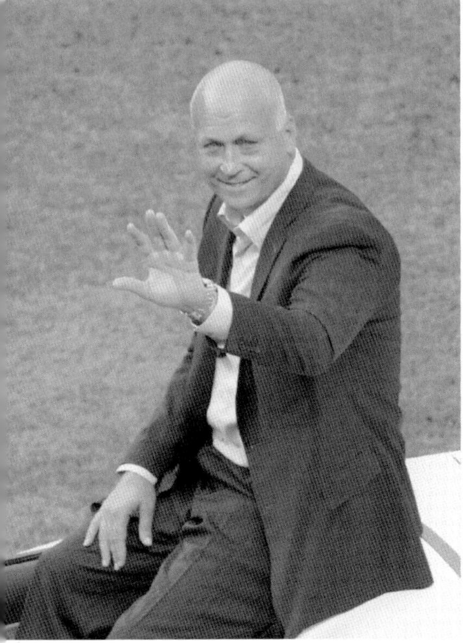

Cal Ripken Jr.
Cal Ripken Jr. spent his summers from 1971 to 1973 as a batboy for what was briefly known as the Asheville Orioles, the city's minor league baseball team. Cal Ripken Sr. was the manager of the team, and Ripken Jr. came to Asheville to learn all that he could about baseball from his dad, especially about pitching and hitting strategy. Ripken, later known as the "Iron Man," went on to play for the Baltimore Orioles for 21 years. In 1995, he surpassed Lou Gehrig's record for the most consecutive games played, with 2,632, a record that still stands today. Ripken was inducted into the Baseball Hall of Fame in 2007. (Photograph by Keith Allison.)

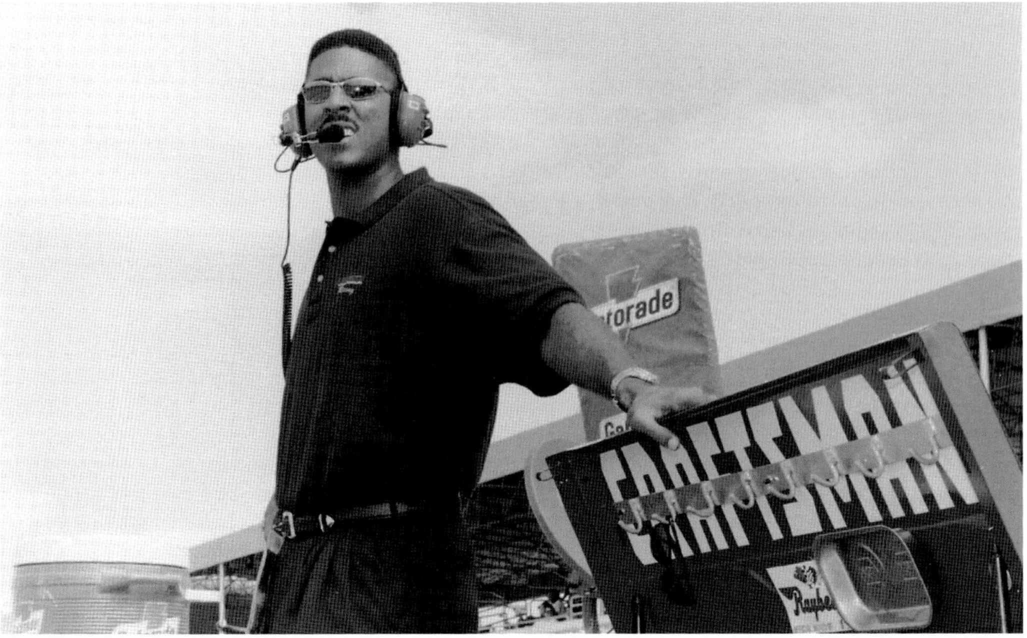

Brad Daugherty

Brad Daugherty played basketball in Asheville at Charles D. Owen High School before beginning his college basketball career under Dean Smith at the University of North Carolina at Chapel Hill. He was a first-round draft pick for the Cleveland Cavaliers in 1986 and played with the team until retiring in 1994 because of back issues. Daugherty now owns several businesses and is a NASCAR racing analyst. (Photograph by Darryl Moran.)

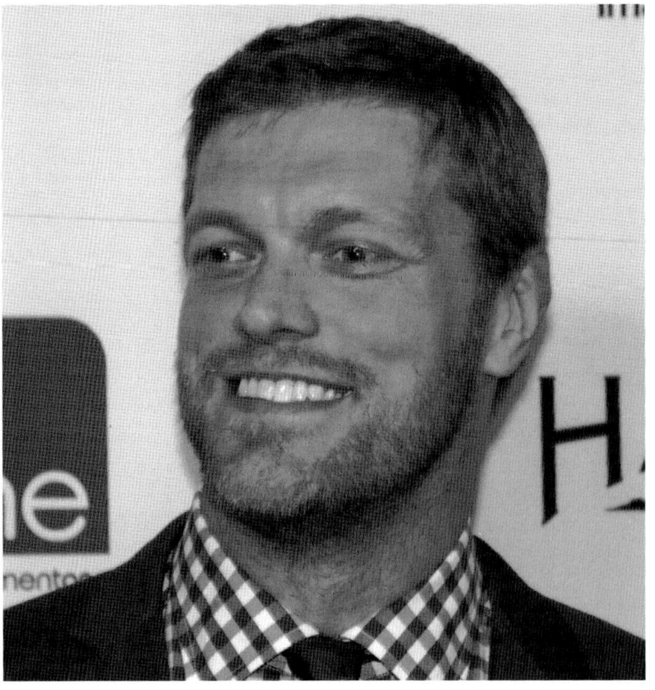

Adam Joseph Copeland

Adam Copeland is a professional wrestler for World Wrestling Entertainment (WWE) who performs under the name The Edge. Copeland's wrestling career spanned nearly two decades, during which time he won 31 championships, and was one of the youngest people to be inducted into the WWE Hall of Fame. Injuries led him to retire in 2011, but Copeland continues to make cameo appearances at various wrestling matches as well as in acting roles on television and in movies. (Photograph by Keith McDuffee.)

CHAPTER SEVEN

The Rebuilders

After the stock market crashed in 1929, Asheville's economy, already weakened by an exploded housing bubble, began a steady and swift decline. The city's civic building spree during the 1920s, while implementing the Program for Progress, left it and the county with a combined debt of well over $50 million (some $700 million in today's dollars). It was, in fact, the highest municipal debt per capita in the country. To make matters worse, the bank that held both the city's and the county's funds collapsed. For the better part of 50 years, the city's growth was stymied by its massive debt. In 1976, the city finished repaying all of its debts and found itself ready to rebuild. Much of Asheville was boarded up, and many of the buildings that were not housed a number of unsavory businesses.

A retired executive from *Southern Living* magazine, together with the heir to an insurance fortune, saw in Asheville not a diamond in the rough but, instead, a diamond in need of some polish. They, along with a dedicated group of community leaders, began the difficult task of rebuilding Asheville. With more successes than failures, things began to turn around in Asheville. A handful of entrepreneurs took chances and opened stores downtown. The rent was low, but that would mean nothing without customers. Slowly but surely, people began to rediscover Asheville, and, importantly, they also began to move downtown to live. By the late 1980s, Asheville's renaissance was in full swing and downtown Asheville was becoming a destination rather than a place to be avoided. In the years that followed, Asheville was born anew.

Pat and Roger McGuire

One of the central figures in Asheville's redevelopment and rebirth in the late 20th century, Roger McGuire moved to Asheville in 1980 with his wife, Pat, after he retired as an executive for *Southern Living* magazine. The McGuires were planning on a quiet retirement raising sheep, but they quickly developed a deep appreciation for the difficult position Asheville found itself in as it emerged from nearly a half century of stagnation and decline as a result of the economic collapse the city suffered during the Great Depression. Asheville's enormous municipal bond debt from that era had crippled its ability to grow. Roger saw opportunity rather than misfortune and began a series of forums and meetings that initiated the discourse about revitalizing downtown Asheville. He created Asheville-Buncombe Discovery, a private, nonprofit organization designed to preserve and improve the livability of Asheville. From these efforts emerged the Pack Place Education Arts & Science Center (opposite, top), and the preservation of the Grove Arcade. Pat became the founding chair of WCQS public radio. The McGuires also created the City Assets Corporation, which developed 60 Haywood Street as a mixed-use project, adding residences downtown for the first time in decades and kick-starting significant residential growth within the downtown corridor. Roger died in 1994 and was honored a decade later by the city with the naming of the green in front of city hall and the county courthouse in the redeveloped Pack Square (opposite, bottom), a project he had suggested some 20 years earlier. (Below, courtesy of Kim McGuire; opposite, both photographs by Aaron Dahlstrom.)

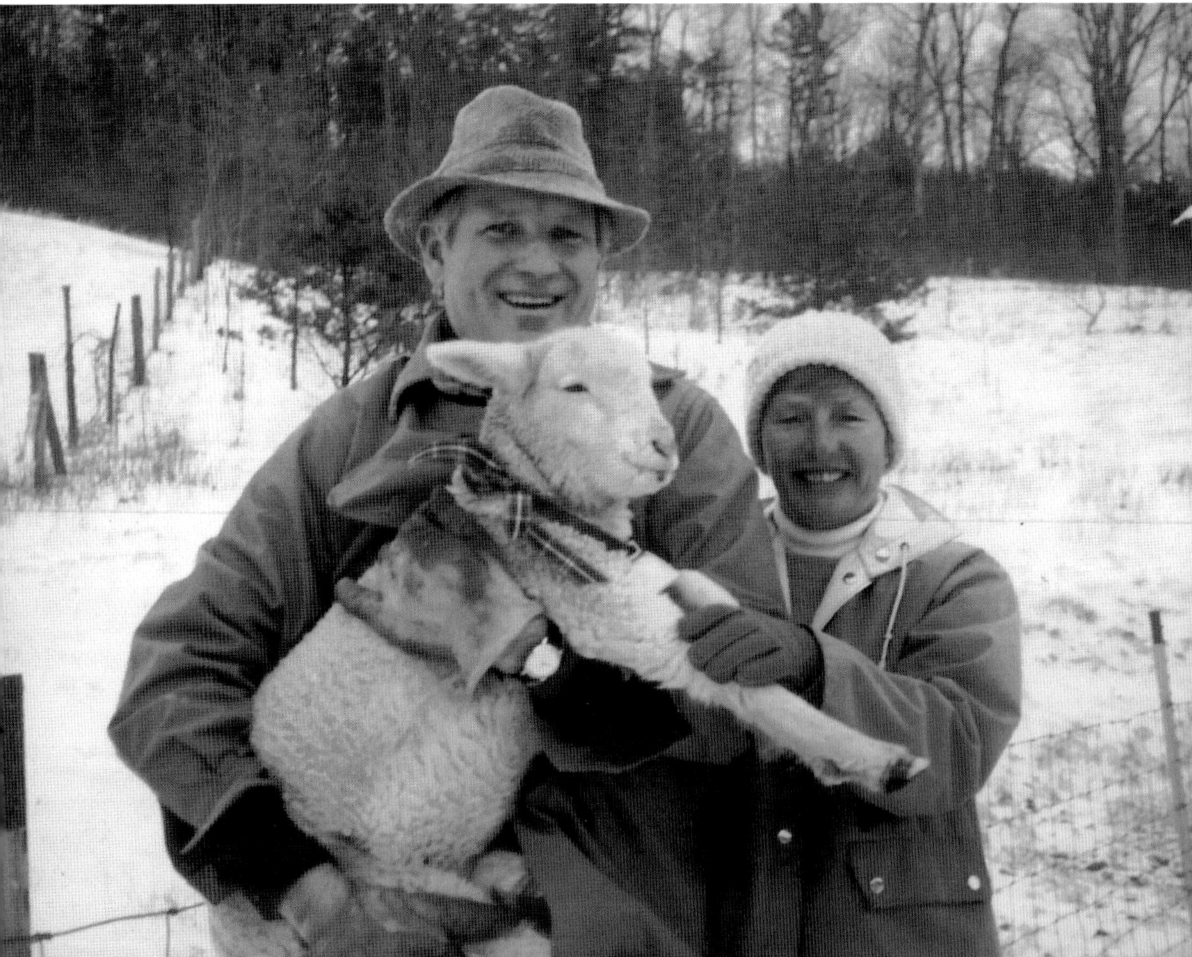

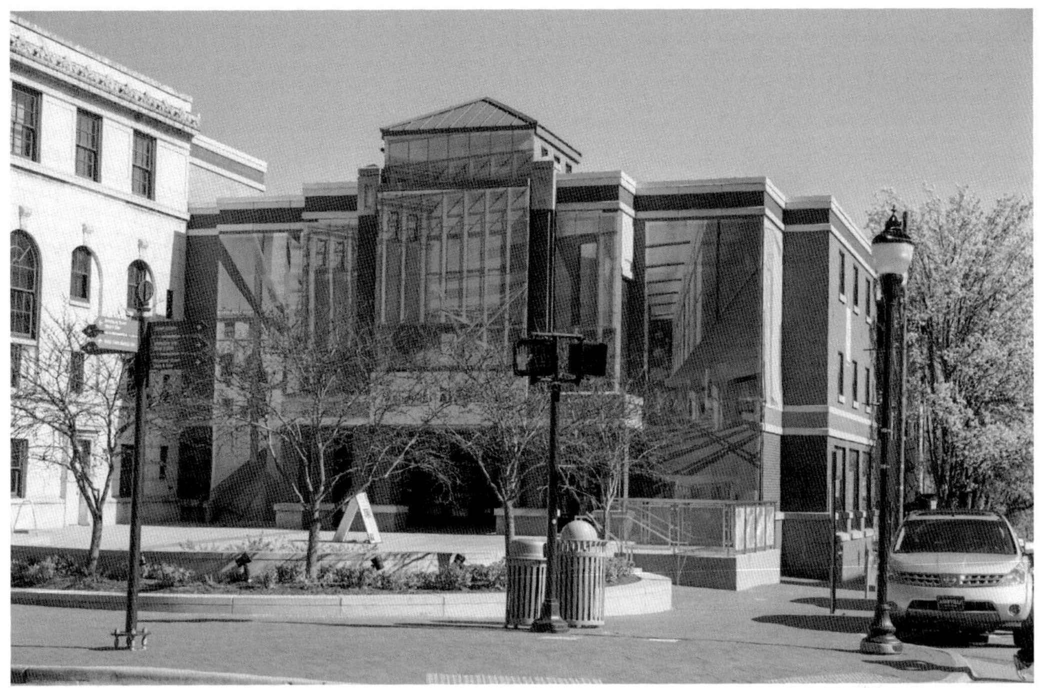

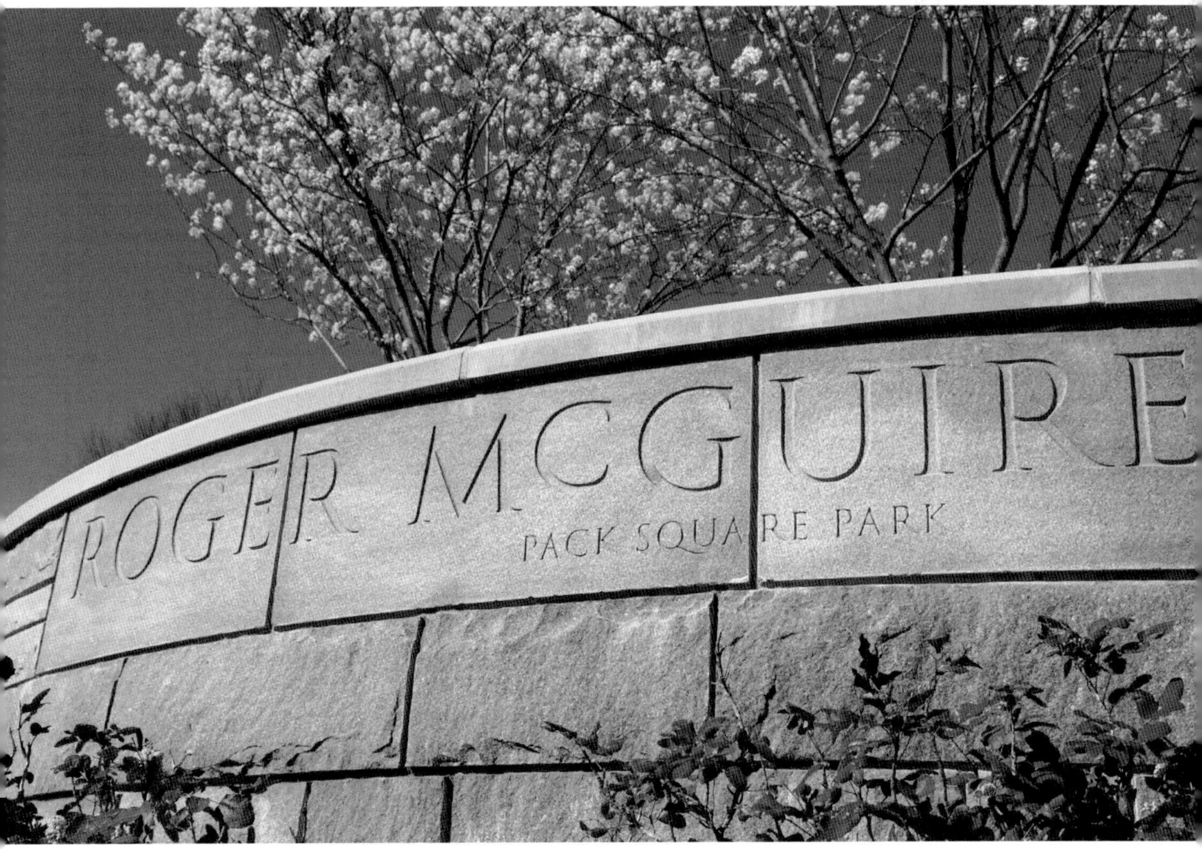

ROGER MCGUIRE
PACK SQUARE PARK

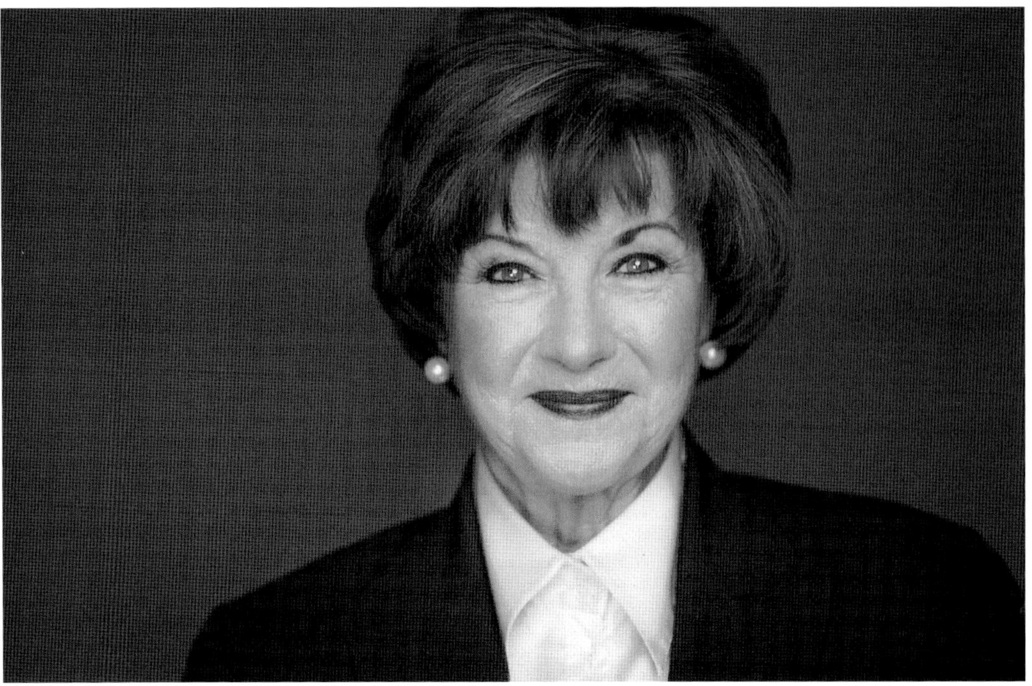

Karen Tessier
After painter Karen Tessier moved to Asheville in the late 1970s, she quickly learned that artists had few opportunities to sell their work and that downtown was all but deserted. This began a multi-decade crusade to revitalize downtown Asheville. In 1984, she participated in a now-famous bus trip that inspired a generation of leaders to rethink downtown. A year later, she went to work with Roger McGuire and served as the executive director of Asheville-Buncombe Discovery, which, as one of its programs, brought fourth-graders downtown for eight years to build future interest in the city. Additionally, Tessier was involved in the creation of Pack Place and the reorganization of Mountain BizWorks and was a founding member of the Pack Square Conservancy, which renovated Pack Square Park. (Courtesy of Karen Tessier.)

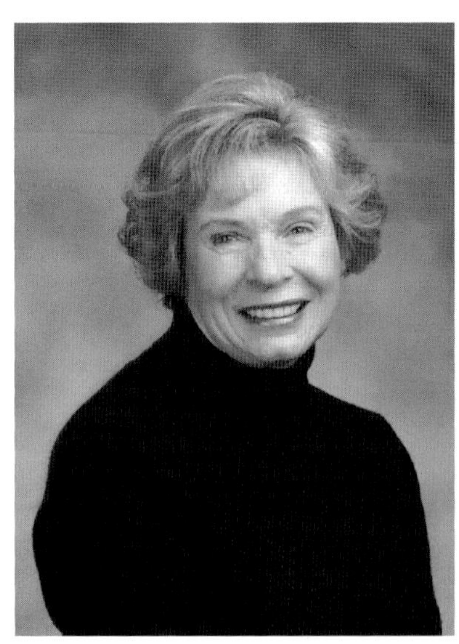

Becky Anderson
Asheville's first downtown development director, Becky Anderson played a leading role in the redevelopment that began in the 1980s. Building upon the community spirit that emerged after a failed bond referendum that would have razed blocks of downtown for a shopping mall, Anderson built strong coalitions that led to Asheville's first Downtown Commission. Anderson later served in leadership roles with the Asheville Chamber of Commerce and the Land of Sky Regional Council and was also the founding director of HandMade in America. (Courtesy of Becky Anderson.)

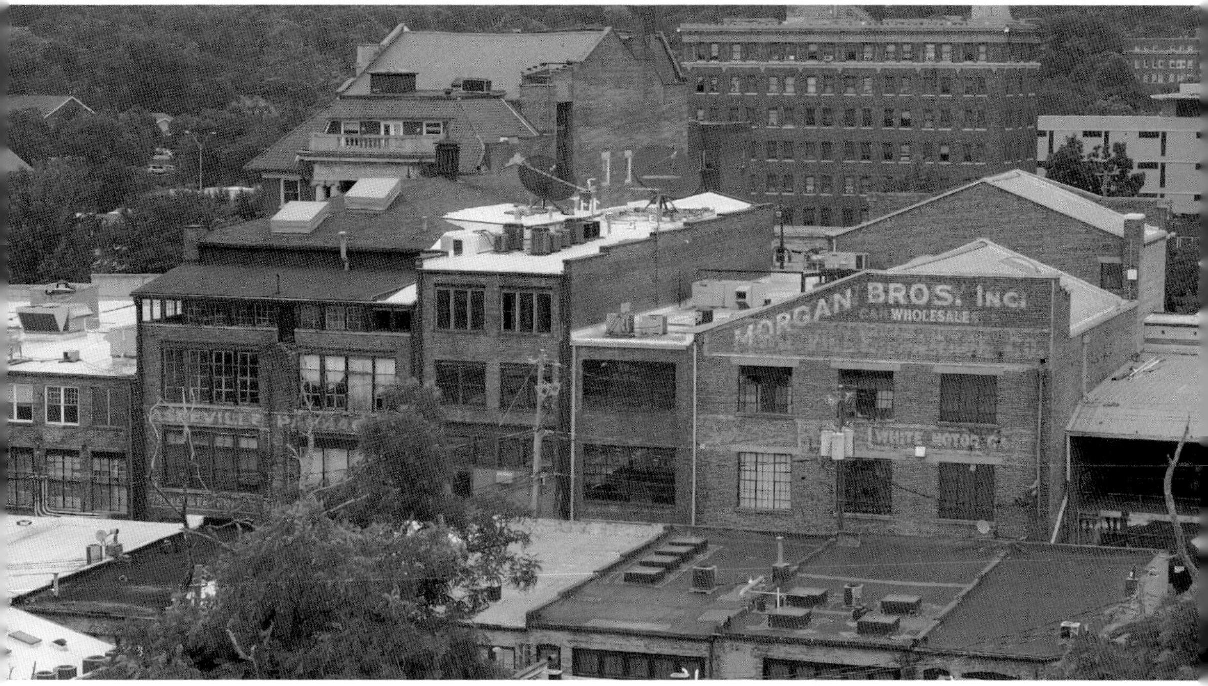

Wayne Caldwell and John Lantzius

In the late 1970s, John Lantzius began buying up much of North Lexington Avenue, one of the city's most blighted streets. In 1980, as Lantzius began to renovate and develop what he called Lexington Park, the Asheville Revitalization and Economic Redevelopment Commission proposed leveling more than 11 blocks of downtown, including Lexington Park, for a second indoor shopping mall. One of the business owners in the affected area, Wayne Caldwell, organized Save Downtown Asheville, and led a campaign that successfully defeated the bond referendum necessary for the new mall to come to fruition. Caldwell's leadership and Lantzius's investment shifted the city from a path of demolition to one centered on preservation and renovation. (Photograph by Aaron Dahlstrom.)

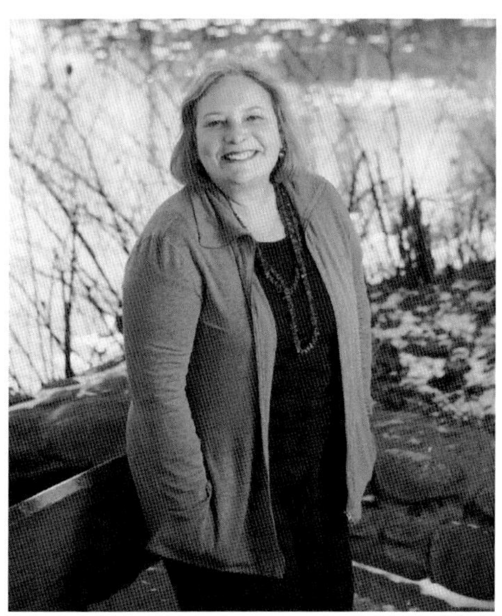

Karen Cragnolin

In 1989, Karen Cragnolin, under the auspices of the Asheville Chamber of Commerce and the French Broad River Foundation, brought together a group of citizens to develop a plan for the Asheville riverfront. From those meetings emerged RiverLink, which, in the years that have followed, under Cragnolin's leadership, has transformed the Asheville riverfront. It now includes such features as the Wilma Dykeman Greenway, which connects a collection of riverside parks, and the beloved River Arts District, home to dozens of Asheville artists. (Photograph by Matt Rose.)

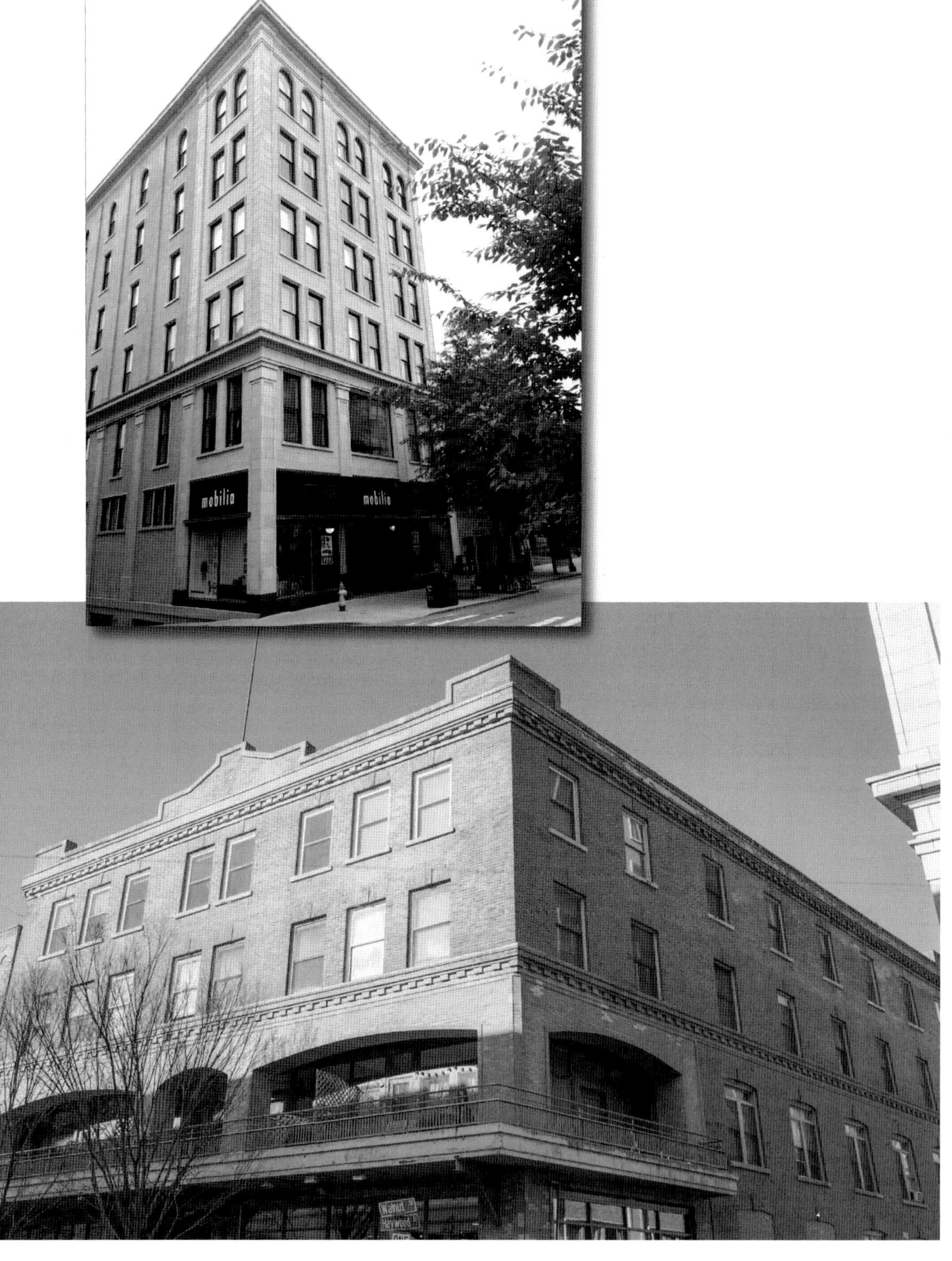
mobilia
mobilia

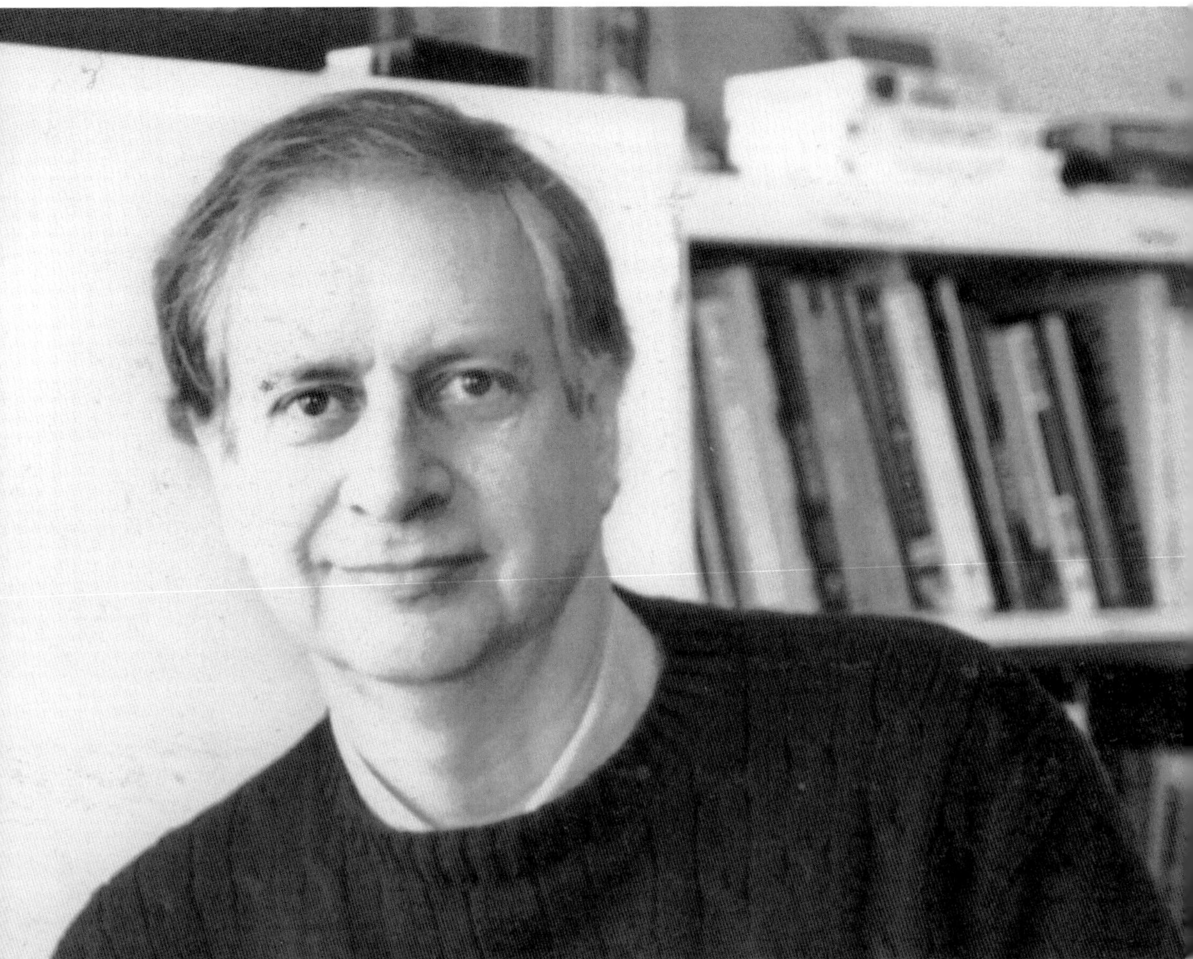

Julian Price

Julian Price, born into a wealthy Greensboro insurance family, decided to move to Asheville in 1990 when a chance visit convinced him that his heart was in the mountain city. Price realized that he wanted to help rebuild Asheville after its 50-year decline following the Great Depression. Two months after he moved to Asheville, he met his second wife, Meg McLeod, and, with her support, he began transforming Asheville. He started by founding Public Interest Projects (PIP), a for-profit entity to encourage downtown redevelopment. Price hired local attorney Pat Whalen to head PIP; since its founding, the group has invested more than $15 million into businesses as varied as Malaprop's Bookstore and the Laughing Seed Café. It has initiated numerous large-scale development projects, such as the Asheville Hotel (opposite, bottom), the Carolina Apartments, and the J.C. Penney Building condominium conversions (opposite, top). Price also created the Dogwood Fund of the Community Foundation of Western North Carolina, which has given more than $2 million in over 200 grants to support revitalization, affordable housing, the environment, and alternative transportation. Additionally, he invested in numerous other projects, including the Self-Help Credit Union, Mountain BizWorks, the *Mountain Xpress*, and RiverLink. Price was known to stop in businesses that he liked and leave behind checks for tens of thousands of dollars as further investment in their growth and future. Price, who died in 2001, was an unlikely benefactor who, in less than 11 years, dramatically transformed downtown Asheville and helped usher in its renaissance. (Above, photograph courtesy of Ramsey Library Special Collections; opposite, both photographs by Aaron Dahlstrom.)

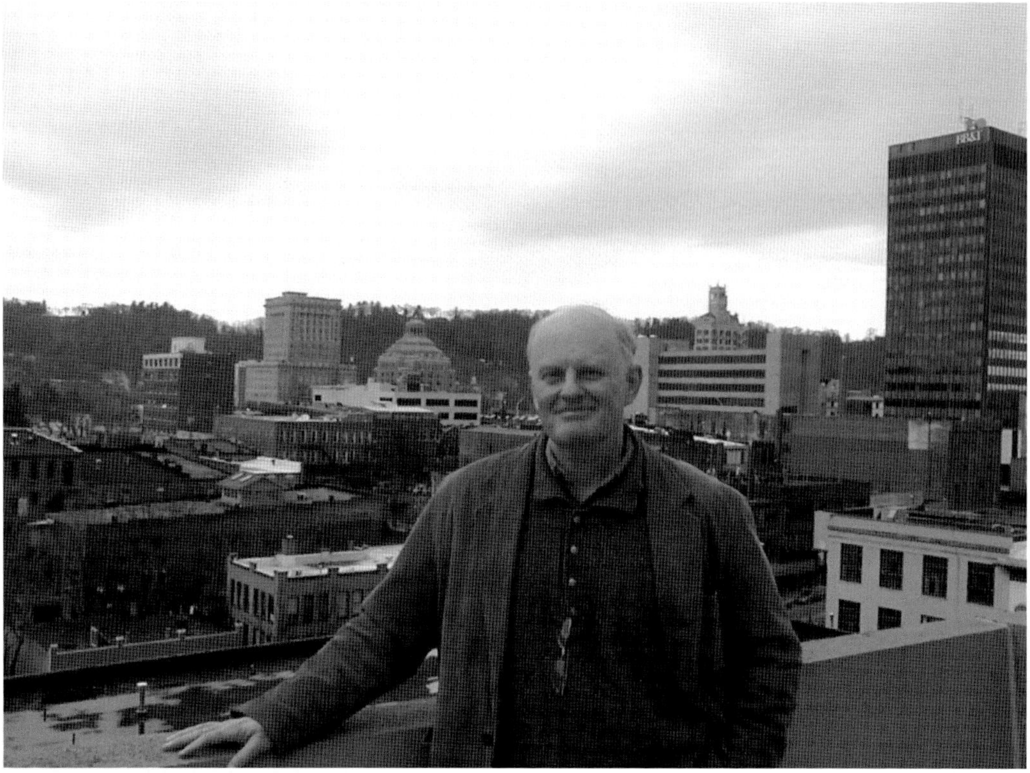

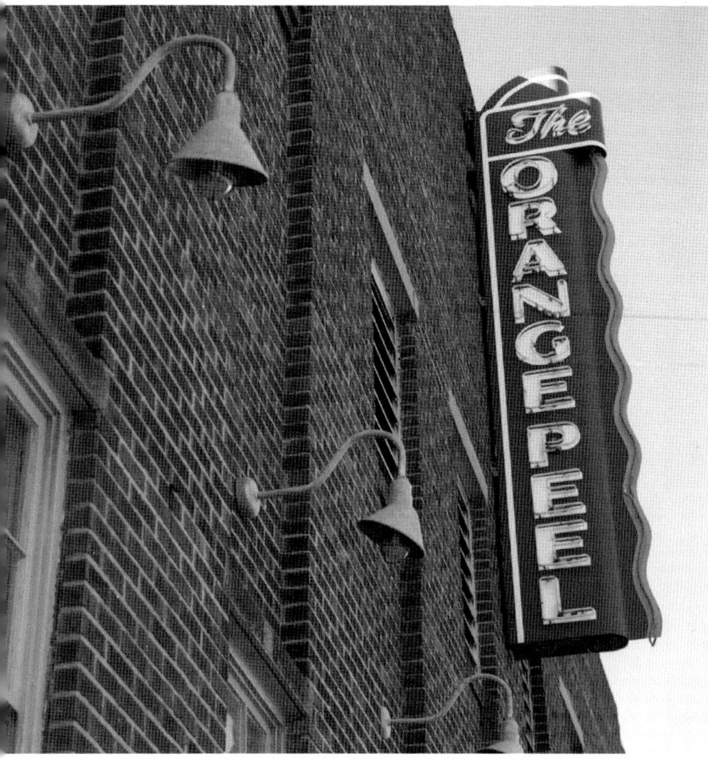

Pat Whalen

While Pat Whalen is always quick to give credit to Julian Price for transforming downtown Asheville, as the president of the development firm Public Interest Projects, founded by Price in 1990, Whalen himself has been instrumental in Asheville's rebirth. Whalen, an attorney, has led the renovation of 12 downtown buildings and 16 retail spaces, salvaged 123 low-income housing units for the elderly, and provided financial support for 18 downtown businesses, including the Orange Peel Social Aid and Pleasure Club, which Whalen himself owns and which *Rolling Stone* named one of the top five rock venues in the country. (Top, photograph courtesy of Public Interest Projects; left, photograph by Aaron Dahlstrom.)

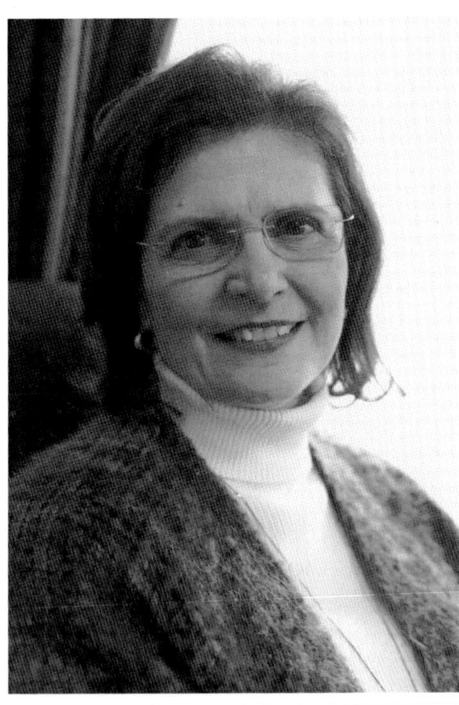

Carol L. King
An accountant by trade, Carol King served as the founding chair of the Pack Square Conservancy. During the first decade of the 21st century, the Conservancy led a public-private partnership that redeveloped Asheville's city center, Pack Square. The multimillion-dollar project transformed the public park, which stretches from the Vance monument to the front of city hall and the county courthouse to better accommodate both major events and people simply passing through. King, also an active Rotarian, has been recognized for her leadership with numerous awards, including the Francine Delany Alumni Award for Service to the Community from her alma mater, UNC Asheville. (Left, courtesy of UNC Asheville Communication and Marketing; below, photograph by Aaron Dahlstrom.)

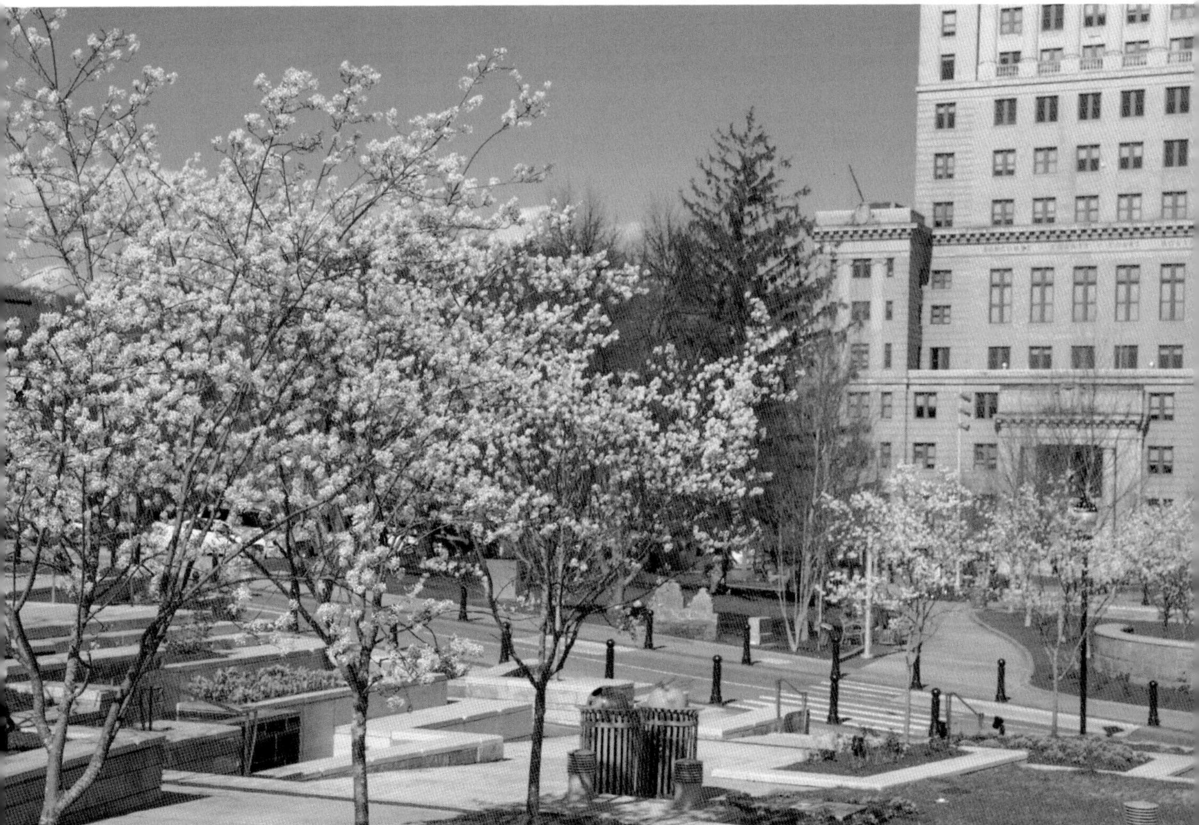

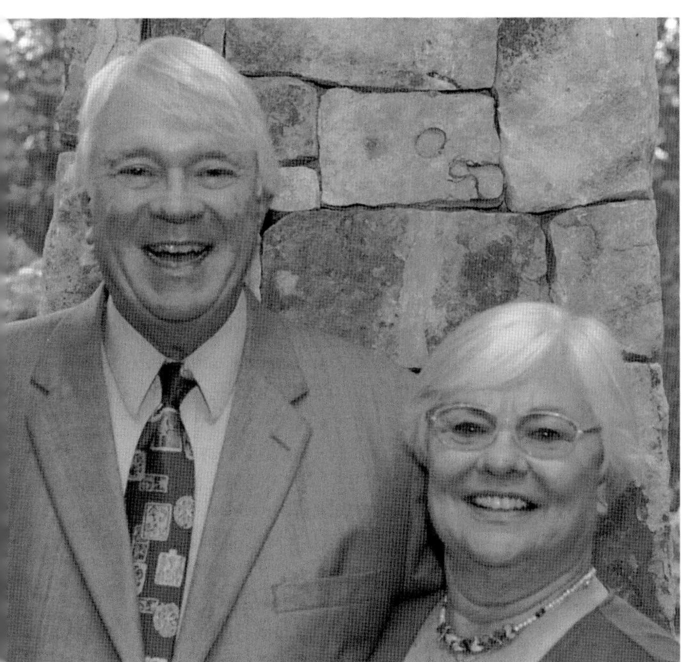

W. Louis Bissette Jr.
Lou Bissette is the first mayor in Asheville to be elected by popular vote. He held office from 1985 to 1989, during which time he helped lay the groundwork for changes in city government that would support Asheville's emerging renaissance. An attorney by trade, Bissette's service, extending beyond political office, is legendary, as he has served on dozens of boards and community organizations including the Grove Arcade Foundation, the Asheville Chamber of Commerce, the Blue Ridge Parkway Foundation, and the Buncombe County Economic Development Commission. In 2013, he was recognized by the Asheville Downtown Association as a Downtown Hero for his work in revitalizing the city. (Photograph by Perry Hebbard; courtesy of UNC Asheville Communication and Marketing.)

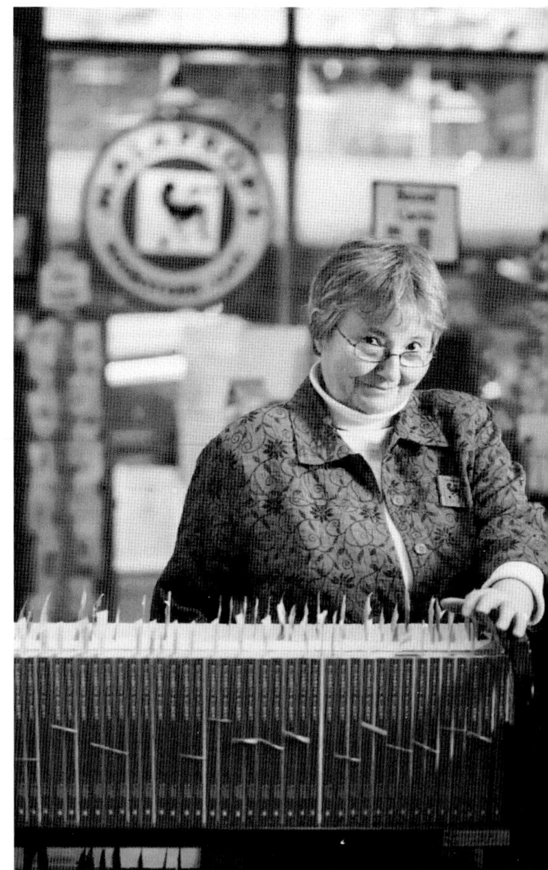

Emöke B'Racz
On June 1, 1982, with only $10,000 and no financial backing, Emöke B'Racz opened Malaprop's Bookstore in downtown. Originally from Hungary, B'Racz grew up during the Cold War in a nation where books and writers were controlled. Her own father, a poet, was taken away in the dead of night for his poetry. When B'Racz opened her first location on Haywood Street, most of the block was boarded up. By the time she moved a few doors down, 15 years later, Asheville had begun its renaissance. B'Racz took a risk and helped pioneer Asheville's rebirth. Over the years, Malaprop's has received numerous national awards, but it is the renewed sense of community that B'Racz has found the most rewarding. (Photograph by Matt Rose.)

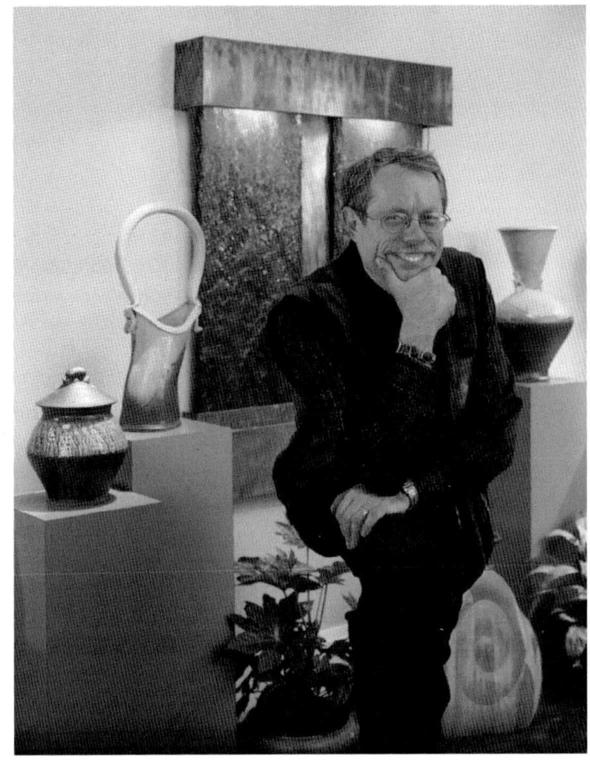

John E. Cram
John Cram pioneered Asheville's fine arts and crafts movement, not only with the opening of his nationally acclaimed New Morning Gallery in Historic Biltmore Village in the 1970s, but also with the opening of Blue Spiral 1 Gallery in the 1990s, at a time when much of downtown Asheville was still deserted. Cram's investment in downtown paid off, and Blue Spiral became the cornerstone of Asheville's vibrant art gallery scene. (Courtesy of New Morning Gallery.)

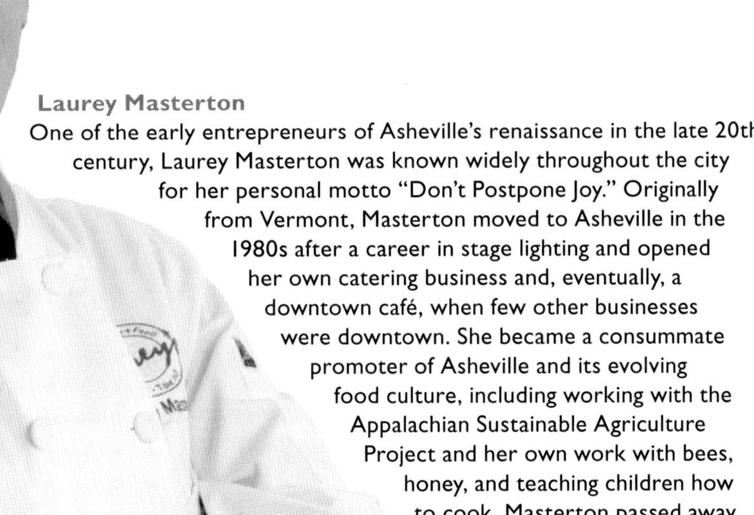

Laurey Masterton
One of the early entrepreneurs of Asheville's renaissance in the late 20th century, Laurey Masterton was known widely throughout the city for her personal motto "Don't Postpone Joy." Originally from Vermont, Masterton moved to Asheville in the 1980s after a career in stage lighting and opened her own catering business and, eventually, a downtown café, when few other businesses were downtown. She became a consummate promoter of Asheville and its evolving food culture, including working with the Appalachian Sustainable Agriculture Project and her own work with bees, honey, and teaching children how to cook. Masterton passed away in 2014. (Courtesy of Heather Masterton.)

INDEX

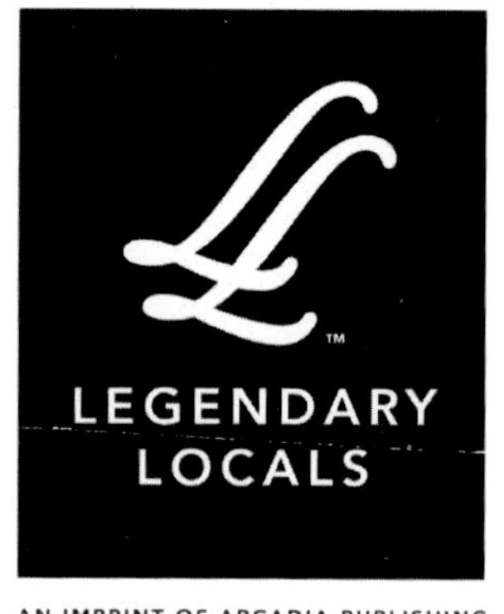
LEGENDARY
LOCALS